REPORT ON THE ISLAND

&

DIOCESE OF PUERTO RICO

(1647)

BY

CANON DIEGO DE TORRES Y VARGAS

T0351402

ECOS

Historical Series
of
Documents from Hispanic Caribbean Religion

Ecos is a publication series of religious documents from the Caribbean, intended to supply translation of Spanish language texts that are keys to understanding religion among peoples of the Hispanic Caribbean islands of Puerto Rico, Cuba and the Dominican Republic. The series' title is taken from the Spanish word for "echoes," and expresses the goal: to preserve the relevance of the past as it touches the contemporary world. Designed for both a general and an academic public, the series responds to an increasingly significant presence of people of Latino heritage living in the United States. At the same time, these volumes provide non-Latino and secular scholars with a reliable resource that explains religious and ecclesiastical facets of the history of people from this region of the world.

General Editors:
Anthony M. Stevens-Arroyo
Professor Emeritus of Puerto Rican & Latino Studies,
Brooklyn College, CUNY

&

Ana María Díaz-Stevens
Professor Emerita of Church and Society,
Union Theological Seminary

* * *

This publication is made possible with assistance from
The Program for the Analysis of Religion Among Latinos/as
PARAL
through support from
The Lilly Endowment

REPORT ON THE ISLAND
&
DIOCESE OF PUERTO RICO
(1647)

BY

CANON DIEGO DE
TORRES Y VARGAS

An Annotated Translation into English
by
Jaime R. Vidal

With Historical Essays and Commentary
by
Anthony M. Stevens-Arroyo

University of Scranton Press
Scranton and London
Volume I of *Ecos*

Library of Congress Cataloging-in-Publication Data

Torres y Vargas, Diego de, 17th cent.

[Descripción de la isla y ciudad de Puerto-Rico, y de su vecindad y poblaciones, pre-sidio, gobernadores y obispos, frutas y minerales.] English

Report on the island & Diocese of Puerto Rico (1647) / by Diego de Torres y Vargas ; an annotated translation into English by Jaime R. Vidal ; with historical essays and commentary by Anthony M. Stevens-Arroyo.

p. cm. -- (Ecos ; v. 1)

Includes bibliographical references and index.

ISBN 978-1-58966-189-9 (pbk.)

1. Puerto Rico--History--Early works to 1800. 2. Puerto Rico--Description and travel--Early works to 1800. 3. Puerto Rico--Geography--Early works to 1800. 4. Catholic Church. Diocese of Puerto Rico--History--Early works to 1800. 5. Puerto Rico--Church history--Early works to 1800. 6. Torres y Vargas, Diego de, 17th cent. I. Vidal, Jaime R. II. Stevens Arroyo, Anthony M. III. Title. IV. Title: Report on the island and Diocese of Puerto Rico (1647).

F1973.T6813 2009
972.95'03--dc22

2009033068

Distribution:
University of Scranton Press
Chicago Distribution Center
11030 S. Langley
Chicago, IL 60628

PRINTED IN THE UNITED STATES OF AMERICA

Dedication

To Father Richard Rousseau, S.J.

Mentor, Colleague, Visionary;

for inspiring us all

to explore the possibilities,

to recognize the needs,

to dream the dreams

that further

the work of Catholicism

and

the maturity of faith

in all languages and cultures.

Ad Majorem Dei Gloriam

TABLE OF CONTENTS

ACKNOWLEDGMENTS

On a fateful day in February of 2003, while snow still covered the mountain peaks of Pennsylvania, the idea of *Ecos* was born. At the invitation of the Jesuit priest, Richard Rousseau of the University of Scranton Press, we and a handful of far-sighted colleagues explored one of the intellectual needs of young people of Caribbean and Latin heritage. Recognizing that this new growing wave of Latinos and Latinas were faced with mature decisions about their Catholic heritage, we resolved to provide a published series of documents that would illuminate the key role of religion and religious leaders in the development of our people's culture and history. Ironically, the religious history of three green tropical islands found their echo in the far-off landscape of hardscrabble Pennsylvania.

Father Rousseau guided our discussion by stating that when history is published in book form it consecrates its importance to posterity. Accordingly, this book as the first in a series is intended to foster Catholicism and religion among our peoples by having our stories told, our ideas published and our identities supported. The name *"ecos"* — literally "echoes" — has been chosen to suggest that while the series is focused on historical documents from the past, the message is intended to be heard in the present day so as to shape the future of tomorrow. Father Rousseau wedded his personal commitments to the Society of Jesus and its Ignatian legacy.

Ecos is expected to enrich our people and the churches in multiple ways: to contribute to pastoral care, to ministry, to the development of Caribbean spirituality and, most importantly, to the education of how faith impacts history and culture. We hope the series will provide a sound academic contribution that will bring a religious perspective to the study of the people of the Caribbean nations of Puerto Rico, the Dominican Republic, and Cuba. Moreover, because these people form a distinct part of a larger group of Latinos and Latinas resident in the United States, these publications will widen the appeal of these books beyond the islands of our heritage. Finally, because our religious story is a major part of the Catholic story in all the Americas, the translated texts are also presented in the original Spanish to make such primary documents accessible to the widest possible public.

With the appearance of this first volume on the work of Diego de Torres y Vargas, we wish to express our gratitude to Father Rousseau and to Glenn Pellino, then Director of Urban and Governmental Affairs at the University of Scranton. Together they opened the door to a three-day seminar in August of 2003 at the university to develop the parameters for the series. These early efforts at defining the series were supported with organizational and financial assistance from the Program for the Analysis of Religion Among Latinos and Latinas (PARAL), then located in the City University of New York (CUNY). At the University of Scranton meeting and subsequent consultations at Fordham University in New York (October 2003) and at the Centro de Estudios Avanzados in Puerto Rico (May 2005), an impressive list of important persons counseled our efforts.

From Puerto Rico, we gratefully acknowledge the input of Anibal Colón Rosado, Jorge Duany, Alfonso Guzmán OFM, Amérigo López Ortiz, Fr. Floyd McCoy, Fernando Picó S.J., Fr. Mario Rodríguez León OP, Samuel Silva-Gotay, and Else Zayas León, archivist for the Archdiocese of San Juan. A special *gracias* goes to Manuel Domenech Ball, who not only participated in the May 2005 Puerto Rico meeting, but was the reviewer of this volume. His comments and gracious identification with the project are highly appreciated. We were aided in developing the project with scholars from the Dominican Republic, such as Carlos Andújar, Alexis Gómez Rosa, Orlando Inoa, and Fr. Ricardo Fajardo. From the Latinos and Latinas residing in the States, we benefited from the keen observations of Teresa Delgado, Anneris Goris, Christina Hip-Flores, Margarita Mooney, Milagros Peña, Yolanda Prieto, Rudy Vargas, and Jesuit Father, William Rickle — who is 'virtually' Latino after his years of service to our people. It was also from these U.S. based Latinos that we heard the voices of Cubans. Each of these consultations helped us envision not only how to identify texts relevant to each of these groupings, but how to connect them as a series that would merit academic visibility.

Action upon the advice flowing from these first series of seminars was stalled by Fr. Rousseau's serious illness that forced his retirement. His replacement as director of the University of Scranton Press, Jeff Gainey, brought his enhusiasm to the project, even though it had not been his own brain child. He quickly grasped the importance of the series and envisioned its unique role in supplying for a linkage between the published resources available to Catholic Studies at a university level and the growing awareness that the future of U.S. Catholicism depends in large measure upon development of Latino leadership within the Church. His expertise in the nuts and bolts of editing was augmented by the attentions of the production manager, Patty Mecadon, whose presence in the office was invaluable. The attractive cover for this book and jacket design for the series came from the talented hand and expert computer skills of Trinka Pettinato.

The final catalyst for this translation of the narrative of Diego de Torres y Vargas came in October of 2006, when PARAL funded the opportunity to attend one of the most important symposia held in Puerto Rico in anticipation of the 500th Anniversary of the foundation in San Juan of the first Christian diocese in the New World. This was a scholarly event of great magnitude and its focus upon the 17th Century confirmed the advice that had been given to us by our advisors in Puerto Rico to publish this bilingual edition of the work of Canon Diego de Torres y Vargas as the first of the series. We personally met with scholars of insight such as Pío Medrano Herrero, author of an original study based on invaluable research of primary sources about Torres y Vargas, and Arturo Dávila, whose many years of service to church history cannot be exaggerated. Additionally, we were encouraged by the kind welcome extended by Dr. Manuel Alvarado Morales, Director of the Department of History at the University of Puerto Rico, who was directing the symposium for the Archdiocese and its collaborating institutions. Along with his colleague, María Dolores Luque de Sánchez, herself co-author of a most important text on the general history of Puerto Rico, the warm quality of Puerto Rican hospitality enriched the academic exchanges.

In the first half of 2007, we set about careful examination of the text and a format for this book. The retirement of Anthony M. Stevens-Arroyo from the university that February augmented the intensity of those labors. The compilation of a critical text proved to be daunting, as remarked in the section on the notes. Moreover, as part of our detailed examination of text, we searched for tell-tale signs of redaction. Previous scholars had indicated generally that Diego de Torres y Vargas had consulted other works when writing his own. We began to search out and specify such sources. The expertise of Ana María Díaz-

Stevens in the study of literature helped us identify passages where the lexicon or style differed from the body of the text, where personal pronouns or family references suggested personal observations from the canon himself, and where references to nautical or commercial data indicated still another source. Although this sort of analysis is generally reserved to literary and even to biblical studies, it was useful here and we consider it a relevant consideration for readers. However, we wanted to keep the focus upon the whole work, rather than the scholarly details of textual criticism. Accordingly, we have not offered our textual analysis as definitive.

Finally, it was decided to compose several essays to provide background information on each of three topics: colonial Puerto Rico, the Caribbean during the Thirty Years War and the life of Diego de Torres y Vargas. While we considered inviting different distinguished scholars to write on those topics, we ultimately settled on a style suited to the university students we have both taught over nearly three decades of professional experience as professors of Puerto Rican Studies and of the Sociology of Religion. The three essays are intended for classroom use and as background guides for informed readers.

The most important part of this publication is the translation, of course. For the intimidating task of a first-time-ever publication in English of an American product of the Baroque period, we turned to Jaime R. Vidal, a native of Ponce, our colleague at Fordham University and a scholar of vast knowledge who possesses expansive interests and considerable editorial experience. In addition to his insightful participation at the 2003 meeting, he gracefully embraced the daunting task of this translation as a labor of love. His emails over a relatively short ninety days carried attachments with pages of his work, allowing us to collaborate with him on each installment despite the distance of half a continent. We would speak late at night by telephone, discussing how and where the historical details uncovered in his translation best fit the volume. Biblical references from the Vulgate, passages from Livy and Virgil, arcane ecclesiastical practices and vestiges preserved in Puerto Rico's churches and museums figured frequently in these conversations. It was at Dr. Vidal's suggestion that we decided upon sidebars rather than long academic footnotes for the translation text. We came to consider that the sidebar format would make the information more accessible to readers. What information did not belong in the sidebars was inserted within the historical essays. Jaime R. Vidal merits our heart-felt praise for his acumen, collegiality and wisdom.

It is our dearest wish that our efforts in this first volume of the series contribute to an appreciation in the United States for the historic role of Puerto Rico as the birthplace of American Catholicism. If in any way our efforts advance the vision of our colleagues in Puerto Rico, we are abundantly thankful. We trust that this first volume in the series, which is focused on 17th Century Puerto Rico, will set a standard that will be matched by subsequent publications about a region of the Americas that may be small in geographic size, but is rich in religious legacy.

Ana María Díaz-Stevens and Anthony M. Stevens-Arroyo

The Stroudsburgs, Pennsylvania

December 8, 2008

Feast of the Immaculate Conception of the Blessed Virgin Mary

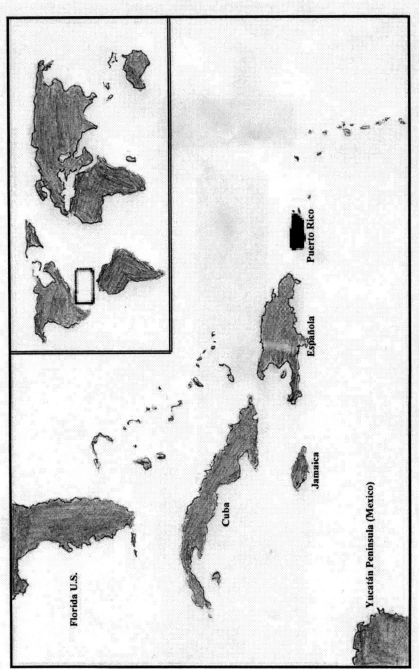

Map of Puerto Rico and the Caribbean: World Map insert.

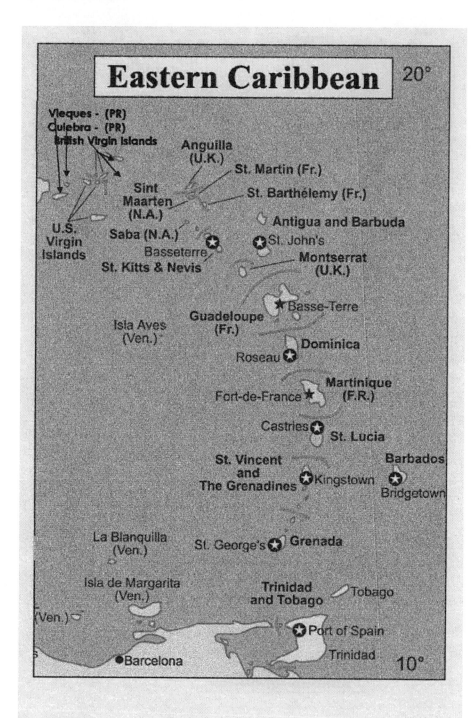

Eastern Caribbean

20°

Vieques - (PR)
Culebra - (PR)
British Virgin Islands

Anguilla
(U.K.)

St. Martin (Fr.)

Sint
Maarten
(N.A.)

St. Barthélemy (Fr.)

U.S.
Virgin
Islands

Saba (N.A.)

Antigua and Barbuda

St. John's

Basseterre

Montserrat
(U.K.)

St. Kitts & Nevis

Isla Aves
(Ven.)

Guadeloupe
(Fr.)

Basse-Terre

Dominica

Roseau

Martinique
(F.R.)

Fort-de-France

Castries

St. Lucia

St. Vincent
and
The Grenadines

Kingstown

Barbados

Bridgetown

La Blanquilla
(Ven.)

St. George's

Grenada

Isla de Margarita
(Ven.)

Trinidad
and Tobago

Tobago

(Ven.)

Port of Spain

Trinidad

Barcelona

10°

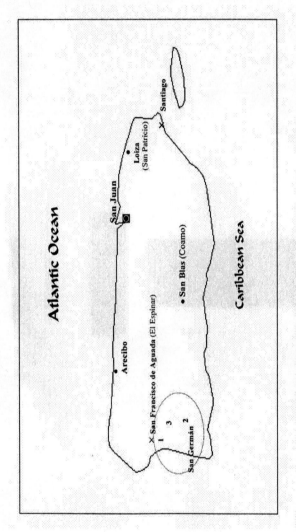

Map of Towns and Settlements Mentioned in Torres y Vargas

Legend

1   San Germán (1512)
2   San Germán el Nuevo (1556) relocated by order of King Philip II
3   Nueva Salamanca, location of San Germán since 1570
×   Abandoned settlements

UNDERSTANDING THE WORK
OF
DIEGO De TORRES Y VARGAS

When something is the "first," that is usually enough reason to consider it important. Other writers had produced reports and chronicles about Puerto Rico before Don Diego de Torres y Vargas[1] put pen to paper in 1647 (#17),[2] so in a strict sense, his was not the first written history of Puerto Rico. But because most of the authors before him were either Spanish colonizers or foreign visitors to the island, we may consider Torres y Vargas to have written the first "Puerto Rican history," meaning it was the first history written about the Island seen through the eyes of someone born in Puerto Rico. However, while Don Diego would have called Puerto Rico in Spanish his "*lugar de nacimiento,*" (the "place of birth"); it is not certain how or if he would he have used the words "*patria,*" i.e., "motherland" for Puerto Rico.

Torres y Vargas was a fourth generation *criollo*, born and raised in Puerto Rico. While some history books equate "criollo" with "Puerto Rican," it is useful to recognize that during the times of Don Diego there was not as yet a modern concept of "citizenship." Under the Spanish monarchy, each person was a royal subject, no matter where they lived; rejection of the king was equivalent to treason. The constant references to "His Majesty" in the document written by Torres y Vargas reflect this commitment to be a Spanish subject. This loyalty to the Spanish king, however, does not mean that subjects like Torres y Vargas did not feel emotionally attached to the different regions where they were born. We might compare this to how a person living in New York considers the United States as his country, while still holding special affection for New York. Being a "New Yorker" does not negate also being an "American." In somewhat the same way, for Torres y Vargas and the criollos of his time, Spain was the *patria,* but the Island of Puerto Rico was the *patria chica,* i.e., the "little motherland."

---

[1] His name is listed as "de Torres y Vargas," however, we have exercised editorial license to drop the "de" in most references.

[2] The reference #17 is to the text of Torres y Vargas. The sign # is used throughout this and other essays to guide the reader to relevant sections of his narrative as edited in this volume.

The most accurate label for Torres y Vargas' history of Puerto Rico is: "The first that was completely authored by a non-European." While today "non-European" often means "non-white," this perspective on race does not necessarily apply to Torres y Vargas. In his day, people recognized racial differences for blacks and people of mixed race, that is, either *mestizos* from Spanish-Indian descent; or *mulatos* from Spanish-African mixture. A criollo like Torres y Vargas, however, was just as white racially as any Spaniard born in Spain. In fact, he should be considered "high-born," since he was a direct descendant of Juan Ponce de León, the founder of the colony of Puerto Rico.

With these cautions in mind, we can better focus upon the unique perspectives provided in this narrative about Puerto Rico. Even if Torres y Vargas did not think of his "Puerto Ricanness" in the political terms of today or to have been racially different from the white Spanish-born bishops he served, his document reflects important social and cultural changes taking place in Puerto Rico as early as the seventeenth century. In a sense, his work is all the more indicative of social change precisely because he was of the same race as the Europeans. The differences between Spaniards and Puerto Rico's criollos are rooted in upbringing and life experiences that were beginning to be felt. If an upper-class white like Torres y Vargas saw differences among those born in Puerto Rico and other Spaniards, then we may consider this evidence of an emerging national identity, even if not fully formed when he wrote.

In the document of Torres y Vargas, there are passages where we glimpse how his perspectives differ from those of authors before him. In small but important ways, he writes about Puerto Rico with feelings unique to someone born and raised on the island, calling attention to details that visitors might miss (see #8). For instance, for someone born in Puerto Rico, the warm temperature is normal (#1): a Spanish visitor, on the other hand, would likely complain about the heat. Torres y Vargas describes Puerto Rico's beauty (#2, #7–8), and the wholesomeness of its people (#84), and the heroism (#85, #124–127) and holiness (#24–26) of famous inhabitants. What literary experts call "local color" affords this document an important place in Puerto Rican historiography.

Torres y Vargas composed this history in response to a request from Gil González Dávila (1570–1658), a professor at Salamanca, who had been named

Royal Chronicler of the Indies in 1643. The historian had already produced several comprehensive volumes on church related matters for various regions of Spain. His new book was to be focused on Mexico and the Caribbean, as indicated in the title of the collection: *Teatro eclesiástico de la primitiva Iglesia de las Indias Occidentales, vidas de sus arzobispos, obispos y cosas memorables de sus sedes* [Ecclesiastical Theatre of the Early Church of the West Indies; Lives of its Archbishops, Bishops and Memorable Events of Its Sees]. With Torres y Vargas' history, Puerto Rico was put "on the map," alongside New Spain as a significant Spanish colony. Moreover, King Philip IV of Spain had recently come to recognize the importance of Puerto Rico in defending his American possessions (#6), which made its inclusion so necessary to the Spanish collection, along with smaller islands in the Eastern Caribbean, then part of the Diocese of Puerto Rico.

González Dávila's work — "*Teatro*" in Spanish — would likely be called today "an encyclopedia." It serves as an example of ecclesiastical history during the Baroque period. The chronicler sent out a formulary,[3] indicating what information should be included in the summaries sent to him. Each author was presumed to be an expert on the history of his own locality. Largely because the Council of Trent (1543–1563) had stressed the education of priests, there was a confidence by the seventeenth century that Catholic clerics in the Spanish Empire understood the criollo societies in which they lived and that they were educated enough to produce insightful and reliable histories. González Dávila took the information he wanted from these submissions with a focus on the names of the bishops and dates of their service and published the first part of his collection in Madrid in 1649. Undisturbed by tardy contributors (some reports did not arrive in time to be used for the 1649 publication), González Dávila would consult other sources to supply or correct the data. The bulk of Torres y Vargas' work is not found in the book published in the *Teatro*. As sole author, González Dávila contented himself with listing the bishops of each place, adding a few comments.

---

[3] The source is in *Cuestionario para la formación de las relaciones geográficas de Indias: Siglos XVI–XIX*, a 1988 publication from the Consejo Superior de Investigación (CSI). Cf. Pio Medrano "Damián López de Haro y Diego de Torres y Vargas ¿Escritorese encontrados?" *Focus II*, 2 (2003) 29–42.

Not only did the official court historian drain away most personalized details from the narratives sent to him, he did not include the names of the clerics and other contributors whose information he used. A notable exception to this rule was the mention by name of Torres y Vargas and a compliment to the quality of the report on Puerto Rico. Gonzalez Dávila wrote: "*Desta isla hizo vna descripción muy curiosa con las memorias de sus obispos y gouernadores, frutos y minerales, el licenciado don Diego de Torres y Vargas, canónigo desta s[anta] iglesia, y della he tomado muchas luzes, para mejor acertar en lo perteneciente a ella.*"[4] [Master Don Diego de Torres y Vargas, Canon of that holy church, made a very interesting description of this island with recollections of its bishops and governors, fruits and minerals and from it, I have taken many insights to better decide what is relevant about {Puerto Rico}.] The admission, "**I have taken many insights from it,**" recommends Torres y Vargas history of Puerto Rico as one of the most noteworthy contributions to the important compilation of royal history in the middle of the seventeenth century. Yet, the Spanish historian ignored the plea from Torres y Vargas to include a description of Marian devotion on the island (#15), contenting himself with a sparse listing of officials and ecclesiastics. Writing in the introduction to the critical edition to González Dávila's first volume that includes the description of Puerto Rico, Jesús Paniagua Pérez and María Isabel Viforcos Marinas call the *Teatro* "a mere work of compilation and not one of creation."[5] Ironically, the work of Don Diego, which remained only in written manuscript form for another two centuries, was more creative and comprehensive than the work of the official historian of Spain.

In the spirit of the age, Torres y Vargas carefully examined religious devotions (#33, 48, #115–116), with special attention to apparitions and miracles reported in Puerto Rico (#15, 22, #25–26, 28, #101–102, 111), including a case of spirit possession (#65). In that century, readers expected that the colonies in the Indies would reflect the positive influence of the Catholic religion on Spanish society. Unlike Protestantism, which was divided into multiple factions, Spanish

---

[4] *Teatro*, (2004) Tomo I:518 [285–287 in the 1649 original edition].
[5] Colección, Tradición clásica y humanística en España e Iberoamérica: Universidad de León (2004) Introducción, (2004) 51.

Catholic culture was united by the overarching construct of Catholic universality. This unitary Spanish Catholic civilization certainly exhibited local variations, as for instance, devotions and miracles particular to each place. However, these local experiences magnified the global reach God had granted to Catholic Spain because they were consonant with Catholic teaching.

Torres y Vargas' work cites some marvelous aspects of piety in Puerto Rico, thus reflecting a tendency in Catholicism after the Council of Trent. During that age, miracles within the Catholic Church proved to many that it alone was the true Church of Christ and was superior to any Protestant Church. Yet piety is not the same as superstition. Torres y Vargas was a believer in an age of belief, but he was also a university-educated scholar. He is careful to distinguish between miracles resulting from rumors and those which have been scrutinized (#26). His discretion produced a history that, while avoiding unsubstantiated exaggerations, shows that miraculous instances of heaven's favor had been reported in the lives of persons in Puerto Rico, thus enriching the island with holiness comparable to what was honored in the universal Church (see #24).

For Torres y Vargas, victories in warfare were signs of Divine Favor and a heavenly reward for holiness. Heroism in religion (#41–48), like heroism in battle (#58), results from the finger of God touching earthly history. And because the wars at that time were framed by Catholic vs. Protestant antagonisms, each battle was also viewed as one waged with "God on our side." What a secular author might consider the "bad luck" of disease and illness is viewed in this history as part of divine punishment for sin or inconstancy (see #99). Thus, when the report of Torres y Vargas suggests that virtue is ultimately rewarded by God, it is reflecting the moral tone of the baroque era history.

Allusions to the classics imbue his history with a moral message larger than that of Catholicism alone. It was the sort of device expected of writers during this time of history when the Enlightenment was still dawning. In fact, it might be argued that if Torres y Vargas had not used this baroque style of writing, his European editor might not have been so impressed with the history. Moreover, familiarity with the literature of his own times is evident in Torres y Vargas' reference to the work of Lope de la Vega, a leading dramatist of the Spanish Empire in the seventeenth century (#55). Thus, even if a modern-day reader may become distracted by such allusions to theology and literature, they nonetheless situate Torres y Vargas' work within his times.

This document, however, is not an exclusively religious one. In order to widen the scope of his narrative about Puerto Rico, Torres y Vargas makes effusive references to the famous figures of history in the classical age of Greece and Rome (#64, 72, 81, 85). He touches upon both church and military history, while offering considerable information about the geography of Puerto Rico in the seventeenth century. Torres y Vargas does not skip over the social and economic changes Puerto Rico due to Spain's decline. We find reflected here the fading values of feudalism and the difficulty of the baroque era to embrace an emerging global economy. Readers of Miguel de Cervantes' *Don Quixote de la Mancha,* (published in 1605) will recognize that the history by a Puerto Rican priest across the Atlantic is washed by the same currents in Spanish history that marveled at the heroism found in books of chivalry (see #58).

In addition to these literary and stylistic considerations, it needs to be stressed that this document is a source for historical information about events that otherwise would have been lost. When Torres y Vargas wrote his history, virtually all communications were hand-written and sent to the *Consejo de las Indias* in Spain. Approval was needed for even simple matters like constructing a building or establishing a school. Usually multiple copies of each request or approval were sent on different ships, so as to insure that at least one version arrived. The Consejo was careful to conserve records of all transactions that awaited the signature of the crown to finalize the decision. Often the Consejo offered detailed comments or conducted an investigation before offering the document for a signature. In an effort to preserve people's rights, all the hand-copied[6] correspondence was filed in archives kept by the relevant agency or tribunal. Such care to completely document each case also brought bureaucratic delay to colonial administration. It took months for the letter written in a place like Puerto

---

[6] Unless a document was labeled "by my/his own hand," it presumably was dictated to a clerk who transcribed the document in a clearly legible handwriting style, often with standardized abbreviations for certain entries. Cf. the text's use of italics.

Rico to be taken to Spain on a ship, months more or even years before it was processed and weeks of transport time were required to deliver the permission back in the place of origin. Nonetheless, buried in case portfolios, historians still find documents once considered lost. Spain's archives have often figured in important research on Puerto Rico.

SPANISH ECHOES IN PUERTO RICAN CULTURE

The Chancellor for Carlos V of Spain was Guillermo de Croy (1458–1521) from Flanders. The title to his lands made him "Lord of Chievres," sometimes written as "Xebres." While Carlos was still very young, this chancellor exercised considerable influence over decisions, especially those concerning the grants in the American Colonies. His signature, "Chievres" on a document meant that things were approved.

Puerto Ricans today say something is "chévere" to mean it is OK, and it appears that this sixteenth century chancellor's signature is the reason.

Confer: José Juan Arrom, 2000. "A propósito de la palabra chévere." In *Estudios de Lexicología Antillana*. Río Piedras: Editorial de la Universidad de Puerto Rico. Second edition: 147–154.

Documents in Puerto Rico were exceptionally hard to preserve because of everyday heat and humidity, and also because periodic hurricanes demolished public buildings. Seventeenth century Puerto Rico not only had to worry about these effects of climate, but also had to face up to the special effects of war. Torres y Vargas composed his history after San Juan had lost most of its public records because the city had been burned by the Dutch (1625). As will be explained below, this meant that he had to find reliable ways of discovering the historical events and identifying the persons responsible for the decisions made. Reading his text today (see #45) gives us a window on other documents long since lost to time and calamity.

We can summarize the special characteristics of the document written by Torres y Vargas by highlighting the following:

- It bridges the time between the establishment of the colony in 1508 by Juan Ponce de León and its development a hundred and twenty-five years later into a strategic military bastion to defend Spanish interests.
- It emphasizes the military importance of Puerto Rico and the heroism of its residents in defending Spanish rule effectively.

- It extols the achievements in religious, military, and civil careers of Puerto Ricans (criollos) who went on to higher posts within the Spanish Empire.
- It provides description of buildings and the layout of the City of San Juan as well as of other parts of Puerto Rico, often giving the dates of construction and the names of some public figures linked to these places.

Sometimes Torres y Vargas relied on the memory of people he interviewed rather than on documents. For instance, the narrative confuses Luis de Vallejo and Antonio de la Gama, by joining the names into a fictional "Antonio de la Llama Vallejo (see #48).[7] Because "Gama" and "Llama" sound alike, it might be a mistake that derives from oral history. He also misidentifies an attack as perpetrated by the English, when it fact it was the French (#50).[8] These inaccuracies become forgivable when we recognize that with few other books or documents to "check facts," the memories of those interviewed by Torres y Vargas were relatively accurate.

The general outline of Torres y Vargas' work seems to repeat the topics in the report on Puerto Rico by Juan II Troche Ponce de León, his relative, prepared in 1582 for the Spanish governor, Juan López de Melgarejo. Torres y Vargas also lists the bishops and governors of Puerto Rico, adding facts from oral history for those who had lived before his time and personal observations from his own experience of those under whom he had served. Additionally, he had visited many of the towns and parishes in Puerto Rico, supplying his own description with information from local residents. Since Catholic culture makes a sacrament out of last confession on a deathbed, facts placed on a person's grave were considered to be special proofs of veracity. In more than one place in the text, Torres y Vargas repeats an epitaph, stressing his eye-witness clarity (#41, 43). These segments of Torres y Vargas' narrative appear to be "oral history," in contrast to other sections that seem to be taken from literary sources like the *Historia general de los hechos de los Castellanos en las islas y tierra firme del Mar*

---

[7] Commented upon by Salvador Perea, *Historia de Puerto Rico, 1537–1700,* (1972) 79ff.
[8] Perea, *op. cit.* p. 106.

Océano published in four volumes by Antonio de Herrera beginning in 1601. Finally, there are some nautical facts about distances and coastlines, and commercial details about port traffic, that likely were taken from yearly reports. In sum, there is evidence of different types of sources used by Torres y Vargas in compiling his history:

- Previous written histories: specifically, Herrera's, which was the best overall history and one recently published; as well as the report from Governor Juan López Melgarejo, composed by Torres y Vargas' relative, Juan Troche Ponce de León in 1582. [For example, #1–9]
- List of the bishops of Puerto Rico [#27–43]
- List of the governors of Puerto Rico [#44–82]
- Commercial records [#83–84]
- Oral testimony from San Juan residents about the bishops and governors [interspersed #27–82, but see especially #46, 48, 56]
- Personal observations of towns, places and events [e.g. #15, 23]
- Personal comments about friends and family [e.g. #61, 72]

It is sometimes possible to identify the places in the text where Torres y Vargas stitches together the divergent sources or adds his own comments. He probably dictated parts of his history to clerks who were specially trained to transcribe the manuscript into professional style handwriting. The preferences of each clerk may explain variations in spelling, such as *"ansi"* sometimes, and *"assi"* or *"asi"* elsewhere.

Torres y Vargas strove to dispel Spain's caricatures of the American colonies. He writes in the third person about himself and the heroism of his father, who died defending the city against the Dutch in 1625 (#61, 72). Those familiar with Latin classics will recognize that Julius Caesar wrote his *Gallic Wars* the same way. The use of the third person contrasts with other sections of the narrative where he intentionally interrupts the narrative with the first person (see #35, 43 et passim).

As will be noted in the translator's comments, some of these assertions are not verifiable because no one has found the headstone with the epitaph cited by Torres y Vargas (#35). In another place, his text remarks on the highly unusual hailstorm in 1614 that he says, "I saw" (#69). But when enrolled at Salamanca in September of 1635, the university authorities wrote that Diego Torres y Vargas was "twenty years old," meaning that he might not yet have been born in 1614.[9] Even if he had been born in 1614, would an infant be able to state 30 years later, "I saw"? One explanation is that Torres y Vargas was exaggerating; a second that he didn't write the report; a third that this may be a question of style, since claiming to "have seen with one's own eyes" might be his way of stating, "I was alive when this happened."

Finally, phrases in Latin about classical history or theological commentary on biblical texts remind us that he was a criollo who had been educated at a Spanish university. While not always relevant to the historical event, his classicisms and Latinisms are characteristic of educated manuscripts at that time.

FEUDALISM IN TORRES Y VARGAS

It is easier to say that feudalism as an economic system was disappearing in the seventeenth century than to define what feudalism meant to that century's cultural and social values. Feudalism is commonly identified with the Middle Ages when it functioned as both an economic and social system based on land use and military obligations. However, its vestiges in society and culture endured much longer. One footprint of feudalism in Torres y Vargas is the attention to titles and coats of arms (see #13, 30, 44).

To understand the feudal references in Torres y Vargas, readers today need to recall the difference between the right to use property and the power over it conferred by ownership. Beginning about 800 AD during the rule of Charlemagne, feudal law gave peasant farmers not **ownership** of land, but **use** of it to produce food for the people of the region. At the same time, titled nobility **defended** rather than **owned** land. Feudalism linked the farmers to the lords of the region by ensuring a portion of agricultural produce was given in exchange for protection from bandits or foreign armies. The feudal system also created a series

---

[9] Cited in Medrano, 1999, pg. 150. See our commentary below in "Who Was Diego Torres y Vargas."

of relationships among the nobles. Much as farmers were bound to loyalty toward their lords, each of the lords was similarly bound to a lord who had higher status. The bonds of feudalism were repeated among the nobles until reaching the level of the king. Feudalism, however, was not static. Like other European rulers seeking to centralize the monarchy, the Catholic kings, Fernando of Aragon and Ysabel of Castile,[10] preferred to govern with as few noble lords as possible, going directly to the peasants for support and tribute. Earlier feudal times had depended on a local noble to collect the tribute, take some for himself and eventually send the crown its portion. The centralized monarchy, in contrast, supervised the collection of tribute and took its portion before sending on the rest back to the local lord. Limiting the number of nobles made it easier for royal authority to settle land disputes, control armies and put only loyal subjects in positions of authority. This was one of the ways the new monarchies of fifteenth and sixteenth century Europe took the "power of the purse" away from the nobles, reserving it for themselves.

At the end of the fifteenth century when Columbus was preparing for his transatlantic voyage, civil strife and wars for dynastic rights had challenged the ability of lords to demand tribute. The problem of feudalism in its late stages was that it no longer produced enough income to have the lords live off the rents as once before. The noble title often seemed only to be an excuse to collect rent from people living in the territory designated by a royal document. Sometimes the holdings had been split so many times among heirs that they provided only the most meager of incomes. Spain abounded with *hidalgos*, literally *"hijos de algo"*, i.e., born into a titled noble family (*algo*) but with next to no income from feudal holdings. Moreover, the frequency with which nobles provided income for their children born out of wedlock confused the situation still more.

COLUMBUS AND PONCE DE LEÓN

When Christopher Columbus entered the Spanish court, the monarchs knew that after centuries of internal battles against the Moors, the kingdoms needed to "catch up" with the overseas trading networks of other nations. But

---

[10] To be referred to in the rest of this essay in the English: "Ferdinand and Isabella."

before embarking westward in 1492, Columbus demanded a contract with the monarchy that would allow him hereditary rule over any lands he might discover on the way to China. Queen Isabella was reluctant to grant this feudal privilege because it went against the existing policy that had been successfully launched in an earlier colonization of the Canary Islands. Isabella simply appointed the governor of the Canaries, who could be removed from command without prejudice. Columbus was insistent on hereditary rights, however, and might easily have sought patronage for his expedition from another country. Reluctantly, Queen Isabella drew up the *Capitulaciones de Santa Fé* that conferred hereditary feudal powers upon the explorer. As a result, Columbus claimed Española, and eventually Puerto Rico and Cuba as "proprietary colonies." The title meant that the Columbus' family had the right to make grants of land, while the monarchy was bound to obligations such as defense of the colonies if attacked. These policy decisions and the contract with Columbus affected the earliest history of Puerto Rico and Juan Ponce de León.

Columbus intended to finance his colonies by having the settlers pay for the land granted to them. He attracted hidalgos who had no chance for territory in Spain, where virtually all lands had already been claimed. Columbus' proprietary colony was an arrangement similar to what the English would later award to the Lord of Baltimore for the Maryland colony and to William Penn in Pennsylvania. Although the economic vitality of feudalism was receding, holding a title could guarantee income from inherited lands. We know from many sources, not the least of which is Cervantes' *Quixote*, that the adventurous *"indianos"* (persons who had lived in the Indies, i.e., the Americas) returned to the mother country and used their wealth accumulated in the colonies to marry daughters of titled, but often impoverished families. There was a prejudice against them as if they were *nouveau riche* because in many instances, they were uneducated and crude, even if wealthy. Such prejudice probably reflects the jealousy the Spanish lesser nobility felt against these well-to-do persons from the colonies. Ironically, settlers in rich colonies like Mexico and Peru often became wealthier with higher incomes than actual nobility in Spain who depended on residual pensions. In this scenario, titles were important to the American settlers: they provided prestige, allowing the adventurers to claim status as nobility, while escaping stigmatization as pretentious indianos.

THE CANARY ISLANDS AND THE CARIBBEAN ISLANDS

After 1477, Queen Isabella implemented a colonization policy for the Canary Islands that gave her the right to name a military ruler as governor. When using the army to suppress native revolts, the governor answered directly to the monarchy. He had no feudal rights of his own. The Canarian natives who laid down their arms and converted were not enslaved as enemies, but were treated rather as peasants under their own native chiefs. The chiefs who became Christians were allowed to rule the land as nobles, making the same oath of loyalty to the monarchy as Spanish lords, and not to the governor. Although the converted chiefs could manage affairs for their peoples, they lacked the power to marshal troops, as had been done by feudal lords. Under this approach, the native chief, Guanarteme of Gran Canaria was baptized at court in 1481. He took the name, "Fernando," with the king as his godfather, professing loyalty to the Spanish kings. The same policy was intended to be applied to the neighboring Canarian island of Tenerife, whose military campaign began in 1496. It makes sense, then, that when Columbus reported his discovery of new islands in 1492, the Queen wanted to use the existing Canarian policy for Española and Puerto Rico.

In this feudal model, conversion to Catholicism depended on the native ruler: once baptized and pledging fealty, it was expected that the chief's "subjects" would become Christians. This group conversion by fiat was later considered to be inferior to evangelization that required converts seeking baptism to be examined individually for their understanding of the faith. This individual commitment is the model used today in Catholicism.

See: Anthony M. Stevens-Arroyo. 1993. "The Inter-Atlantic Paradigm: The Failure of Spanish Medieval Colonization of the Canary and Caribbean Islands" *Comparative Studies in Society and History* 35:3 (July 1993) 515–543.

Catholic piety was another trait expected of people from truly established Spanish noble families. Noble Spanish families had ancestors who had defended the Catholic faith in wars against Muslims and Protestants. This is reflected in how Torres y Vargas connects governors and commanders in Puerto Rico to wars with religious linkage in Europe. Social status was often increased by practicing one's religion faithfully, unlike the attitudes of a hundred years later when the French Enlightenment expected religious skepticism from elites. Thus, Torres y Vargas provides details not only of administrative achievements but testimony about religious piety from leading figures (#46, 53, 64, 68, 76, 78), even telling us about one governor's virginity (#112).

We will see that Torres y Vargas had studied in Spain and likely knew first hand of Spanish prejudice against those born in the Americas. He missed few opportunities to show that criollos were equal to Spaniards, stressing heroism and titles derived or deserved (see #85, #124–127). Equality with Spanish noblity explains Torres y Vargas' focus upon persons with titles. This baroque emphasis on the grandeur of the criollos may be interpreted as a necessary step towards a Puerto Rican nationalism. The notion that Puerto Ricans were equals is found in Torres y Vargas and later writers would elaborate that idea into an affirmation of patriotic attachment to Puerto Rico.

We should recall that Don Diego came from a class of land holders in Puerto Rico. By the time he wrote, the feudal obligations of farmer to nobles and kings, like that of nobles to each other and to the king, could be satisfied by paying tribute in gold or silver. Even though the Spanish crown tried to limit the influence and growth of titled nobles, however, they could not immediately overturn the centuries' old practices of awarding rents, that is, guaranteed income, for those who held a title. This practice had such deep roots that as late as the seventeenth century, people zealously preserved such claims. Moreover, the upper class in Puerto Rico was more dependent on the income from such titles than settlers in richer colonies like Mexico where wealth generated locally from mines, land-holdings and commerce was markedly higher. The notion that one could be noble but also poor was not only common in Puerto Rico, it was also the experience of many in Spain. Additionally, the idea that rank brought income applied as well to the clergy of the church. In his own case, Don Diego was a canon of the cathedral, which meant that he was given income from government funds as a salary. The higher the title, the greater the income, so the maximum position of Dean of the Cathedral was more than just an honorary title: it also meant higher pay.

WHY ALL THOSE LAST NAMES?

If there was income from the land holdings of a family with the Ramírez name, as well as from a Díaz name, the family inherited claims to the wealth of both families. The first child of a marriage in which Mr. Ramírez married Miss Díaz, would inherit this claim from his or her parents. But there was an option for the second child to use "Díaz" as a last name, so that while the older child would inherit the wealth from the Ramírez side, the younger child would be guaranteed income from the Díaz side. On this account, the well-born would continue to use two, three and even four last names from the maternal and paternal sides in order to keep the flow of income to the offspring.

The land-holding class was not the only important one. Don Diego pays special attention to Spaniards with military achievements, showing that brave and noble soldiers were to be found in Puerto Rico (see #58, #124–127). Just as in Spain, where the indianos sought to intermarry with the established families, Spanish officers in Puerto Rico often chose to marry the daughter of a local land owner. This strategy bestowed social importance by matching the European status of an army officer to the wealth of a criollo land-holder. In this light, we need to interpret Torres y Vargas' observations about the eligible women in Puerto Rico (#84) as testimony to a general opinion throughout the Spanish Empire. There were many marriageable daughters in these social circumstances and military officers knew it. More importantly, such was the case with Torres y Vargas' own family.

We should not be surprised that there is little mention of native Taínos in this document. The Taínos of Boriké[11] were generally considered to have been Christianized by 1647 when Torres y Vargas wrote. Most historians now recognize that despite the suppression of native uprisings and the fatal impact of various epidemics, Taínos and Taínas survived genetically within the population of Puerto Rico. However, culturally and religiously, they were considered by Torres y Vargas to have assimilated as loyal subjects of the king. All had been baptized with Christian names by 1647. They wore European-style clothes, spoke Spanish and often had married into Spanish families, thus gaining equality within the system, albeit at a non-elite level. Torres y Vargas was aware of Spanish prejudices against Taínos and Taínas. In fact, he suggests that the Spanish custom of avoiding the original Indian names for places in Puerto Rico is quaint (#9) and one not preferred by criollos.

Torres y Vargas reserves the category of "Indians" to the inhabitants of other Caribbean islands that were under the jurisdiction of the diocese, where these groups lived apart and had not adopted Spanish dress or language (#86–98). He also claims that some Indians were culturally disposed to barbarism (#89), prone to violence (#92), to deceit (#96) and even to cannibalism (#98). The sav-

---

[11] Boriké has become a favorite spelling to reproduce the native language: the more traditional form in Spanish is "Borinquen." Torres y Vargas uses "Boriqueña" (#4).

ing grace is that Torres y Vargas reserves such labels to only some specific groups and incidents and not to all Indians.

COLONIAL SAN JUAN AND THE SYSTEM OF TRADE

The term "civilization" is related to "the building of cities." Clearly, cities concentrated many people into a relatively small area, meaning that in the city markets, buying and selling would offer better opportunities for commerce. Trade had always depended on cities, not only for the Greeks and Romans, but as an integral part of the feudal system as well. By the seventeenth century, commercial wealth and intermarriage had allowed city merchants to enter the circle of Spain's social register of noble birth and acquire titled agricultural land. In order to follow the same path to upward mobility, settlers in the colonies relied on wealth generated by American cities.

Juan Ponce de León, Torres y Vargas' ancestor and the eventual founder of the colony of Puerto Rico, was a hidalgo, the son of a noble but with no clear title to inherited lands in Spain for himself. When he came with Columbus in 1493, Ponce de León expected to replicate Spanish feudal control of land and workers in America by invoking the *encomienda*. This was based on a medieval institution (*behetría*) of Spain's effort to take back territory from the Moors. It allowed residents of newly conquered territories with no Christian lord to legally choose a defender, who could exercise the virtual powers of a feudal lord. When Spain intensified the colonization of the Canary Islands in the fifteenth century, it had recourse to this precedent by fashioning a rule in 1477 to obligate the natives to work the land as a form of tribute to a land holder that the crown had designated — but without hereditary title. Such was the origin of the encomienda that was eventually used in the Caribbean by Spain.

Very early, Columbus' plan to colonize the Indies by making land grants with an encomienda of Taíno workers ran into trouble with hidalgos like Ponce de León.

- There was not very much arable land to be granted on the islands.
- Little profit could be generated from trade because few of the products that grew in the tropics had commercial value on European markets

HOW CITIES FOSTERED COMMERCE

Cities provided the place where raw materials could be elaborated and made into saleable products. For instance, the city resident buys wool at the market from the shepherd. In his house, the city dweller uses a spinning wheel to turn the wool into yarn. The same, or other city residents, turn the yarn into cloth, dye it, turn the cloth into a jacket, or some other article of clothing and sell it at the market. In the United States, we still see last names such as "Fuller" for those who cleaned the wool, "Weaver" for those who made the cloth, "Taylor" for those who made clothing, etc.

Not only were cities places to buy and sell raw materials and products, they eventually became places to store materials, products and, eventually, money. Merchants worked together in town councils to prevent unfair practices and cheating in the markets. Banks were created to safeguard money and loans.

Merchants realized that they could make a greater profit if their products were hard to get in a particular region. For instance, you buy a jacket made of wool cheaply because wool is everywhere in your region. But if you take the wool jacket to a region where there are few sheep, it becomes uncommon. The same principle of common-uncommon applies to growing flax, from which linen is made. The best garment for summer is a linen garment, while wool is best for winter. Merchants transported goods between the sheep-herding region and the flax-growing areas. By selling linen where wool is easily available, a merchant could sell the linen jackets at price high enough to buy two wool shirts with the profit from his sale. The same merchant returns to the first flax-producing region, and sells the two wool jackets for four linen shirts. Once again, the price is greater where the product is uncommon. The merchant becomes richer than the suppliers as long as he moves the goods to places where the supply is less than the demand. **Such is the Law of Supply and Demand.**

The richest trade consisted of importing and exchanging goods from as far away as possible. Thus, for example, Marco Polo leaves Venice and goes to China. Cities like Venice monopolized trade with Muslims in the cities of the Holy Land who sold goods that came in from far away places under Muslim rule.

Portugal, with no coast on the Mediterranean, began a process of sailing south along the African coast in order to round the African continent on the way to India and China. They set up way stations or *factorías* where the ships could stop to take on food and fresh water on the long journey. Columbus had married into a Portuguese family that had holdings on the island of Madeira, which was part of the African sailing route. Watching the tides and rethinking his own previous experiences on ships sailing northward near Iceland, however, Columbus concluded that one could instead sail west across the Atlantic to reach China and Japan (Cipango), places described by Marco Polo and other travelers.

Columbus thought the Caribbean Islands — he called them the "Indies" because he supposed they were close to India — would be a stop-off before trade with China. Much like a store on a turnpike has a monopoly on travelers, Columbus hoped his islands would be indispensable way stations on the Atlantic route to China. He would make money from the travelers of his route to the Indies.

and neither the natives nor the colonists had money to buy what merchants from Europe would bring.

• Commerce with the native Taínos was based upon exchanges of shiny brass and glass beads to be used as jewelry, usually in exchange for food.

Since neither land grants nor trade provided enough funds to run his proprietary colony, Columbus looked for quick profits. The surest path was gold, and to satisfy the labor needs for gold mining Columbus opted for enslaving the Taínos. Queen Isabella interfered with this plan. She prohibited making the Taínos into slaves, insisting that the natives be held under an encomienda. Later, she would order those already sold in Spanish slave markets to be returned to

---

THE ENCOMIENDA AND SLAVERY

The encomienda was intended to ensure agricultural labor on the new lands that the Spaniards claimed in the Americas. Legally, there was a significant difference between the encomienda and slavery. Yet, in practice, forcing the natives to work the land approximated their enslavement. Church leaders, and not only Bartolomé de Las Casas, were outspoken in denouncing mistreatment of the Indians. Early on, the Spanish Queen prohibited slavery for the Taínos and Taínas: she forbade making them property to be bought and sold. However, if the natives refused to work or worse — if they revolted against the Spanish colonial authority — the law allowed the rebels to be punished with slavery. This, after all, had been a practice since the time of the Roman Empire.

The colonization of the Americas provided new legal challenges at a time when feudal laws were under great stress. Profession of the Catholic faith was hugely important in the colonies for fashioning a secure status for the American natives within its economic and political order. While today conversion is often viewed as having been a violation of the Indians' freedom of religion, at that time Christendom depended on a single faith as basis for Christian temporal authority. When defenders of native rights urged conversion for the Taínos and Taínas, therefore, it was a path towards securing equality for them under existing law.

Las Casas went a step further because he also wanted the crown to recognize the Indian chiefs as "native lords." This would have made the Taíno caciques akin to Spanish nobles with hereditary title to rule over a given territory. The proposal made Las Casas very unpopular. The monarchy opposed creating additional feudal lords because it would have diluted the centralized power of the crown. Royal opposition to the claims of Columbus' heirs was rooted in this policy of shrinking feudal lordship. The same policy explains why Juan Ponce de León was given only administrative and military titles, but not one that would have made him the Lord of Puerto Rico. Even in the time of Torres y Vargas, the lack of a secure feudal basis for the social and political power of colonial elites caused tensions with their Spanish counterparts, who often presumed that the criollos lacked titles because they were inferior.

the Indies. To prevent future excesses, she also created the *Consejo de las Indias* to collect relevant data on the colonies, process requests, and advise the crown about policy in the colonies.

Back in Española, things went even more ominously for Columbus because the native Taínos did not accept the authority of the Spanish to make them work at finding gold or to feed Spaniards as a form of tribute. Finally, sensing the unrest both among frustrated settlers and angry natives, a soldier named Francisco de Roldán engineered a major revolt against the Columbus' family in 1497 by joining forces with Española's *caciques*, or Taíno chiefs. The revolts, the abuses, the intrigues and the general decline of the native population, especially by imported diseases meant that by 1499, the colonization effort under Columbus was failing.

The sad trajectory of Columbus' efforts to become a feudal lord in the New World is the backdrop for the settlement of Puerto Rico. Confusion at court about the Columbus family's claim once the Admiral had died opened the door for Ponce to establish his own stake. The reputation and fame of Juan Ponce de León, after all, was of interest to Torres y Vargas who was a direct descendant of Puerto Rico's founder. Ponce, who already held title to property in Española, may be considered to have tried to "wipe the slate clean" in order to start colonization with a better understanding with the natives on the island of Boriké to the east of Española. After scouting the coastline of Puerto Rico in 1506, the year of Columbus' death, Ponce secured the support of the crown's appointed governor, Nicolás de Ovando, for his new enterprise. Ponce landed a colonizing expedition on the shores of Puerto Rico in 1508 (#44). Meeting with Agüeybaná, the local chief of the southern region, he sought to avoid the mistakes of excessive contact with native Taínos that had provoked the native uprisings in Española. This is one reason that his first settlement was far away on the north shore. Flattering his sponsor, Ponce called it "Caparra," after a place in Spain, near Governor Ovando's birthplace (#9).

Juan Ponce de León entertained the same feudal aspirations in Puerto Rico as Columbus had in Española. The Taínos of Boriké revolted in 1511, however, and Ponce's necessary armed defense wound up creating the same scenario of hostility with the natives that had so weakened the Santo Domingo colony.

Upon receiving news of the success in putting down the native revolt in 1511, the crown granted Puerto Rico a feudal coat of arms, one described in the text of Torres y Vargas (#11, 105). It was the sort of recognition that had been afforded victorious generals who had defeated the Moors in Medieval Castile. It represented a great honor for a hidalgo like Ponce de León. Lawyers in Spain, however, got a restoration of the Columbus' family control over Puerto Rico in 1512.

The Colonizing Efforts of Juan Ponce de León

When the Columbus' family rule was restored in 1512, Ponce lost his own claim to a feudal title. His family's good name before King Fernando helped him get a commission as *"Adelantado."* This title was used to describe a person who literally "went before the king's rule." It gave him a right to become an explorer who would claim discovered lands in the king's name. The appointment was intended as compensation for having lost title of Puerto Rico. The reason Ponce searched for Biminí/Florida (discovered on Easter Sunday 1513), was to secure rights over a territory.

The story that Juan Ponce de León was a fool seeking the "Fountain of Youth" seems more legend than fact. Oviedo, who is not always reliable in attributing motives, alleged Ponce sought the water to enhance his sexual potency. A more likely explanation is that Ponce was looking for a place the Taínos called "Biminí", famous for abundant water — possibly a reference to Florida's Everglades. The idea of a Fountain of Youth came from European fables of the time.

See Peck, Douglas T. "Anatomy of an Historical Fantasy: The Ponce de León-Fountain of Youth Legend," *Revista de Historia de America*, 123 (1998), Instituto Panamericano de Geografía e Historia, Mexico City.

Ponce left Puerto Rico for Spain in 1514 to report his discovery and secure feudal title to Florida from the king, not trusting in written documents alone. He returned to the island on June 15, 1515 to plan a colonizing expedition to Florida. The effort was made more difficult with the death of his wife, Leonor, in 1519. Ponce made various trips back and forth to Spain and the Florida coast before being fatally wounded by Florida's Ticumúa Indians in 1521. Taken to the nearest Spanish colony in Havana, Cuba, Ponce died from his wounds. His properties and title as *alcaide*, or governor of the fortress, stayed in Puerto Rico with his heirs.

This abruptly ended Ponce's rule. Even when the monarchy issued a royal document giving Ponce control over the military defense of the island with the title of Captain, he was not offered a hereditary feudal title as the island's ruler.

Once the Admiral's original feudal grant had been restored by the courts, the Columbus family set about undermining the authority of Ponce de León in Puerto Rico. To compete with Caparra, they ordered a new settlement in 1512 near the Daguao River (close to present day Fajardo), and named it "Santiago."

They began to cancel land grants and reassign native workers under encomienda in order to lessen loyalty to Ponce. Because it was vulnerable to attack from angry Taínos, however, the Santiago settlement folded. A later settlement near the Arecibo River (1515) was to be more successful and carried the Taíno name of the river onto the town (#23).

That same year of 1512, the Columbus family sent a lawyer, Sancho Velázquez, to investigate what Ponce had done in the time he governed Puerto Rico. Velázquez charged Ponce with keeping 50% of the gold due the Columbus' family. Claiming authorization from the *Capitulaciones de Santa Fé*, Velázquez tried to strip away Ponce's titles. A contentious official, Velázquez also fought with the new Bishop, Alonso Manso, who arrived in 1513. At issue in this dispute was how the Bishop invoked Church law to combat public scandals. With such dissension, the colony floundered.

While feudal-sounding titles provided some claim to social privileges in Puerto Rico, the lack of an economic base undermined prosperity in the colony. Although there were settlers in farms scattered around the island, the only source of wealth was trade. Caparra was miles from the sea and a port was needed with more ready access to sailing vessels. On this account, in 1519 the settlers chose a new site for a city, closer to the ocean than Caparra. The process of building and moving took place over a couple of years, 1519–1521. To make transfers

---

HOLDING ONTO PROPERTY AND TITLE FOR THE PONCE DE LEÓN FAMILY

The Ponce de León family may not have held onto hereditary feudal power, but the descendants had a family coat of arms, large land holding and social prestige. To replace the family home in Caparra that had been built of stone, the family oversaw the 1521 construction of a house built out of wood on the small harbor island of San Juan, opening to the Atlantic Ocean. Destroyed by a storm, it was rebuilt from stone and became the "Casa Blanca," the residence for the Ponce family.

Ponce's only son, Luis, was underage when his father died. In order to preserve whatever inheritance rights that might be restored, Juan Ponce de León's son-in-law, García Troche, assumed representation for Luis. Later, Luis took vows as a Dominican friar and appears to be the first native born American criollo to be ordained a priest (Murga Sanz, 1971: 243; 251–253). Fray Luis' name is listed among the friars in Santo Domingo in 1544. Eventually he was stationed in Peru where he passed away.

Nephews of Luis and grandchildren of Juan Ponce de León held onto the rebuilt Casa Blanca (1523) as family property for over a hundred years.

from Caparra and the hinterland easier, a stone-cutter named Martín Peña, built a bridge over a narrow channel that bears his name today. It allowed passage through a common pasture land (*Hato Rey*) just south of the city site, instead of a much longer journey eastward to get around the waterway. A second bridge named in honor of St. Anthony was built from this peninsula onto the small San Juan Island (*isleta)* and is referred to as the "Bridge of the Soldiers" by Torres y Vargas (#10, 81).

There is a historical question as to whether the name of the island is "San Juan" and the city is "Puerto Rico." However, if we recognize that "civilization" meant "building a city", we can rest with the notion that "the Puerto Rico of the Island of San Juan Bautista" represented the entire colony.

To officially elevate a settlement to status as a city, Spanish law required the establishment of several institutions. A church and a school were essential. The family of Ponce de León donated land in the new city site where the Dominicans began to build their monastery/convent named for St. Thomas Aquinas in 1523. The members of the Dominican Order were teachers and confessors for the educated classes. Other institutions required for city status were to follow. In 1524, Pedro Herrera donated money for a hospital named in honor of the Immaculate Conception (see #11–19). Finally, a city brothel was established in 1526

CITY GOVERNMENT IN THE TIME OF TORRES Y VARGAS

San Juan's management was officially controlled by the *cabildo*. This was a city council with a precedent in medieval Spain. It represented the *vecinos* or people with property in the city, usually by choosing a council of twelve aldermen or *regidores* who decided issues of city administration. Matters like the water supply, police, preservation of records on property, and supervision of the city's market fell under their responsibilities. They taxed residents to clean the streets, employed the magistrate (*alguacil*) and police, kept commercial records and responded to kings and nobles. The cabildo included the *alcalde*, who was chosen by the members of the cabildo for a set term.

Additionally, there was the title of *"alcaide,"* a word taken from the same Arabic root but with a different application. The alcaide was governor of the military fortress, responsible for its physical upkeep. The Ponce de León family sought and secured the title of "alcaide of San Juan" since this could be passed on in the family and remained a title. If the governor was absent, his role could be filled temporarily by the alcaide, as happened later when Juan Troche Ponce de León briefly assumed the governor's duties (see #50).

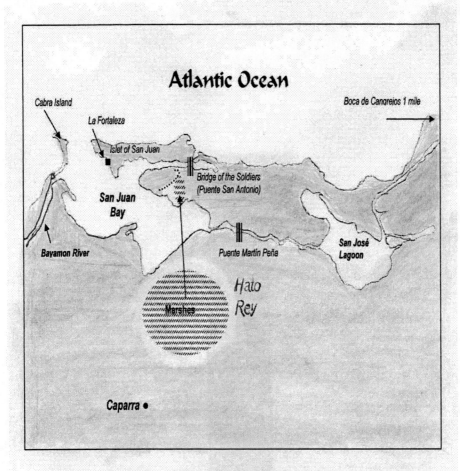

Map i : Early Settlement of Caparra and the San Juan Islet with key bridges

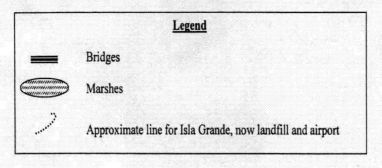

under Bartolomé Conejo, as holder of a prostitution license, an event the priest Torres y Vargas discretely omits.

While the Columbus family was proprietor of Puerto Rico, it appointed the governors. Sebastián Ramírez de Fuenleal, who was also Bishop of Santo Domingo, administered the island from 1526 to 1529. He found the city's population split between factions loyal to the Ponce family and those favoring the Columbus family. Often one group was unwilling to follow the orders of their rivals, and the resulting gossip, petulant social feuds and general mischief factionalized the colony. These city elites guarded inherited prerogatives within jealous nepotistic circles, a trait some say is still found in Puerto Rican society today. Those who were outsiders, such as Cacique Juan de Humacao, a Taíno convert, were often victimized. The rivalries were fed by the power of the cabildo to decide matters benefiting one or other faction. Only the passage of time and intermarriage among rival families mollified conflicts. A royal official from outside would have threatened such machinations, but a total white population of about 500 people did not seem large enough to finance such an office.

Meanwhile, the island settlements were not always safe from attack. In 1528, the town of San Germán was raided by the French and the village was burned, eventually forcing the settlers inland to a hilly location further south where the modern city now stands. Taking advantage of the colony's vulnerabilities, Indians, described as Caribs, burned the hermitage at Aguada named El Espinar in 1528, and martyred five Franciscan friars (#21). The Caribs attacked San Juan itself from canoes in 1529 (see #44, 54).

Bishop Fuenleal named Francisco Manuel de Lando as governor in 1529. The new official took a census in 1530 and wrote convincingly about Puerto Rico's strategic importance. Since it was the first major island encountered after crossing the Atlantic, or the last seen before setting upon the high seas, he said, it was ideally placed to protect the sea lanes. On that account, de Lando voiced a need for better defenses. In 1533, a stone fortification named "Santa Catalina" was ordered to be built (La Fortaleza), but there was not enough money to finish the construction, nor were there funds to buy cannons or hire soldiers, making the building useless as a fort.

While de Lando was governor (1530–1537), the gold mines in Puerto

Rico petered out more or less at the same time that the Spaniards began to exploit the silver and gold of Mexico and Peru. Colonists in Puerto Rico wanted to leave the island for the continents where they could be a part of trade and commerce. *"¡Dios me lleve al Perú!"* [May God take me to Peru!] was a cry reported to be on the lips of many. The governor felt forced to issue a decree that threatened extreme punishment for illegal departure. The chronic complainers in the population promptly sent off letters of protest to the king. As if these were not bad enough conditions, periodic hurricanes often wiped out all building progress, forcing people to begin all over again.

DEVELOPMENT OF THE COLONY

For this first-third of the sixteenth century, many people stayed in Puerto Rico because they had been ordered to do so. A quickening of commerce came in 1537 when the Columbus family finally surrendered its claims to rule the Indies. In exchange for its feudal rights, the family received a perpetual pension guaranteed to the Admiral's descendants. Despite freedom from a governor appointed by the Columbus' family, the habits of fighting with each other proved to be stubbornly ingrained among the cabildo members. The next seven years were rife with factionalism, each side appealing to the king against the other. In 1544 the king began to appoint governors to "clean up" the factionalism. Twenty years later in 1564, the governors began to be military men who were prepared for the problem of attacks on Puerto Rico from foreign powers.

When the legal settlement with the Columbus family placed the colony completely under royal rule in 1537, however, it brought much needed royal spending on city defenses. The monarchy moved towards investments in defense of the island, because until then it had seemed foolish to spend the crown's money on a colony whose sole proprietors were Columbus family members. In 1538 orders came to complete La Fortaleza. Some experts advised the king that de Lando had made a bad choice of location to guard the harbor. Gonzálo Fernández de Oviedo wrote: "only blind men would have chosen such a site for a fort." Torres y Vargas dismisses this criticism, however, observing that the site had been adequate when the attackers were Indians. He then praises the spectacular view from its windows, comparing the scenery to "a Flemish landscape" (#54).

A better military location overlooking the entry to the harbor in 1539 was chosen for what was to become El Morro Castle. Authorization was also given to rebuild the Cathedral with stone, since a hurricane in 1529 had destroyed the previous place of worship made of wood and thatch. Despite these improvements in the city of San Juan, the economy of Puerto Rico remained relatively stagnant, especially when compared to Mexico and Peru. One poet wrote: "*Este que siglos ha fue Puerto Rico/ hoy debiera llamarse Puerto Pobre.*" [This, which ages ago was a *Rich Port* / should now be called *Poor Port*.]

The embarrassing early failures in leadership from the *vecinos* of Puerto Rico are not related in the text of Torres y Vargas. It may be that he lacked documents about the conflicts. But since his text does contain oral testimony about other events during those early years from 1537 until 1564, another explanation seems more likely. He probably decided that since his historical purpose was to praise Puerto Rico and its people, it would be counterproductive to dwell upon some ugly moments. Thus, Torres y Vargas would be neither the first nor the last historian to be selective about his reporting.

We know that by 1550 commerce had begun to increase. Boats stopped for fresh water and food supplies, wood and rope were sold to restock the ships and leather (from hides) — the sixteenth century equivalent of plastic — brought in some currency. There was also an effort to establish sugar cultivation and processing. Ginger was a reliable cash crop since it produced a yellow dye for cloth manufactured elsewhere. Life in the Puerto Rican colony had become more bearable.

Nonetheless, the overall neglect and underdevelopment of the colony is inescapable, even for a favorably disposed historian like Torres y Vargas. The passage of nearly a hundred years had intensified the conditions of scarcity. The Thirty Years' War that was being waged when he wrote still prevented peaceful trade and expansion, further impeding the island's economic development. The Spanish Bishop of Puerto Rico, Damián López de Haro whom Torres y Vargas served, wrote a report that included a sonnet about the sparse population, the rapacious speculation, the lack of urban infrastructure (not even wells for drinking water), rampant poverty, lack of cultural refinement of women and the infernal heat in San Juan.

POEM CITED BY BISHOP DAMIÁN LÓPEZ DE HARO

Esta es Señora una pequeña Islilla
falta de bastimientos y dineros,
andan los negros, como en esa, en cueros,
y hay más gente que en la carcel de Sevilla:

Aquí están los blasones de Castilla
en pocas casas muchos caballeros,
todos tratantes de xinxibre y cueros
los Mendozas, Guzmanes y el Padilla;

ay agua en los algibes si a llovido,
Iglesia Catedral, clérigos pocos,
hermosas damas faltas de donaire,
la ambición y la embidia aquí an nacido,
mucho calor y sombra de los cocos,
y es lo mejor de todo un poco de ayre.

* * *

This is, lady, a small island
With few supplies and little money,
Negroes walk around clad only in their skins,
and you'll find more people in the Seville jail;

Here are the coats of arms of Castile
In a few houses, many gentlemen,
All of them dealing in ginger and hides –
The Mendozas, Guzmanes and Padilla;

There is water in the reservoirs when it rains.
We have a Cathedral and few clergy,

Beautiful ladies with little elegance,
Ambition and envy have been born here.
There is great heat and shade from the coconut palms,
And, best of all, a little breeze.[12]

Some might say this poem portrays Spanish prejudice against Puerto Ricans. However, we ought to note that the composition was not original to the bishop, but likely from popular culture: these may even have been the words of a tavern song. It is not clear if the bishop intended to caricature Puerto Rico or repeated the poem just to give other Spaniards an idea of what he was up against. Even if we do not know the full story, however, the contrast between the visions of Spaniards and those born in Puerto Rico is plain. Torres y Vargas did not risk ridicule of his homeland before a Spanish public, whereas apparently the bishop felt no such restraint.

TORRES Y VARGAS, CULTURE AND CIVILIZATION

Gonzalez Dávila had stated the purposes of his work in a letter of presentation to the king: *"Contiene este primer tomo las hazañas de la Fe Católica, la memoria inmortal de sus verdaderos triunfos y lo glorioso de sus vitorias diuinas y ganadas con el poderoso braço del Señor de los Exércitos, en el Nueuo Mundo de las Indias, donde la ignorancia de la idolatría era absoluta señora de sus coronas y reyes, fingiendo inmortalidad en dioses vanos, ofreciéndoles (como si pudieran algo) en vez de animales brutos, coraçones humanos, en tanto número, que causa horror y admiración el oírlo. "*[13] [This first volume contains the great deeds of the Catholic faith, the immortal memory of her true triumphs and the glorious {aspect} of her divine victories won with the powerful arm of the Lord of Hosts in the New World of the Indies where the ignorance of idolatry held absolute sway over its rulers and kings, spun immortality for its empty gods,

---

[12] English translation adapted by the editors.
[13] *Teatro* (2004) 59 [folio A2 in 1649 original].

(as if it could), sacrificing human hearts instead of {those of} dumb animals and in such quantity that it causes horror and wonder to hear of it.]

In contrast with this pejorative opinion of natives and the corresponding exaltation of Spanish achievements implicit in the words of the Royal Historian, Torres y Vargas is highly focused on the criollos of the Island of Puerto Rico and the City of San Juan. Even while recognizing that the criollos considered themselves Spaniards, the contrast with the attitude of the Spanish historian is clear. Had the entire account of Torres y Vargas been published by González Dávila, readers in Spain would have been shown a very positive side of all the residents of Puerto Rico, and not just the colonizers, commanders or governors from Spain. Moreover, Torres y Vargas' focus on his native city anticipates the contrast between the city populace and mountain farmers, or *jíbaros*, who later become symbols of the island's authentic culture.

The painstaking efforts that Torres y Vargas took to compile a complete historical narrative provide readers with many insights into the seventeenth century. Torres y Vargas shows deference and appreciation to his sources, some of which were probably persons acquainted with historical personages (#82) and friends or family members (see #73, 80). For instance, he "treads lightly" on scandals, such as attached to Governor Juan de Vargas, who in 1623 arranged for his stepson, Luis de Castro, to transport the Situado from Mexico to Puerto Rico. Shamefully, de Castro substituted lead for the gold in the boat destined for Puerto Rico and absconded with the money. The swindle threatened financial ruin to the investors who had paid for the expedition to Mexico, and the creditors in Puerto Rico demanded justice. The governor was confined to house arrest and the subsequent sad deaths of de Vargas and his wife are described sympathetically by Torres y Vargas (#70), who perhaps heard the story from family members. He does not dwell on the shameful events, however.

We can also discern in this narrative the importance of military families in the Spanish Empire. As indicated above, service to the King in the army was a signal distinction within the society of time, and this was repeated for Torres y Vargas who himself came from a military family. Even though he had chosen a career in service of the Church, Don Diego is knowledgeable about military details. He speaks insightfully of cavaliers in the Castle (#59, 63) and of a revellin (#59) — items of defensive warfare in the sixteenth century. He praises the defensive measures of new forts (#64, 66) and of converting the Bridge of Soldiers into a draw-bridge (#81) to better protect the city. He laments the carelessness that produced an explosion of gunpowder in the castle (#73); praises defensive measures to protect a vital bridge when under attack (#81); denounces payment to soldiers in credits (#60) and measures distances by "a musket shot" (#90).

Torres y Vargas' praise for Puerto Rico's "ordinary" inhabitants has a literary echo (see #122). The seventeenth century was to produce fictionalized biographies that described how common people could prove their worth "by their wits," instead of depending on noble birth. Named "picaresque," this literature featured characters who overcame humble beginnings to survive and even overachieve in a changing social order.

THE PÍCARO IN PUERTO RICAN CULTURE

Most experts consider the novel, *Lazarillo de Tormes* (1554) to be the prototype of the *pícaro* literature that became increasingly popular in Spain. Certainly, the style had taken shape in the publication in 1599 by Mateo Alemán (1547–1615?) of *Guzmán de Alforache*. The pícaro is of humble birth — in *Guzmán* he is, like his author, a converted Jew. He has a gift for language to get himself out of trouble and sometimes approaches the cleverness of today's "con-man." As a satire that plays on exaggerations, both of the establishment and the pícaro, it is not always clear which side is being ridiculed. This lends the picaresque literature a certain subversive, and even, revolutionary character. The earliest Spanish prose reproduces issues of religious orthodoxy. These were repeated in the aftermath of the Thirty Years' War in German works such as Hans Jakob Grimmelshausen's *Simplicius Simplicissimus* (1669). The eighteenth century novels, *Moll Flanders* (1722) by Daniel Defoe and *Candide* (1757) by Voltaire have less of a religious message and reflect trends of economic and social mobility.

The picaro became a stock character in Spanish theatre in the seventeenth century and appears frequently in eighteenth century operas. The picaros in Mozart's "Marriage of Figaro" and "The Magic Flute," for instance, anticipate the new thinking about the common people taking hold against the decaying old regime. In Puerto Rican literature of the nineteenth century, the mountain peasant jíbaro inherits these functions of the pícaro and eventually becomes an icon of authentic Puerto Rican culture.

The linkage between Torres y Vargas' work and what would later become Puerto Rican national pride is important. Living in a society that had known attacks and destruction from Spain's enemies for more than a hundred years, Torres y Vargas describes the chain of events that gradually led to Puerto Rico's acquired status as the Caribbean military bastion for the entire Spanish Empire. The pride in local achievements rivaling those of Spaniards would seem at first to detract from a uniquely Puerto Rican identity and to foster attachment to Spain. However, without the first step of depicting Puerto Ricans as equals of Spaniards in patriotic efforts during the seventeenth century, the nineteenth century would have found it harder to mount sufficient audacity to claim a distinct Puerto Rican nationality. Thus, the document written by Torres y Vargas, clergyman and historian of Puerto Rico, is a monumental first step in shaping a collective personality among the Puerto Rican people and well deserves an indispensable place in the historical study of those times.

SOLDIERS, HERETICS AND PIRATES:
THE THIRTY YEARS' WAR IN THE CARIBBEAN

Canon Diego Torres y Vargas wrote his description of Puerto Rico against the background of the Thirty Years' War. Commonly considered to have begun in 1618 over contested dynastic questions about rule of Bohemia, an entire generation in Spain and its Caribbean colonies would be ground down by the relentless conflict. Spain's foes included not only traditional powers like Austria and France but also emergent nations like Sweden and Denmark. During these struggles, Spain was drained of men and resources and saw its military hegemony eroded. When in 1648 the Treaty of Westphalia put an end to the major conflicts in Europe, it also rang down the curtain on Spanish world hegemony.

Standard North American history books generally provide only limited attention to the Thirty Years' War. After all, the Pilgrims did not arrive at Plymouth Rock until 1621 after the war had begun, so the effects of the European conflict were minimal on the English-speaking part of a future United States. Spanish colonies on the South American continent were similarly beyond most of the backwash of the war, so that standard Latin American history texts also have infrequent treatment of this conflict. In contrast, European histories have a great deal to say about the Thirty Years' War. Unfortunately, much of the focus is upon the continent, generally viewing the Caribbean as a distant appendage and unimportant player in the war. It is not uncommon for many texts to mention the Caribbean islands only as compensation for European powers that exchanged control as part of the peace treaties.

The Thirty Years' War, however, radically reshaped the Caribbean, and Puerto Rico was at the epicenter of the upheavals. The history told by Torres y Vargas is a necessary addition to traditional histories of the Americas, for otherwise the effects of this war in the western hemisphere would go unrecorded. The cleric's text provides not only an account from a Caribbean perspective of this first half of the seventeenth century, but also supplies precious insights into cultural and political changes. Instead of viewing the surrender of islands from one European power to another as merely a matter of changing colors of the possessions for world maps, it must be remembered that these transitions of power affected the lives of tens of thousands of people. Torres y Vargas' narrative provides a perspective on a population otherwise ignored.

A complete history of the Thirty Years' War is not possible here. However, there are various events found in the text of Torres y Vargas that should be understood in the context of this war. Some of these precede the outbreak of hostilities; others coincide with the conflict, while the rest occur in the war's aftermath. The following pages are intended to provide a set of references to this context.

BEFORE THE WAR:
FROM ISLAND WATERING STATION TO MILITARY OUTPOST

After Cortés had set himself up as ruler of Mexico in 1521, bullion had begun to flow in ship caravans from the New World to the Old. Charles, King of Spain and Hapsburg Emperor, used this gold and silver to support his armies in an attempt to make his rule hegemonic in Europe. As has already been described in the first essay of this book, the discovery of immense riches in precious metals on the continents eclipsed the meager economic value of Puerto Rico and the other Caribbean islands for sugar, ginger or hides. The role of the Caribbean in Spain's colonial plan was reduced to providing strategic bases to protect the flotillas carrying wealth across the seas.

Since the gold and silver from the Americas helped finance Emperor Charles' armies in Europe, his enemies decided to hijack the cargo before it arrived safely in the Spanish royal treasury. The passage of Mexican and Peruvian bullion through the Caribbean sea lanes, therefore, was menaced by opportunistic enemy ships. These attacks overrode territorial claims because the commanders of the enemy raiders needed to load their vessels with food and water stolen from the islands while trolling for targets of their piracy. From European perspectives, these hostilities in the islands during the 1500s rarely rose beyond the category of skirmishes and merit scant attention in history books. For small colonies such as Puerto Rico, in contrast, these raids had devastating effects on the fragile settlements. The resident population was terrorized by the marauders, who destroyed buildings and stole whatever they wanted with impunity. Fear of the enemy and despair about the failure of Spanish defenses was the common lot of the common folk. The drama of the destruction has been recorded for posterity by Torres y Vargas, thus rescuing these events from the prejudice of those only interested in the European side of the conflicts (see #3, 86, 90, 97).

By 1556, at the end of the rule by Charles V, Christendom had been irrevocably split into Catholic and Protestant realms. Vanished was the passivity of feudal times that had simply imposed the religion of the ruler on the subjects. Instead of insuring unity under the mantle of a single Christendom as under feudalism, faith had become a choice to be made by individual believers, dividing not only nations, but also families. This was the sad result of the inability of most political states in the sixteenth century to allow the freedom of religious choice. What ought to have been religious dissent in matters of faith was treated as the specter of treasonous revolt against a monarch with a different religion. All too often, religious dissent was met with state persecution: Catholics vs. Protestants, and Protestants vs. Catholics and even sometimes, both against their own kind. Charles' reliance on mercenary armies to put down the populace was doomed to failure, since gold and silver could purchase men's arms, but it could not possess their hearts.

Emperor Charles fostered reform of Catholicism in the hope it might bring order to his realms by accommodating the demands of the Reformation. Ironically, the Council of Trent (1545–1563) may have prolonged the conflicts instead because Trent transformed a shaky institutional Catholicism into a formidable and vigorous foe to Protestantism. Luther and Calvin had denounced a corrupt hierarchy and lax faith among believers. But Trent countered with reformist bishops and well-trained Jesuits whose zeal renewed Church institutions and restored Catholicism as a formidable religious force in the seventeenth century. Sadly, religious hostilities between Catholics and Protestants became ingrained during the Thirty Years' War, and some have stubbornly persisted to our own days.

The remoteness of the Caribbean from European control often left the inhabitants to their own devices. In 1570, for instance, King Philip II of Spain ordered the inhabitants of the town of San Germán in Puerto Rico to move inland to avoid attacks by the French. Such a measure did little to abate the raids in the Caribbean which grew in scale, especially after the failed 1588 invasion of England by the Spanish Armada. The English attacks of 1595 and 1598 on San Juan, for example, were ordered by the English Queen as an American reprisal for European attacks by Spain. But even though San Juan ultimately remained under Spanish rule, the attacks exposed the vulnerability of the Caribbean islands that served as a line of defense for Spain's caravans from the mainland.

The blame for converting religion into a source of division rather than the cause of Christian unity lies partly with Europe's rulers. They often hid their greedy desires for territory and hegemony by proclaiming that they were defenders of religion. By embracing the Lutheran or Anglican Church, for instance, taxes could be refused to a Catholic monarch on the basis of religion. Correspondingly, efforts at extracting back taxes from Protestants could be masked as necessary to restore Catholic rule. Surely, it was easier to motivate soldiers to risk their lives or to mobilize townspeople to finance armies by claiming that the war was necessary to defend the faith. Religion — although stripped of much institutional influence over kings — was increasingly to be offered to the ordinary people as the noble cause to go to war. This was the European dimension of religious conflict that freed faith from feudalism, but also antagonized Christians against each other.

It is impossible to understand this historical period without considering the shattering effect of religious division. The Thirty Years' War, it might be said, was violent on two levels: the earthly and the divine. Soldiers or sailors were also heretics or martyrs. The war was fought not only for territory or wealth, but also for salvation and redemption. The absence of a single religious authority to preserve Christian morality or rules of engagement in war allowed for brutal excesses on both sides. While the horrors of the Thirty Years' War were found both in Europe and the Caribbean, the war might actually have been worse in the islands precisely because the smaller populations suffered more devastating effects from the conflict. In contrast to Europe, where blood was shed to overthrow feudal rights, in the islands there was no real feudal nobility to displace or extensive church lands to confiscate. Hostilities in the Caribbean were characterized instead by a systematic and destructive intent with bloody results and — at times — of extirpation. There were vicious raids on settlements with the attackers going far beyond the replenishment of food and water in order to slaughter, kill, burn and destroy. In the seventeenth century, the Caribbean had become, in the celebrated phrase of Eric Williams, "the cockpit of Europe."

The religious and theological dimensions to the Thirty Years' War ought not to be ignored. It cheats the reader to ignore the religious concepts in play, because religious identity as Protestant or Catholic often served as a surrogate for nationality. Modem concepts of nationhood defined by culture and language were incubated in this war, emerging in the second half of the eighteenth century as definitions of the nation state. The subtlety of his difference can perhaps be appreciated by the difference between being "King of France" and "King of the French." The first notion makes the crown and the region determinative, with the people reduced to objects occupying a space. In the second, the people are the source of the monarch's authority. It may have taken another century for the dawning of the European Enlightenment to philosophize about this difference, but the Thirty Years' War compelled modern thinking about nation and nationality, religion and tolerance. The battles and theological wars served to finally separate church from state, allowing both to survive.

Although distant across the Atlantic, and a relatively small dot on a world map, Puerto Rico was a key participant in this war, as evidenced by the description of Torres y Vargas. Before the war would end, many islands in the Eastern Caribbean would be permanently transferred away from Spain and would fall under the rule of England, France, Holland, Denmark and Sweden. Since the Diocese of Puerto Rico was responsible for most of these smaller islands, the circumstances that resulted in transferred loyalties occupy a significant part of Torres y Vargas' narrative about his diocese. Europe was trapped in a war to make national identity non-transferable, yet in the Caribbean, the tiny island colonies were repeatedly surrendered or reclaimed in European treaties, as if there were no real persons living on those islands. Moreover, each transfer also represented a victory or loss for the rival Catholicism and Protestantism. Thus, the narrative by Torres y Vargas is written against the backdrop of issues significantly different from those encountered in Europe and often omitted from North or South American history.

As a believer, Torres y Vargas writes sincerely about religion. In such desperate times, miracles and signs from God were eagerly awaited as testimony to the meaning of suffering. But if he gives testimony to the positive side of belief, Torres y Vargas also offers a glimpse of the negative effects of war over religion. Military victories by warring states carried within themselves the seeds of destruction because the violence used to win the battle created deep seated opposition from the defeated that would lead to a new war. The atrocities committed by one side against the other became religious "proof" of the godlessness of a competing faith. Defeat in battle required an explanation of divine punishment for sin, and no mercy needed to be shown to foes unwilling to recant their heresy. As part of his intolerant age, Torres y Vargas does not enshrine the ecumenical values of today's world. Rather than import today's premises to a reading of this text, however, the reader is advised to take account of those times and troubles.

UNDER KING PHILIP II (1556–1598)

A cluster of pre-war events find their way into the narrative of Torres y Vargas:.

- The dynastic struggle between Protestants (Huguenots) and Catholics in France occasioned attacks in the Eastern Caribbean by the French on the Spanish for control of certain islands described by Torres y Vargas. [#3]
- The Spanish effort to control the Netherlands produced the "Army of Flanders," cited repeatedly in the Torres y Vargas' narrative. In fact, his father had been a member of this elite force. [#61, et passim.]
- The English attacks by Sir Francis Drake in 1595 (#55), and the successful one by the Earl of Cumberland in 1598 (#57), occupy a major part of the narrative. These attacks before the Thirty Years' War stimulated the build up of island defenses and helped preserve Puerto Rico as a Spanish colony against later assaults (#59–60, #63–64).

While England is seen today as a mostly Protestant country and France as a mostly Catholic one, both England and France had episodes of rule with the opposite loyalties before the Thirty Years' War. Charles was still Emperor when Mary Tudor, the Catholic daughter of Henry. VIII, ruled England. (In fact, she was married to Charles' son, who later became Philip II). France at that time was torn asunder by war between Catholics and Protestants (Huguenots) vying for the crown. Ironically, the victor in France was Henry of Bourbon, a Protestant, who switched religions in 1596 so as to consolidate his power. In this tug of religious war, Spain alternately saw England and France as friend or foe. But in 1556, Charles V abdicated his throne, leaving the difficult choreography of alliances to his son, Philip II (1556–1598).

In the first years of Philip II's rule, French Huguenots cast an envious eye on Spain's control of the Caribbean. While waging a dynastic war to snatch the crown of France for a Protestant lord, the Spanish colonies represented easy

---

CONFLICT WITH FRANCE

The first French effort for an American colony was in Florida. The Huguenot minister to the French king, Gaspard de Coligny, sent Jean Ribault to explore the Florida coast near Jacksonville and north to what became South Carolina. In 1564, Fort Caroline was built on the St. John's River, near present day Jacksonville. Anxious to prevent encroachment on Florida, the Spanish commander, Pedro Menéndez de Avilés was sent to expel the invaders, leaving from Puerto Rico in September of 1565. *It appears that while preparing his forces, Menéndez was favorably impressed with Juan II Troche Ponce de León, grandson of Puerto Rico's founder, helping the younger Ponce de León to secure a command for the expedition.*The French settlement was destroyed by the Spanish after a series of bloody encounters. The religious factor helped contribute to the slaughter that finally stained the hands of all, even though Spanish settlements at St. Augustine on the Atlantic Coast and Pensacola on the Gulf of Mexico prevented the French reentry into Florida. French interests then were refocused southward on the Caribbean islands.

In 1569, as they had in 1528, the French attacked Puerto Rico's outlying town of San Germán, then located near Añasco. The inhabitants relocated the settlement inland to its present location in 1573, following a royal decree to move inland in 1570 as one of Philip II's defensive measures. Nonetheless, San Germán was again attacked by the French in 1576.

Once the Bourbon Dynasty consolidated power as France's Catholic monarchy in 1596, the French concentrated on colonies in Canada.
- Samuel Champlain explored the St. Lawrence River in 1603
- Champlain founded Mont Royal (Montréal) in 1605
- Quebec City was founded in 1608

During the Thirty Years' War, the French once again targeted the Spanish Caribbean.

booty and quick wealth. Moreover, an effort was made to establish a base of operations in Florida from which to attack the Spanish.

Philip II was attentive to improved administration of the empire and was supportive of Catholic Church reforms issued by the Council of Trent. He inherited the policy of waging war in the name of Catholicism and using silver and gold from the Americas to pay the armies in Europe. He decided on a strategy to defend his American possessions by building fortifications against marauders. The Caribbean in general and Puerto Rico in particular, became the defensive line against attacks by sea against Mexico or the South American colonies on the Atlantic coast. Although very expensive, the construction of such defenses allowed his troops to become aggressive in Europe.

However, Philip II's enemies decided to build permanent bases in the Caribbean to keep pressure on the source of Spain's wealth, stealing the gold and silver whenever possible. In a sense, these enemies adopted a mirror strategy: if Philip was aggressive in Europe, they would be defensive there: if Philip was defensive in the Caribbean, his enemies decided to be aggressive. Philip II tried to attack and defeat his enemies one by one: in turn, they formed alliances to fight together. This was the background for the alliances during the Thirty Years' War that ended in 1648 with defeat for Spain under Philip IV, the king's grandson.

The details of this period are the subject of many fine histories, and can only be outlined here. However, hostilities with the French, English, Dutch, Portuguese and Swedes form the background of Torres y Vargas' history. The island of Puerto Rico became contested space in a global struggle. Don Diego wrote about the battles not only as defense of his native Puerto Rico, but more clearly as a defense of a vital part of the Spanish Empire.

SPAIN, PORTUGAL AND THE NETHERLANDS

The first Hapsburg, father to Charles V and grandfather to Philip II, had ruled in the Netherlands under a feudal title derived from marriages involving the rulers of Burgundy. However, joining Flanders with Castile presented problems to the Spanish Hapsburgs. Spain's Romance language and Mediterranean culture was very different from the heritage of the Flemings and Dutch who lived in a northern clime and spoke Germanic tongues. Moreover, the level there of commercial development and the degree of urbanization for the general population was dramatically different from Spain. Rule over these separate regions of the Empire would have required considerable adjustments to ensure mutual benefits. To further burden accommodation, the Protestant faith took root in the Netherlands before these major differences could be addressed. Social differences were magnified by religious conflict, and such religious differences made the military conflicts that ensued all the more cruel.

COMMERCIAL DEVELOPMENT IN THE NETHERLANDS

The Netherlands, or Low Countries, so called because so much of the region was at or below sea level, enjoyed excellent transportation in the sixteenth century. This was partly because man-made canals were used instead of roads to move food and goods. Unlike the mud and rocks that could cause wagons to break down, materials could be shipped on barges moved over rivers and down canals. The reduced friction factor also meant that less horsepower (literally understood) was necessary to move goods on these floating barges than on the bulky overland wagons.

Easier transportation for importing food enabled an increase in size of many cities in the Netherlands, while in turn the larger city populations enabled industry to grow. Most typical was the cloth industry that not only wove from wool and flax, but also could dye and embroider cloth. Prosperity for the merchants in the cities made them impatient with taxes and commercial restrictions imposed by the Spanish monarchs.

In the sixteenth century, the Protestant faith appealed to the many merchants because of an emphasis on individual conscience in decisions about faith. This preaching mirrored the business practice of many "burgers" as the city dwellers were called. Gradually, the control of the Protestant church by councils of elders became a model for city governance in political and commercial affairs. There had always been such things as "chamber of commerce," e.g. the *cabildo* in Spain. Among Dutch Protestants, however, the merchant wealth meant that these town councils were equal to or even more important than the monarch's power. Moreover, the amount of wealth created was no longer confined to the city's trade, but depended on increasing the distances across nations and continents. Thus, the Dutch cities became extremely interested in trade with the Caribbean, Asia and Africa. The long-distances around the globe would increase profits for the local Dutch cities.

The effort by King Philip II to maintain rule over these lands on the northern border of France would greatly contribute to the eventual decline of Spanish hegemony. The conflict was also important to the development of modern states because the war precipitated the emergence of republican forms of government, limiting powers of the monarch. Spain was Catholic and spoke Romance languages: Holland was Protestant and spoke a Germanic tongue. Even a partial observer had to conclude that although they had one ruler, these were different nations. Thus, the sixteenth century's Eighty Years' War in Flanders was an eerie projection of the seventeenth century's Thirty Years' War that redefined the European nation-state in terms of language, culture and religion.

Philip II also made the fateful decision in 1581 to annex Portugal to his empire. At a time when fewer conflicts would have helped, the assertion of dynastic claim to the throne in Lisbon was doomed from the beginning. The issue was succession to the Portuguese throne, and there were grounds for Philip's rights to rule just as there had been credibility to Portuguese claims to the crown of Castile in the time of Queen Isabella. Resistance to the Hapsburg claim came from the Duke of Bragança. The Duke and his descendants continually undermined Spanish rule for the next half century. They encouraged local uprisings and sought support from Spain's enemies, even from Protestants like Elizabeth of England. Spanish troops were needed to thwart the revolt, but maintaining

---

CONFLICT WITH THE NETHERLANDS

The Dutch revolt against Spain began in 1566 over restrictions on the towns and their commerce as placed by the king's half-sister, Margaret of Parma, the Spanish Regent. King Philip II sent a military man, the Duke of Alba in 1567 to deal with dissent. The Duke's solutions to conflict were frequently brutal and bloody. He alienated much of the populace when he executed Counts Egmont and Hoorn (both Catholics) who were seeking concessions from Spain within the framework of Philip's rule. Netherlanders, both Catholic and Protestant, revolted against the harsh rule by the Spanish monarchy in hostilities called "The Eighty Years' War," lasting into the seventeenth century.

In 1573, the brutal Duke of Alba was replaced by a more diplomatic ruler, Requesens (d. 1576), who in turn was replaced by Alexander Farnese, Duke of Parma in 1578. In 1579, the League of Arras reconciled southern Catholics to Spanish authority (eventually, today's Belgium). The Northern provinces (today's Holland) proclaimed the Union of Utrecht to align Protestants against Catholics and Spain. Shortly thereafter, in 1581 the Protestant cities proclaimed themselves free from Spanish rule and formed the Dutch Republic, in imitation of the Greek republic as described by Plato. A Protestant nobleman, William (the Silent) of Nassau, Prince of Orange (1533–1584), was proclaimed as Stadtholder, or protector of the Dutch Republic. This represented a variation of the feudal pattern because the city dwellers set limits beforehand upon the powers of the new ruler defending them. Eventually a later descendant, William III (1650–1702), would become King of England.

Spanish control proved both costly and futile. It should also be remembered that Portugal had established settlements in Brazil, along the African coasts and even in India, making the conflict world-wide. Annexation by King Philip II gave Spain's enemies an excuse to attack overseas colonies. The Portuguese matter presented more problems than benefits to the already strained Spanish troops and a deflated treasury. In retrospect, annexing Portugal to Spain was a vexing illusion, not unlike the later desire in 1776 for a new United States to annex Canada.

At war virtually around the globe, King Philip II's good news came in 1570 when his brother, Don Juan of Austria (see #93), combined with Greek sailors to defeat the Turks on October 7th. This is the origin of the Feast of the Holy Rosary. In gratitude, the pope granted all Spanish subjects exemption from fasting from meat on Fridays, which remained a custom until the II Vatican Council. Meanwhile, Puerto Rico had grown sufficiently during that decade to found a new town in 1579 for the settlers already living on the banks of the Coamo River, near hot water springs. Named after St. Blaise (San Blas, in Spanish), Coamo was the third incorporated city in Puerto Rico (see #8).

Perhaps the best news for Philip II was the implementation of the reforms of the Council of Trent around the world. These efforts strengthened the Catholic Church by installing a Catholic Reformation. A key role was performed by the Society of Jesus, founded by a veteran Spanish soldier, Ignatius of Loyola (1491–1556). The Jesuits became "soldiers of faith" and would win more battles for Catholicism than the troops in Philip's armies. Meanwhile there was a reformation of convent and monastery life, most notable for the Carmelite nuns of St. Teresa of Avila (1515–1582). Reacting against the medieval custom of placing widows or unmarried young women of the upper classes into convents — even if these women demonstrated no religious vocation — St. Teresa instituted much needed reforms coupled with a thirst for spirituality. All nuns were dedicated to strict observance, providing for no distractions within the convent. This was the organizing principle for the "Discalced" (literally, "barefoot") Carmelites. The reform also demonstrated vigor in sanctity and mysticism, not only for St. Teresa and St. John of the Cross among the Carmelites, but in a general climate for reform that was often animated by saintly mystics whose visions incited Catholic piety.

Torres y Vargas reflects on how the reforms of the council and the renovation of Catholic life arrived in Puerto Rico, even during a long and exhausting war. He writes admiringly of the Synod held by his bishop, López de Haro, (#42) and of a previous assembly of reforming clerics (#39) held in Santo Domingo. He praises the virtue of bishops and governors who practiced their faith (see #46, 53, etc.). An important episode in his history is the founding of the first cloistered convent of nuns in Puerto Rico (#17). He writes effusively of the Puerto Rican woman, Gregoria Hernández (#24). He relates her life and virtue in terms similar to those of a famous Italian visionary nun, Venerable Maria Raggi (1552–1600) whose biography had been published in Spanish (1604) shortly after her death by her confessor, Fra Pedro Juan Zaragosa Heredia. It seems Torres y Vargas and also the spiritual director of Gregoria Hernández had read this book. Maria Raggi was a widow, driven from the Genovese colony of Chios by invading Turks.[1] Miracles attributed to her fascinated the age and Bernini fashioned a remarkable memorial to her, placed in a Roman church in 1643. Most likely similarities to Maria Raggi in her married station and attacks by the Turks on her family became an interpretative lens in Torres y Vargas' history in describing Gregoria Hernández' spiritual life. Ironically, the Puerto Rican Carmelite convent admitted widows and unmarried upper class women in the "old" style that St. Teresa of Avila had reformed. It was funded with a donation from Ana de Lanzós, a wealthy widow who expressed concern for the economic plight of unmarried upper class women in colonial Puerto Rico, some of whom were related to her. Canon Torres y Vargas was later to hold the first canonical scrutiny for new Puerto Rican nuns, and the Carmelite foundation continues to exist today, although the original convent building has been turned into a fashionable hotel, named appropriately enough, "El Convento."

THE PAIN OF DEFENDING CATHOLICISM WORLD WIDE

There was a price to pay for Philip II's linkage of Spanish military power

---

[1] See: Judith Bernstock, "Bernini's Memorial to Maria Raggi" *The Art Bulletin.* 62:2 (June, 1980) 243–255.

as defense of Catholic rights in Europe. Spain was forced to declare national bankruptcy in 1576 and again in 1596, because the wars were too expensive for the government to maintain its obligations to pay suppliers and soldiers. Ironically, the importation of gold and silver from the Americas actually caused "poverty," because there was more bullion than goods for sale. The problem was inflation, because when the supply of money is greater than the demand for goods and services, the price paid for those goods and services rises. Soldiers with pounds of gold coins bid against each other to buy a loaf of bread. Sometimes the weight of the gold was more than the weight of the purchase, literally making some items "worth their weight in gold."

Spanish scholars like Juan de Mariana, SJ, (1536–1624) criticized Spain's financial reliance on America's precious metals. Mariana's *De Monetae Mitatione* (1605) considered inflation (although he did not use that word) to be a form of theft, since it reduced the value of the money held by the populace. Mariana had already developed a theory that allowed the people to take power away from a tyrannical monarch: adding inflation to the list of offenses had revolutionary repercussions.

King Philip II was wise enough to recognize the need for sweeping economic reforms. He decided to pay for the defenses of Puerto Rico, Española and Cuba by giving each colony a percentage of the gold and silver shipped from Mexico and Peru. This funding did not have to be processed in Spain and then reshipped back to Puerto Rico, but went directly to support the military installations on the islands. Called the "Situado," it was established by law in 1582. The rationale was that since the island colonies were necessary to defend the shipments back to Spain, a share of the cargo would be dropped off in the island to pay for its defense.

Before the Thirty Years' War, the major threat to Spanish seaports and naval convoys sailing in the Caribbean came not from army troops, but from privateers. A privateer was captain of a boat given a letter of "marque" that allowed raids on hostile nations with the tacit approval from his own country. This letter served as sort of warrant that kept the attack from constituting mere piracy, but also stopped short of making the hostilities an act of war. The French called the authorization *Lettre de Course* ("racing letter" or "racing commission"), and the term "corsair" is roughly equivalent to "privateer." These practices were already established in Europe, but were now extended to the Americas.

Spain usually transferred the Situado to Puerto Rico in large convoys, guarded by warships. The convoys would sail from Mexico and stay as close as possible to the shoreline of Cuba, Española and Puerto Rico in order to be protected by shore batteries and patrolling costal guard ships. This route became known as "the Spanish Main." The aggressions came from the non-Spanish privateers preying on Spanish galleons laden with gold and silver. High jacking the Situado was one of motives of Drake's attack on San Juan in 1595 (#55).

Not all privateers remained loyal to their countries. They would sometimes succumb to the temptation to forget their duty to turn part of their loot over to the king who had written the letter of marque. Instead, they would rob any and everyone. As such, they became unabashed pirates who acted outside the law. Knowledge of channels, sea lanes and tides enabled pirates to elude capture at sea. Hijacking just one vessel carrying Spanish gold could make a ship's crew rich for life — they just could not spend the money in the Spanish colonies without being found out. Unable to function within legitimate society, the pirates could nonetheless sell their booty as contraband, smuggled into the islands. Ordinary people, deprived of scarce commodities such as cloth or tools because of the war, would often buy these "hot" items at bargain prices. Since this was at times the only way to obtain needed items, the public tolerance for smuggling and piracy was quite high in the Caribbean of Torres y Vargas. Still, there was general fear of these marauders. Often these pirate captains recruited to their outlaw gangs any misfit, deserter, mutineer, or criminal seeking loot. Torres y Vargas was disgusted with their disdain of religious symbols sacred to Christians (#90) and ordinary people feared them on account of frequent displays of cruel savagery.

The Thirty Years' War opened the door for organized armies to steal the Situado — if pirates did not get it first. In 1628, without firing a shot, the Dutch Piet Heyn captured the entire Spanish fleet with its cargo and bullion destined for Spain. Pirates from Tortuga stole Puerto Rico's part in 1637 and 1641. The end of the war in 1648, however, would reassign control over key islands to the

English, French and Dutch. Spain's foes came to realize that they no longer needed to rely on pirates or privateers to establish footholds in the Caribbean. In fact, the pirates of the Caribbean would become a menace to all the parties in-

---

THE 'REAL' PIRATES OF THE CARIBBEAN

As outlaws from ordinary society, the sea bandits or pirates lived on islands where the access was difficult because of rocks and the like. The most famous of these islands was Tortuga, so named because it was shaped like a turtle's back. The small islands near Bermuda were refuges for the same sort of pirate life tolerated by the British. Authorities "looked the other way" as long as the pirates made the Spanish their targets.

The pirates, for their part, could not easily re-enter legitimate society. The stereotype of the pirate with an eye-patch, peg-leg or hook for a hand represents how in some cases thieves were branded for life: e.g. chop off the hand for stealing, cut off the leg to prevent escape, etc.

The Thirty Years' War invited competing powers to joust for control of Tortuga, which by 1629 had been transformed from an occasional hide-out from patrol ships into a year-round settlement or "Pirate Kingdom."
"

Tortuga became the point of departure for periodic landings on the northern coast of the Spanish colony of Española, which had been virtually abandoned under royal decree in 1603. In search of provisions for food, timber to repair ships and leather to be used for clothing and cord, the pirates sent out expeditions to land on uninhabited sections of northwestern Española. Camped out for weeks, these pirates used smoldering fires called "boucan" in the Indian language. This is the probable origin of the term "buccaneer."

Spaniards successfully retook Tortuga in 1631, but left a tiny garrison of only 25 soldiers. Spanish Tortuga was quickly demolished by Sir Anthony Hilton, head of the Providence Company and English Governor of Nevis, an island that had been captured in 1628. Hilton allowed both French and English pirates to continue to occupy Tortuga while he attempted to govern both Nevis and Tortuga from the English base on the island of Barbados.

The British and the French could not get along, however, helping ensure the success of the Spanish counterattack in 1635. A remnant of the French settlers took refuge on the mainland of Española — an ominous prophecy of the eventual establishment of a French-speaking colony. French reinforcements arrived on Española from Saint Christophe, another island taken from the Spanish. The combined forces assaulted the former pirate kingdom and Tortuga was once again held by the French.

After the Thirty Years' War, Betrand D'Ogeron (1615–1675) developed Tortuga as a legitimate colony, with amnesty to former pirates in exchange for allegiance with France. The promise of agricultural expansion on Española led to the formation in 1664 of the French West India Company. With such sponsorship, colonists left tiny Tortuga to settle on the Spanish territory of Santo Domingo Island. By the end of the century, the Treaty of Ryswick (1697) would formally transfer rule of the western part of Española to the French (today's Haiti).

volved. As the seventeenth century blended into the eighteenth, all of the former rivals began to coordinate their clamp-downs on pirates and smugglers. This elimination of lawlessness, however, came too late to the Caribbean to prevent a cultural legacy that allowed a pirate to claim fame as some kind of Robin Hood. (See pp. 30–31 above for this legacy in Puerto Rican culture).

The most famous of Philip's aggressions against his enemies, now defined as "Protestant heretics," was the Spanish Armada of 1588 sent against Queen Elizabeth of England. As mentioned above, the failure of the Armada led to attacks of reprisal on Puerto Rico: by the British under Sir Francis Drake in 1595 and the eventual conquest of San Juan by the Earl of Cumberland, George Clifford, in 1597.

CONFLICT WITH ENGLAND

Philip's wife (and cousin) Mary Tudor died in 1559, leaving the English throne to Elizabeth I. As the child of Anne Boleyn, Henry VIII's second child, Catholics regarded Elizabeth as a bastard child without the right to rule. Elizabeth consolidated her power by aligning instead with Protestants, passing the Acts of Supremacy and Uniformity and installing the Book of Prayer to supplant Catholic rituals. Catholics were persecuted, often as traitors, because they usually supported a Catholic claimant to the throne of England.

Because she was both Catholic and family to the royals, Mary Stuart, Queen of Scots, became involved in various intrigues to take the throne away from Elizabeth. As widow of a French prince, Mary's claim involved a foreign power. While French support alienated many of the English, it was a significant threat. When formally excommunicated in 1570, Elizabeth feared a revolt would soon follow. She imprisoned Mary Stuart, eventually executing her in 1587. King Philip II sent the Armada in 1588 to redress this execution by invading England so as to depose Elizabeth and restore a Catholic monarch.

The Armada is cited in English-language histories as a great victory over Spain and Catholicism. The defeat, however, was not because the Spaniards lacked nautical skills: the major problem was the weather. With visibility reduced, the English ships found it easier to attack the larger, bulky convoys filled with soldiers, avoiding the protecting Spanish gun ships that could not maneuver in the choppy seas. The 1944 Allied invasion on D-Day was postponed twice because of the same kind of weather.

In the aftermath of the successful English defense of their island, Elizabeth authorized attacks on Spanish colonies in the Americas by Sir Francis Drake.

As stated above, Sir Francis Drake was a privateer when he attacked San Juan, Puerto Rico in 1595 with another enterprising sea captain, Sir John

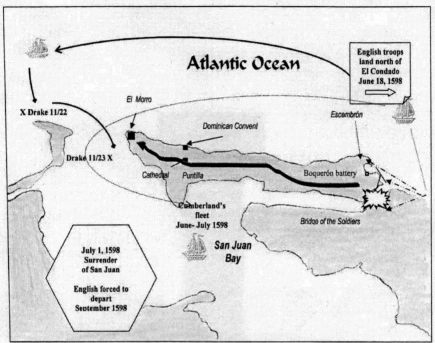

Map ii: Attacks by Drake and Cumberland upon the Islet of San Juan

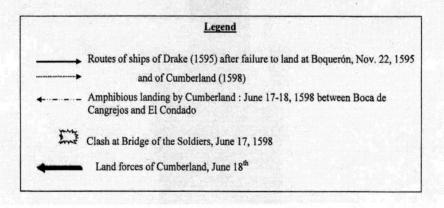

Legend

Routes of ships of Drake (1595) after failure to land at Boquerón, Nov. 22, 1595 and of Cumberland (1598)

Amphibious landing by Cumberland : June 17-18, 1598 between Boca de Cangrejos and El Condado

Clash at Bridge of the Soldiers, June 17, 1598

Land forces of Cumberland, June 18th

Hawkins.[2] Already famous for earlier attacks on Spanish possessions, Drake was unpleasantly surprised by the level of opposition he found in Puerto Rico. He nearly was killed the first day of the attack, when a cannonball fired by El Morro Castle burst through his cabin window, knocking him off a chair where he was drinking beer. The shot killed two and wounded many (#55).

Drake's strategy was to land troops on beaches outside of the line of fire of the recently completed El Morro Castle. Once the city was taken, thought Drake, the Spanish soldiers defending the fort could be starved out by a siege, since the garrison depended on food and water from the people. Drake was unable to follow this strategy and sailed away without having taken his prize. As mentioned above, Torres y Vargas cites the famous Spanish dramatist, Lope de Vega, who wrote of Drake's defeat (#55, see pp 27–28). However, despite his defeat Drake's testing of the island's defenses had exposed its weaknesses.

In 1598, George Clifford, Earl of Cumberland, had the ultimate success.[3] His initial landing was on June 16th near the Boca de Cangrejos in present-day Carolina. Marching down past the lagoon (Condado), one squadron pinned down the defenders of the Bridge of the Soldiers that guarded entrance to the San Juan islet,[4] killing Bernabé de Serralta, the captain of the defenders and two native brothers, Juan and Simón de Sanabria (#122), and forcing Spanish retreat to El Morro. Other English troops waited until low tide to cross the water of El Boquerón further north near the sea, although their ship ran aground (see #122). These maneuvers allowed Clifford to place troops on the beaches of Escambrón to the west of the city of San Juan by the 18th of June. Not only was the landing beyond the range of the canons of El Morro Castle, it opened the city to English occupation since walls had not yet been built. In the confusion created within the castle, Clifford sailed under the nose of El Morro into the bay, landing at San Juan's harbor (Puntilla) the same day, the 18th of June. Within a week, canons

---

[2] More detailed data is referenced in Salvador Perea, *Historia de Puerto Rico 1557–1700*, (1972) 111ff. where he cites English sources.

[3] These events are related in Perea, *op. cit.*, 121ff. He cites the English account by Dr. John Layfield.

[4] The Spanish *"isleta"* or "tiny island" allows no easy English translation. We have used "islet" nonetheless-Ed.

were placed in line to begin to batter the castle walls on the 29th of June. Without reinforcements or supplies, the situation inside the fort became impossible, especially with a devastating outbreak of dysentery. The Spanish garrison surrendered on July 1st (see #56).

The English victors disarmed the Spanish soldiers and sent them away on the 17th of July with the Governor of Puerto Rico on one of the Spanish ships, since the English were wary of trying to hold prisoners when their own position was so recently established. The out-going Governor, Pedro Suárez Coronel, however, did not sail away with the vanquished troops, but escaped to the Puerto Rican hinterland where militias were still able to fight a guerrilla was against the English invaders who ventured out of the city in search of provisions. Torres y Vargas comments on how such exploits helped Suárez gain a new post as Governor of Cumaná (#57).

If the Earl of Cumberland had been able to hold the city until another expedition could have been sent from England, Puerto Rico might have become English as later would Jamaica and Trinidad. However, English soldiers suffered greatly from the heat and an inability to secure supplies of fresh water and food from the local people. They soon succumbed to the same dysentery that had debilitated the Spanish defenders. This was the slow defeat inflicted on the English victors by the common folk of Puerto Rico who did everything possible to harass the invaders. Clifford sailed away from San Juan on August 27th, taking most of his forces, but leaving behind Sir John Barkley's troops to hold the city. However, Barkley soon had to evacuate San Juan in the first week of September 1598. After menacing other settlements on the coast of Puerto Rico, he also left the waters of Puerto Rico for good on the 23rd of November (#57). When King Philip II learned that Puerto Rico had been taken, he was already in his death throes and never heard that the island had been restored to Spanish rule before year's end. These English attacks are described by Torres y Vargas, and it appears that he included many details and perspectives gleaned from living memory of the events some fifty years before (#55–58). Don Diego's familiarity with military matters also enters into this part of his narrative. San Juan's residents knew, even if the moribund king had not, that the victory really belonged to Puerto Rico's populace that had so harassed the English.

PHILIP III AND PHILIP IV: THE THIRTY YEARS' WAR

Philip III (1598–1621) inherited the unresolved problems of his father. But whereas Philip II had tried to continue the outreach of the empire begun by Charles V, this younger Philip began a process of shrinkage. In 1603, he ordered all inhabitants of the north shore of Española to retreat inland and south because he could not protect them from raiders, any more than his father who had been unable to protect the settlers of San Germán, Puerto Rico in 1570. Philip III confronted the rising power the Dutch Protestants, who had organized themselves

---

A REPUBLIC AS A CORPORATION

The Dutch Republic formed the East India Company in 1602. The Dutch company was less bureaucratic than the Spanish "Casa de Contratación," which was more or less an office that simply recorded commercial arrangements for trade between Spain and the colonies. The Spanish Casa and the Consejo de las Indias, its successor, were more interested in regulation and insuring the monarchy's rights and percentage of income than in planning ventures. In contrast, the Dutch companies were more like "investment houses" that speculated on possible profits for each commercial venture.

The name "company" was adopted for these corporations because of the similarity between the sale of shares and the military practice of organizing a troops. A military company was paid from by the "spoils" of war: many victories meant much booty. For the Dutch merchants, this example explained the rewards of commercial investment. Among Catholics, the same word "company" was used to describe the formation of the Jesuits of Ignatius Loyola. He intended the "Compañía de Jesús" to respond to the needs of the pope with military-like obedience, being rewarded only by the spiritual "conquests" for the faith.

The Dutch company functioned like a giant corporation that hired its own explorers and soldiers, without depending on the monarch. The explorers and soldiers were paid according to the profits resulting from their efforts. The Dutch East India Company also founded trading stations around the world such as the colonies in Indonesia (1611), in Japan (1641) and South Africa (1652).

The Englishman, Henry Hudson (1570?–1611), was employed by the company to find a Northwest Passage from the Atlantic to the Pacific. This was how he sailed up the Hudson River in 1609. The potential for a fur trade alongside the river banks led to the founding in 1625 of New Amsterdam at the mouth of Hudson on an island the Indians called "Manhattan."

Eventually the Dutch formed a West India Company in 1621 because they saw the need to strengthen their foothold in the Caribbean. They had already founded Suriname on the northern coast of Brazil (1602) and later took the island of Curaçao (1634). The Dutch briefly held the Brazilian city of Bahía in 1625. They went to war with England (II Anglo-Dutch War, 1665–1667) and sailed up the Thames River in 1667, destroying much of the English fleet.

in a league of seven merchant cities. This became a Protestant United Netherlands in opposition to the provinces that sided with Catholicism. As the Dutch Republic, these cities launched sea attacks on Spanish colonies, including Brazil (1599), which was now a target because of the annexation of Portugal. The Dutch Republic also founded a Dutch East India Company in 1602, by structuring a committee of supervisors more or less akin to medieval town councils and Reformed Church elders. This board of directors supervised the foreign interests of the republic. Not surprisingly, the Dutch Republic became a model of government without royal control.

EVENTS DURING THE WAR NARRATED BY TORRES Y VARGAS

Diego Torres y Vargas lived during a time that was both bloody and glorious for Spain. The battles for possession of the island are famous. Of note within his narrative are observations about events during the war about key public figures.

- The Dutch attack of 1625 and the role of people born in Puerto Rico defending the city [#70–73].
- The leadership of Catholic bishops in developing the resources of city and performing works of mercy to benefit the people [#31, 37, 40 et passim].
- The defense of the Eastern Caribbean by governors of Puerto Rico [#81, 99].
- The eventual loss of Spanish island colonies in the Eastern Caribbean [#96–100].

Left unmentioned were the great impediments placed upon Puerto Rico's progress during the war. Supplies were scarce because Spain dedicated most of its resources to the military and because constant raids and piracy prevented the arrival of valuable cargo to Puerto Rico. People went without cloth for clothes, churches were deprived of statues or candles, libraries were bereft of books, store shelves were bare of imported products like wheat that could not be grown in a tropical climate, and so forth. The city of San Juan turned shabby in appearance to visitors. Skilled artisans were at a premium, lending a "homemade" quality to most construction. There even was no professionally trained artist to paint official portraits or provide churches with devotional paintings.

Nonetheless, Puerto Rico had a share of Golden Age glory in the person of Bernardo de Balbuena (1561–1627), appointed Bishop of Puerto Rico in 1623 (#38–39). His fame pushed Puerto Rico into the literature of the Golden Age with a poem from the pen of Lope de La Vega.

THE FAME OF BISHOP BALBUENA OF PUERTO RICO

Bernardo del Carpio o La Derrota de Roncevalles, was written by Balbuena in 1585–1600 while he was in Mexico. It is a poem 40,000 lines long, described as "chivalresque epic with fantasy." Written about an historical figure who fought the Franks at the time of Charlemagne, this literary genre is characterized by marvelous powers attached to swords, potions, and the like, each of which give the hero special powers to overcome evil enemies. If this literature appeared today it might be compared to tales of Superman or the X-Men of comic books and movies. Balbuena's work is indirectly mentioned in don Quixote III, 125:26–27: *"Mal la huvistes, francés en essa de Roncevalles."* It provides an example of how a past event, the defeat of the French, can be repeated with a contemporary political meaning. Here, it reminds the Spanish during the Thirty Years' War that they were capable of defeating their French foes because they had done it in the era of Charlemagne. Such comparison is another of the seeds of nationalism during the Baroque period.

Praise for the prelate from Lope de la Vega celebrates the victory over the Dutch attack of Puerto Rico in 1625.

Laurel de Apolo
By Lope de la Vega
Silva II

Y siempre dulce tu memoria sea,
generoso prelado,
Doctísimo Bernardo de Balbuena.
Tenías tú el cayado
de Puerto-Rico cuando el fiero Enrique,
holandés rebelado, robó tu librería,
pero tu ingenio no, que no podía,
aunque las fuerzas del olvido aplique.

¡Qué bien cantaste al español Bernardo!
¡Qué bien al Siglo de oro!
Tú fuiste su prelado y su tesoro,
y tesoro tan rico en Puerto-Rico,
que nunca Puerto-Rico fue tan rico.

* * *

Your memory will always be sweet, generous Prelate,
The great Doctor Bernardo de Balbuena
You held the Bishop's crozier
Of Puerto Rico when the fierce Enrique
Dutch rebel,
Stole your library,
But could not steal your talent, could not
Although the forces of oblivion were applied.
How well you sang to the Spanish, Bernardo!
How well to the Golden Century!
You were their Prelate and their treasure
And their precious treasure in Puerto Rico
So that Puerto Rico had never been so rich before.[5]

When he ascended the Spanish throne, Philip IV (1621–1665) plotted a strategy in the Thirty Years' War by not only strengthening his army defensively in the Spanish Netherlands (Flanders), but also by taking the offensive by attacking France while that country confronted a Huguenot revolt in the City of La Rochelle. Laid to siege under orders from Cardinal Richelieu from 1627 until 1628, the La Rochelle Huguenots were finally defeated in 1629. In another example of the church-state contradictions of these times, Catholic Spain helped

---

[5] English translation in Loida Figueroa: English version, pg. 97.

fund this Protestant revolt against a Catholic French King Louis XIII, to weaken a rival already engaged in a simultaneous war against Sweden. The events are mentioned in the narrative of Torres y Vargas (#3).

The Dutch attack on Puerto Rico in 1625 had an even more personal meaning for Don Diego since, as noted above, his father, García Torres, a Sergeant-Major of the Spanish garrison, was killed by a Dutch musket shot during the defense of the city. Clearly, the Dutch had scouted the island and its fortifications long before the attack. There were Dutch ships patrolling the coastline, and surveillance sorties in preparation for the attack. Dutch maps of the city may have come from spies. In fact, we are told in other sources that Puerto Rican mariners were reluctant to stray far the protection of the coast for fear they would be captured by the Dutch marauders.

In all likelihood, the Dutch intended not just to weaken Spain by destroying the city's fortifications with a frontal attack in 1625, but hoped to occupy the colony and perhaps persuade its inhabitants to switch allegiance from Spain and Catholicism to the Dutch Republic and Protestantism as well. If that seems outlandish, consider that the United States' invasion of Puerto Rico in 1898 that convinced some Puerto Ricans to reject Spanish culture and language to seek annexation as a state of the American union. Had the Dutch triumphed in 1625, Puerto Rico might well have become a Dutch base of operations in the Caribbean.

The invaders, commanded by Bowdoyn Hendrick, appeared on the waters near San Juan on September 24th with 17 ships, 2,500 musket-bearing marines, and more than a dozen canons.[6] Anticipating the attack, the Spanish commander, Juan de Haro, ordered trenches dug on Escambrón and Boquerón, which are the flat beaches on San Juan Islet where the Earl of Cumberland had landed in 1598. He also commanded pickets to mirror the advance of the ships along the coast line, demonstrating that no beachhead could be taken without immediate and stiff resistance. However, imitating the 1595 feat of Sir Francis Drake, Hendrick sailed into the bay in plain daylight on September 25th, right

---

[6] Much of the description that follows is referenced in Perea, *op. cit.*, 151–164.

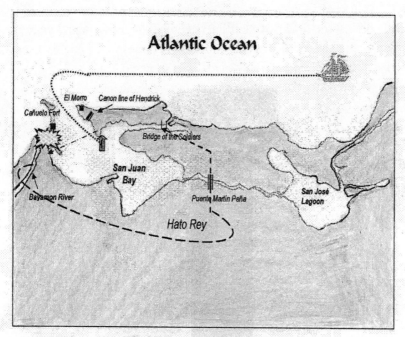

Map iii :Dutch Attack of 1625 with key engagements

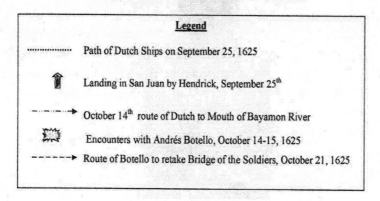

under the nose of the canons of El Morro. The castle's artillery was old and some canons exploded when fired. Also, the artillerymen in El Morro were unskilled and in the rush of battle missed their targets with appalling frequency. Within two days, the Dutch had taken the battery on the harbor island of El Cañuelo, disembarked at the docks of Puntilla, occupied the city and had begun to probe El Morro's defenses with marauding patrols. It was during one of these assaults that Don Diego's father, García Torres, was shot and killed (#61, 72).

In control of the City of San Juan, Hendrick made the Dominican monastery his headquarters, while the Spanish troops retreated behind the walls of El Morro. Laying siege to the garrison, the Dutch general ordered trenches built to protect his artillerymen from the castle's cannonballs. Feeling confident of his position, on September 30th, Hendrick sent an emissary to invite the Spanish to surrender. The response from Governor de Haro was dripping with sarcasm, masked with baroque elegance. Not surprisingly, the Spanish Governor, Juan de Haro, the out-going Governor, Juan de Vargas (#70–71) and the Dutch Hendrick were all veterans of the war in Flanders, as also were many of their officers and troops.

By October 3rd, Hendrick lined up his canons against El Morro Castle, just as had the English Clifford in 1598. However, as narrated by Torres y Vargas, the castle had been better fortified in the intervening decades (#58, 61, 63). At daybreak on October 4th, patrols of about eighty Spanish soldiers scouted the trenches. Inspired by the Feast of the Holy Rosary[7] that commemorated Spain's victory at Lepanto and informed by intelligence gathered the day before, a larger sally of fifty men was led by Juan de Amézquita on Sunday, October 5th. A Puerto Rican native, Juan de Amézquita de Quijano had spent thirty-eight years in the Spanish army and at one time had been held captive by Moors along with Miguel de Cervantes, the author of Don Quixote.[8] His raid killed sixty Dutch soldiers and confiscated weapons and large amounts of ammunition because instead of defending them, the trenches had made the Dutch soldiers like "fish in a barrel."

---

[7] At the time, the feast was celebrated on the first Sunday of October.
[8] See Perea, *op. cit.* p. 163 n. 16.

That night, Puerto Rican sailors stealthily boarded Bowdoyn's flagship moored in the bay, killing eighteen and capturing the ship and two Dutch sailors. Presumably, the Puerto Ricans had learned from the tactics of pirates.

The captured vessel, as well as the militia on the mainland, was under the command of Andrés Botello, an army veteran born in the Canary Islands who had taken up residence in Puerto Rico. He oversaw an effort to infiltrate the line of Dutch ships. The full story assumes something of a "Pirates of the Caribbean" movie script, with the Spanish soldiers in the dead of night on the deck of the captured ship speaking some Dutch phrases they had learned from combat in Flanders in an unsuccessful effort to surprise the invaders' fleet. Meanwhile, back at the siege of the castle, the Dutch unleashed a furious bombardment that finally toppled the tallest tower of El Morro on October 8th.

There was a lull in the fighting for the next week, as both sides assessed their resources. On October 14th, Hendrick decided to send seven launch boats with twenty soldiers each to the mouth of the Bayamón River on the mainland beyond the El Cañuelo Fort, opposite San Juan. This expedition was motivated, no doubt, by the lack of fresh water in the occupied city that is described in Torres y Vargas (see #10). Ironically, the castle under siege possessed a better water supply than the attackers because after the English successful seige in 1598, a large cistern had been built within El Morro (#63). Botello, lying in wait with his forces at the river's mouth, set a trap for the Dutch expedition. After killing some, he sent the rest of the Dutch solders scurrying back in their boats to the city. The next night, October 15th, using the dark of night as a cover for their maneuvers, the Spanish attacked the island fort of El Cañuelo and succeeded in burning it with sixteen Dutch defenders inside.

The final move of Hendrick came on the 18th of October as the Dutch general ordered two ships into the line of fire of El Morro, hoping that the Spaniards would waste their ammunition. But de Haro did not bite. Dutch annals suggest that these failures had led Hendrick to conclude by the 19th of October that he would not be able to take the city. Moreover, the Spanish counterattacked on October 21st with a sally outside the castle by Don Juan de Amézquita, this time with a hundred and fifty men. Meanwhile, Botello circled around the coast of the harbor, crossed the Martín Peña Bridge with fifty men and successfully drove off the Dutch guarding the Bridge of the Soldiers (#74, 85). These and other movements were made possible by the success of scouts carrying messages to the different Spanish commanders. Torres y Vargas tells us that one of these worthy messengers was a Puerto Rican named Francisco Villanueva de Lugo, who swam across the Loiza River to bring his message home (#73). Apparently, the Spanish commanders were confident that the natives were highly qualified for such duties requiring knowledge of the land.

The Spanish had now trapped the Dutch in the city, with the forces of El Morro on one side and the militia with Botello's men on the other. Audaciously, Hendrick sent his final letter demanding surrender to de Haro, threatening to burn San Juan if the Spanish did not give up. The response of de Haro artfully reminded the Dutch general of the resiliency of the Puerto Ricans. With this rejection, the bluff of the beleaguered Hendrick had been called. The next day, the 22nd of October, the Dutch began to retreat to their ships, withdrawing from their cannon line in front of the Dominican convent. Under fire from the castle and Botello's forces coming from the opposite direction, a rout was underway. Hendrick was mortally wounded and another sixty Dutch soldiers were killed. One of the Dutch ships, the Medenblick, was left behind, unmanned for lack of a crew. The Spanish victory would have been complete except that the Dutch torched the city as they left.

> "Valor tienen los vecinos para hacer otras casas, porque les queda la madera en el monte y los materiales en la tierra."
> "The residents have what it takes to build other houses, as long as there is wood in the forest and stone in the ground."
> —*Juan de Haro's response to Hendrick's demand for surrender*

De Haro tried to block the exit of the rest of Dutch ships from the bay by floating tree trunks in the passage to the high seas that lay beneath the guns of El Morro. The governor personally went to the walkways of El Morro to supervise the artillery's effort to destroy the Dutch fleet attempting to escape. One of the guns exploded, however, and de Haro suffered gunpowder burns and twenty-four wounds from shrapnel. Bedridden for nine days, he had nonetheless proven himself an effective leader of his men.

Torres y Vargas is clearly proud of this victory over the Dutch. The forces of Hendrick had lost over four hundred men, while the Spanish casualties were only about twenty. The battle had demonstrated the wisdom of the military governors who had improved the fortifications and the bravery of the defenders who fought brilliantly. Puerto Rico remained a Spanish colony and merited more attention and investment as a military bastion. In fact, the city of San Juan would not be retaken by an enemy until 1898.

OF BELLS AND BULLETS

A curious footnote to this incident touches New York City. The fleeing Dutch stole the bell of the Catholic Cathedral, and took it to New Amsterdam, where it was installed in the belfry of the Second Dutch Reformed Church. When the British attacked New York City to quash the American Revolution, this bell taken from San Juan was melted down into bullets by order of George Washington. Thus Puerto Rico's gift to the American War of Independence was in the form of bullets.

While the Dutch had been repulsed from Puerto Rico, attacks in the Caribbean on Spanish possessions were to intensify. The lesser islands became principal targets because the Spanish troops were occupied in defense of San Juan. Many of these islands formed part of the Diocese of Puerto Rico, and there is a description of them in the history by Torres y Vargas (#86–102). Moreover, because ecclesiastical and civil jurisdictions often overlapped, the military efforts on these islands were usually directed out of Puerto Rico.

THE OTHER ISLANDS

The Spaniards had left the island of San Cristobal under control of its natives, the Kalinago, assigning evangelization to the Diocese of Puerto Rico. Both the French and the English had eyes on this tiny island, with the British trying to occupy it in 1624. The French had better luck in 1625, renaming it "St. Christophe." After a massacre wiped out most of rebelling Kalingo natives in 1626, the island was divided in half in 1627 for both French and English, with the English shortening the island's name to "St. Kitts." By the time Torres y Vargas wrote his history, the Spanish had lost this island (#3). Isla Nuestra Señora de las Nieves, which is a little more than two miles to the southeast of San Cristobal, was also resettled by the English and renamed "Nevis" in 1628. (The future American patriot, Alexander Hamilton was born on Nevis in 1755.) Both islands became bases for attacks on Spanish island colonies. During the Thirty Years' War the Spanish also lost control of the islands Saint Eustatius or Statia (1636), Saint Barthelémy (1648 to the French, who sold it to the Swedes in 1784, before being sold back to France in 1878) and Saint Martin (also, Sint Maarten). All three lie some 150 miles east and south of Puerto Rico.(See map.)

The history of St. Martin figures in the history written by Torres y Vargas (#99–100). After the French settled in 1624 to raise tobacco and the Dutch established a station to gather salt in 1631, the Governor of Puerto Rico ordered an attack in 1633 to drive the invaders out and establish a Spanish town, protected by a military garrison. The St. Martin expedition was complicated because of distrust against the Portuguese troops. Portugal, annexed during the reign of Philip II, had revolted in the last years of the war against Philip IV, aided in part by support from Protestant England. How could Spain rely upon Portuguese troops to defend San Juan? The lack of money to pay the soldiers had heightened the possibility of mutiny. Governor de la Riva entrusted the defense of San Juan to local troops instead, sending the Portuguese troops to rescue the colonists on St. Martin. Although the governor was reprimanded by Spain for letting criollos assume such a task, the natives acquitted themselves well as defenders of their own city. The criticism from the monarch, however, came too late to be included in the report of Don Diego. Instead, Torres y Vargas concentrates on dreadful events that forced the Spanish to abandon the island in 1647, burning the fort and leaving the French and Dutch free to divide St. Martin between them.

THE DOMESTIC REVOLTS AGAINST SPAIN

In 1640, John IV of Bragança declared himself King of Portugal and led forces against the Spanish. Although Portuguese independence would not be officially recognized until 1668, this revolt clearly put to an end to aspirations for permanent control of Portugal by the Spanish royal house.

Encouraged by the assault on the Hapsburgs, in the same year of 1640, the Duke of Catalunya declared war on Philip IV. This was the so-called "Reapers' War," given its popular base among farmers resisting taxes. It lasted until 1659. However, while these hostilities were engaged, Andalusía and Naples revolted against Philip IV in 1641.

Despite reverses in the Caribbean, the islands of Margarita and Cumaná off the coast of Venezuela were successfully defended by Spain. Both became part of Venezuela when that country obtained its independence. Santo Thomé de Guyana, which was also part of the Puerto Rican diocese, was located on the South American mainland. Under constant attack by natives armed by European enemies of the Spanish, this settlement no longer exists. Trinidad was under attack from the Dutch in 1614 even before at the outbreak of the Thirty Years' War. However, it remained in Spanish hands until conquered by the British in 1797, and officially became a British colony in 1802.

Torres y Vargas wrote his history against this background of the taking and retaking of such settlements. Reprisals at each conquest meant desecration of Catholic religious symbols and harsh punishments for enemy colonists. The victories by the French, Dutch and English in these places constituted a serious threat to Spanish dominion. Moreover, the enemies did not content themselves with the smaller islands of the Eastern Caribbean. A third of Española and all of Jamaica would be ripped away from Spain before the century would end.

Philip IV ordered changes in the fortifications of Puerto Rico. After evaluating the Dutch attack strategy, in 1634 the king ordered a new fort built at a redoubt where the city walls ended. "Fortin del Espigón" became San Cristobal Fort. Further down on the islet at Boquerón another fortification was built, named San Geronimo. Meantime the construction of a city wall connecting El Morro with San Cristóbal on the northern part of the city was renewed after 1630. The wall was dotted with guard watch points called "*garetes.*" Jutting out from the wall, these stations allowed the soldier to peer through the narrow slit to see if anyone was trying to scale the walls. Torres y Vargas recognized the military importance of these improvements (#78, 81) that now encircled the city.

Although it was to end in calamitous defeat of Spain, the Thirty Years' War was not without its promising moments. In fact, Spanish forces from the Netherlands invaded France and drove within a few miles of Paris in 1636. This triumph, as well as the ongoing efficiency of these troops made the Army of Flanders more or less similar to the Marines or the Green Berets or Special Forces of the U.S. Importantly, Don Diego's father had been an officer in the Army of Flanders, and his son is careful to stress the glory attached to membership in this military unit. However, it was easier to win a battle than to occupy a country, and after regrouping in 1636, the French forces were able to repel the Spanish. Less than a decade later, the Army of Flanders was to be defeated when, in 1643, the Dutch Republic triumphed at Rocroi. The Army of Flanders, once widely considered the best in the world, had been beaten, signaling that that Spain had no more to give.

EVENTS AFTER THE WAR DURING THE LIFE OF TORRES Y VARGAS

The Thirty Years' War ended in 1648 with the Peace of Westphalia. The treaty limited the Hapsburgs in Germany to portions of the south (Austria). Spain definitively recognized the independence of Holland as the cost of the peace. In general, Westphalia is considered to have established the modern national state structure of Europe. Rather than definition by dynastic claims or religious imperatives, the treaty identified each state as a permanent nationality.

The treaty also forced Spain to open the Caribbean to other countries' trade and colonization. It was the first written surrender by Spain of part of Española to France (Haiti), although in actual fact, pirates and French companies had already established a presence in Española. In 1655, after being repulsed in an effort to take Santo Domingo, Admiral William Penn and General Robert Venables were able to occupy the Spanish island of Jamaica. They established an open city at Port Royal, promising amnesty to pirates and buccaneers who would accept British law. The most famous of the shadowy types attacking and pillaging Spanish colonies under English protection was Henry Morgan (1635–1688).

Spain continued to fight on in a lost cause. Peace with France came with the Treaty of the Pyrenees in 1659. At that time, Spain ceded Roussillon at the Pyrenees to France and also surrendered parts of what is now Belgium. But old feudal ideas died hard. To ensure peace between Spain and France, Philip IV's daughter, Maria Teresa was married to the young French prince, who would become King Louis XIV. It was more than just an historical footnote, however, that Spain was too "broke" to pay the promised dowry. This was to lead to another war, that of the Spanish Succession, at the end of the century. The bankruptcy of

Spain also caused a collection or *Donativo* made for the king and taken up by Torres y Vargas in Puerto Rico in 1659.

The loss of the islands in the Eastern Caribbean had turned Puerto Rico into the most strategic bastion for protecting all of Spanish America. It was large enough to supply considerable troops with provisions, it was heavily fortified and strategically placed to protect the Atlantic sea lanes, and its people had proven both loyal and valiant in defending the Spanish cause. Although Santo Domingo retained much of its primacy administratively and ecclesiastically, the singular military role of Puerto Rico lent it new importance. It is not exaggeration to suggest that Puerto Rico's new role after 1648 began the process of profiling its history as distinct from that of Cuba or Española. By reading the text of Torres y Vargas, one can glimpse the mindset of the Puerto Ricans on whose shoulders rested these historical changes.

THE IMPORTANCE OF PUERTO RICO AFTER WESTPHALIA

Philip IV had recognized how important Puerto Rico had become as a strategic military defense point. In 1645, the, king wrote of the island, **"It is the front and vanguard of all my West Indies and consequently, the most important of them all, and the most coveted by my enemies."** This pronouncement by the King of Spain is featured by Torres y Vargas (#6). However, even more important than this royal edict, were the substantial and notable changes in the quality of life and enhancement of social progress to come.

To buttress Puerto Rico as the "vanguard of all my West Indies," the monarch set in motion an upgrade of facilities, governmental attentions and military personnel to administer the colony. Eventually this would mean that the civil and military officials posted to Puerto Rico would have achieved a significant level of skill and talent. When more soldiers were stationed on the island, the government would pay greater attention to services such as hospital care, quality housing near installations, control of ship traffic, greater funding for defense installations through replacement and repairs. All of this would result in better jobs for local Puerto Ricans: they were needed to build fortifications, service incoming ships, grow food and raise cattle to provide for armed forces stationed on the island, including washing their clothing and repairing their shoes. As the city would grow, its needs for food and supplies would raise production from the hinterland, benefiting farmers around the island. In turn, this gradual quickening of economic life improved the conditions for demographic increase, with more immigration and higher birth rates coupled to lower mortality rates. Even the ascent to the Spanish throne of an incompetent Charles II in 1665, would complicate, but not derail, the march through history of the people of Puerto Rico along a path blazed by the generation of Diego Torres y Vargas.

The transformation of Puerto Rico into the Caribbean bastion of Spain was also to enhance the quality of life for native-born residents. The need to preserve and enhance the fortifications on the island was accompanied by development of its economic and human potential, expanding the availability of cultural and technological resources. Education improved for people living on the island. The Puerto Rican population began to benefit from the artists, musicians and teachers who practiced their professions locally. The city of San Juan witnessed the importation of new books describing innovations in philosophy, theology, politics, and the like. Cumulatively, these improvements raised the quality of life for island elite society. Opportunities would now develop for literary compositions in Puerto Rico and there was patronage for a portrait painters who would depict the highly positioned for posterity.

Towards the end of the seventeenth century Puerto Rico began to enjoy significantly closer ties with Spain and leading cities of Spanish America. With the peace, Puerto Rico would figure in policy decisions made in Spain about protection of all the South American colonies. Puerto Rico was eased into commercial networks, since it was the bulwark in creating safe shipping lanes. Eventually, these factors would induce greater numbers of Puerto Rican criollos to seek education in Spain and to assume more significant roles in governance upon return. The Puerto Rican criollos that came after Torres y Vargas were more likely to travel his path to education, imitate his expressed preference to live in Puerto Rico, and rise to equal Spaniards in talent and achievements.

These improvements were planned after the war between France and Spain finally ended in 1659. An ensuing national bankruptcy, however, frustrated efforts to develop Puerto Rico, followed immediately by the incompetence of

Carlos II during his reign. The War of Spanish Succession would postpone the implementation of this blueprint for Puerto Rico's improvements until that conflict ended in 1713 with the installation of the House of Bourbon on the Spanish throne. Nonetheless, by the last two decades of the seventeenth century, the foundations for change had been set. It would seem safe to say that the changes were structured during the times of Torres y Vargas — even if they were implemented only later. While history books are more likely to date progress and prosperity in Puerto Rico with the middle of the eighteenth century and not the times of Torres y Vargas, a more sober look at events shows that what happened in the 1700s was made possible by the valor and sacrifice of the people of Puerto Rico in the 1600s.

WHO WAS DIEGO DE TORRES Y VARGAS?

Genealogy is the starting point for appreciating the life and service of Diego Torres y Vargas. On his mother's side, he was five generations removed from Juan Ponce de León, the founder and first governor of Puerto Rico. Put another way, his grandmother was the great-grandchild of Juan Ponce de León. Because of this family history, the future priest and author of this history of Puerto Rico had many social and educational opportunities in his life. Without a doubt, he was of the upper class in seventeenth century Puerto Rican society. While today, there may be a built-in resentment against persons born into privilege, the real question in the seventeenth century was what people did with those privileges. To appreciate the record of the Ponce de León family in Puerto Rico, a brief look at the founder's immediate family shows several tendencies among all of them, with a few achieving a record of distinguished service to Puerto Rico (see chart).[1]

Two of Ponce's daughters, Juana and María, had married two Troche brothers, García and Gaspar. This practice, in which couples are related both by marriage and blood, is still found in Puerto Rico. These intermarried siblings were the only branch of the Ponce family in Puerto Rico to produce descendants. Juan Ponce de León's other daughter, Isabel, married Antonio de la Gama, Governor of Puerto Rico under the Columbus family, but she had no children. Juan Ponce de Leon's only male child, Luis, had been born in Española. He had not yet reached legal age as an adult when in 1521 his father died from wounds received while trying to explore Florida. Luis' brother-in-law, García Troche, became temporary executor of the family estate until Luis would become old enough to inherit his father's title, lands and possessions. However, Luis later chose to profess vows as a Dominican friar. Although we are not sure when he was ordained, he may have been the first criollo to become a priest in the Americas. In any case, he neither took titles for himself nor produced heirs to his

---

[1] For more complete data, see Vicente Murga Sanz, *Ponce de León*, 1959, Universidad de Puerto Rico.

Genealogy of Diego de Torres y Vargas

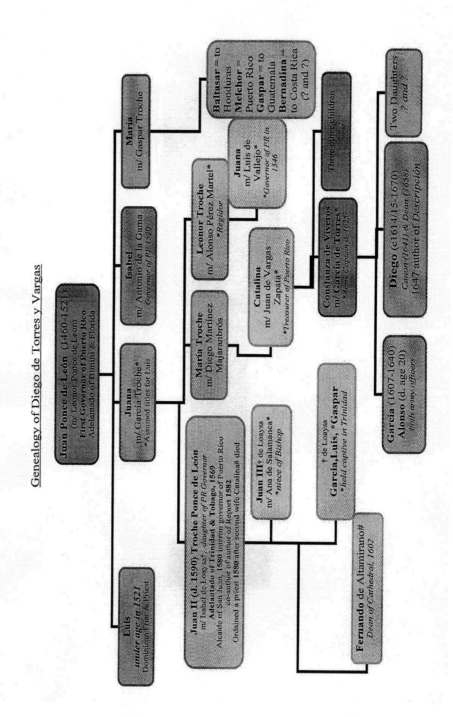

father's line. These would pass through the line of García Troche and his wife, Juana Ponce de León.

The Ponce de León family tree shows certain tendencies that reflect the marriage patterns which were common at the time. **First**, we find considerable intermarriage among prominent families. This had the effect of conserving land holdings and preserving titles like alcaide and places on the cabildo. The Ponce de León women in different generations would often marry governors of the is-land or wealthy residents, so the circle of those elites stayed small. **Second**, we see association with the Spanish military as a career or for marriage of eligible daughters to Spanish soldiers coming to Puerto Rico. **Third**, we find multiple marriages with many children who are half-brothers and sisters to each other. Many of the women married while teenagers, and — with the limitations of med-ical science at the time — it was not unusual for these women to die in childbirth while still relatively young. The husband often married a second time to another young woman, who likely outlived her much older husband. (A study of these colonial women, what they suffered and how they coped is worthy of more at-tention than can be afforded here.) **Finally**, there is often a church career for cer-tain children. Many of Ponce de León descendants were ordained priests and held important ecclesiastical positions, so that Torres y Vargas would not be the first in the extended family to become Dean of the Cathedral.

We might be tempted to view these linkages to the church as proof of deep Catholic conviction, but sometimes they reflected little more than the need for sons without a chance of inheriting land to seek social prestige and guaranteed income through the church. When a religious vocation flows from economic needs, it does not always produce clergy dedicated to priestly ministry. Since he had an older brother who was ahead of him in line to inherit the Torres y Vargas titles and possessions, it appears this mundane tendency influenced Diego's entry into an ecclesiastical career. To his credit, Father Torres y Vargas left a record of service to the church that deserves our admiration: his was not a "false" voca-tion.

García Troche had ensured that the male line of Ponce de León would continue by using his wife's famous last name for his son, Juan, who is usually referred to in history books as "Juan II." This grandson of the first Ponce de León married Isabel, the daughter of Iñigo López Cervantes de Loaysa, a governor who was also a civil judge in Santo Domingo and member of an influential colonial family. The prestige of Juan II, therefore, came from many sources: his grandfather, his uncles and aunts and — through his wife — from his father-in-law.

Juan II found his rights, honors and influence disputed by a new governor from Spain, Franciso Bahamón de Lugo, who had arrived on the island in 1564. Not to be shunted aside by politics, Juan II traveled back to Spain to present his complaints. In the end, Bahamón was transferred out of Puerto Rico to Cartagena in modern day Columbia (#49). Apparently, Juan II knew the power of his last name. Building on the fame of his family, he brought the remains of Juan Ponce de León back to Puerto Rico from Cuba around this time. The founder was re-buried with great pomp in the cathedral, and as the principal heir, Juan II increased his social prominence.

FROM TRAGEDY TO TRIUMPH

The loss of his fortune was not the greatest tragedy to Juan II of the ill-fated attempt 1569 in Trinidad. Tragically, Gaspar, one of his children, was kidnapped by the Caribs, who took the young man away to their island of Dominica. Disheartened by this failure and the loss of his son, he returned to Puerto Rico where he assumed a place on the cabildo. Unexpectedly in 1580, he was given a report that after ten years in captivity, his son was still alive and being held for ransom by the Caribs. Juan II appealed to the Spanish authorities in Santo Domingo for the ransom, but the bureaucracy took four years before finally posting the decree. It does appear that his son found his way back to Puerto Rico years later.

Juan II Ponce de León lived a full life:
•   He took scientific readings during an eclipse to accurately record Puerto Rico's latitude and longitude, sending the information to Spain.
•   When his second wife died, Juan II himself became a priest in 1580.
•   In 1582, he wrote a report about Puerto Rico for Governor Melgarejo with the help of a Spanish clerk, Antonio de Santa Clara. This report containing descriptions of the island, its settlements, institutions and commerce was the first of its kind to be prepared in Puerto Rico and seems to have been used in outlining the longer and more comprehensive history written by his relative, Torres y Vargas in 1647.

The achievements of Juan II Ponce de León in all these different fields gave him an aura in Puerto Rico somewhat like what American colonials were to give to Benjamin Franklin in the eighteenth century. The town of Ponce was named after this Juan II, not his great-grandfather, the first Juan Ponce de León.

See Salvador Perea, *Historia de Puerto Rico 1537–1700*, (1972) 67–87.

Juan II's gifts of leadership also impressed Pedro Menéndez de Avilés while he was using Puerto Rico as the staging ground for a 1565 military expedition to drive the French out of Florida. Menéndez named Juan II a lieutenant for the Florida operation. This helped Juan II to secure the military title of Adelantado of Trinidad and Tobago for himself shortly afterwards. In 1569, he led an effort to colonize those islands. Unfortunately, after spending his fortune on the expedition, it ended badly for Juan II after ten months because the settlers revolted and the native Caribs attacked the colony. Worse still, his son disappeared in the raid by the natives. If these events were not tragic enough, the death of his wife back in Puerto Rico was to follow. However, as often was the case for men of his class, Juan II married again, this time to Catalina Carrillo Altamirano. Fernando, one of their children, would be ordained a priest and would be named Dean of the Cathedral in 1604 before being transferred to Mexico (#85).

As explained in the second essay, Puerto Rico was under constant threats because of European wars. The Spanish governor, Francisco de Ovando y Messía, had left the island to seek medical treatment in Santo Domingo. On the way he was captured and held prisoner on a French frigate. The French wanted to seize slaves and goods and sell them in Puerto Rico for the ransom. The governor sent a letter to Juan II, who as alcaide of the fortress was entitled to act as interim governor. The captive governor wanted Juan II to authorize the French to conduct the sale because that would speed his release. Juan II saw problems in such negotiations and instead offered a simple cash ransom, as related by Torres y Vargas (#50). Before the issue could be resolved, Governor Ovando y Messía died. Thus, Juan II, the native Puerto Rican, governed Puerto Rico until Gerónimo de Aguero Compuzano arrived from Santo Domingo to assume the post (#50). Juan II was concerned with a possible sea attack on Puerto Rico and urged the building of a battery on the small island called El Cañuelo across from El Morro (#66).

Juan III, one of the seven children from Juan II's first marriage, married the niece of Bishop Diego de Salamanca. A daughter, whose name has not yet been uncovered by research, married Juan López de Melgarejo,[2] sent from Santo

---

[2] Perea, 1972: 79, ftn. 61. citing *Boletín Histórico*, XI:6.

Domingo to serve as interim governor of Puerto Rico. Melgarejo asked Juan II to compose a report on Puerto Rico, and some of the information would be used as references in the 1647 narrative by Torres y Vargas. In 1580, shortly after his arrival as permanent governor, Juan de Céspedes asked Juan II to record the effect in Puerto Rico of a solar eclipse with a narrative and drawings, so that the island's latitude and longitude could be accurately charted. When completed, this scientific observation was sent to Spain.

These responsibilities indicate that Juan II as an elder statesman had reestablished his social standing after the disastrous expedition to Trinidad. Moreover, after his second wife passed away, Juan II became a priest and Archdeacon of the Cathedral in 1580. Thus, Juan Troche Ponce de León, actually entered three states of life: marriage with parenthood, the military, and the clergy.

To reach Canon Torres y Vargas, the Ponce de León line passes through Juan de Vargas Zapata, a distinguished military figure in the conquest of Peru. Vargas Zapata was rewarded with the post of treasurer of Puerto Rico. Since his first wife had died, Juan de Vargas Zapata married again after arriving in Puerto Rico. His bride was Catalina, a great-granddaughter of the first Ponce de León, niece of Juan II and future grandmother of Canon Torres y Vargas. Although his second wife was forty-eight years younger than himself, Juan de Vargas[3] had four children with her. One of these was a daughter, Constanza de Viveros, whose additional last name identifies her with a well-known Spanish family. Constanza married García de Torres, a Spanish captain and officer in the renowned Spanish Army of Flanders, who had fought in the war against the Dutch Republic before his posting to Puerto Rico. Among their children, were two sons in the military: García, named after his father and also an army officer (1607–1640), who died at age 33; and Alonso, who died at 26 while in the military (#72). The future priest and author of this history, Diego was apparently their third son, born either in the autumn of 1614 or sometime in 1615, since the university admission records of August of 1635 suggest he was then "twenty years old." Diego was

---

[3] The Spanish branch of the family apparently produced Diego de Vargas Zapata y Luján Ponce de León (1643–1704), governor of the Spanish province of New Mexico in 1692 when Spanish rule was restored.

"Torres" on his father's side and "Vargas" on his mother's. The Vargas name helped distinguish his lineage in as much as there were many relatives in Puerto Rico who were in the Ponce de León family.

Such blue-blood family ties probably helped Diego find people to supply him with information about the high ranking governors and bishops of Puerto Rico in the later composition of his history. Famous people would likely speak to him because he was related to them: persons of lesser station would be flattered to have a member of such a famous family consult with them. As noted in the first essay, these oral testimonies appear alongside of the lists of officials and ecclesiastics. They remain valuable, even if reliance on personal recollections sometimes produces errors.

As noted above, Juan (II) Troche Ponce de León had written a report on Puerto Rico in 1582, sending the original to Spain under the name of the governor. It may be that a version survived the 1625 torching of the city because a relative had kept a personal copy at home, turning it over to Torres y Vargas when composing his history. Thus, in different ways, the high prestige of his famous family apparently assisted Torres y Vargas with oral and written sources that enriched his 1647 history of Puerto Rico.

THE EDUCATION OF DON DIEGO TORRES Y VARGAS[4]

We can surmise that as a child, Diego attended the cathedral school in San Juan while Bishop Balbuena occupied the sea of Puerto Rico. We are certain that Torres y Vargas went to Spain for college in 1635 when he was about 20 years old. At the time, there were three prestigious universities in Spain: Alcalá de Henares, Valladolid and Salamanca with Salamanca being the most respected of the three. We might compare these institutions to the U.S. equivalent of the "Ivy League" Harvard, Princeton and Yale, with Salamanca as Harvard. Note

---

[4] For more details about the facts cited here, see Pío Medrano Herrero. *Don Damián López de Haro y don Diego de Torres y Vargas, dos figuras del Puerto Rico barroco*. Plaza Mayor. San Juan (Puerto Rico) 1999.

that these were the most prestigious in *Spain,* and as a criollo from the island colony of Puerto Rico, the Salamanca degree secured by Diego Torres y Vargas would provide him considerable prestige for his entire life.

We have a description of him from the university records:

> *Don Diego de Torres y Vargas, natural de Puerto Rico, de 20 años, moreno y menudo de rostro, nariz afilada, a cánones en 13 de agosto de 1635. Testigos, el licenciado Calzas y Antonio López.*

> Don Diego de Torres y Vargas, a native of Puerto Rico, 20 years old, olive-skinned and smallish features, narrow nose, [admitted] to [studies of] canon law on August 13, 1635. Witnesses, Master Calzas and Antonio López.[5]

Torres y Vargas graduated with a bachelor's degree in canon law in 1639. There is no suggestion that he was especially distinguished in his studies, but neither was he a marginal student. At graduation and ordination, he was offered a post in other churches, possibly because of the recommendation from the Bishop of Puerto Rico, Juan Alonso de Solís, who had written: "*don Diego es de los más bien nacidos que se han conocido en esta tierra.*" [Don Diego is from the best-born [families] that has been known in this land.].[6] We find another description of him, dated 1639:

> *Es hijo del capitán y sargento mayor García de Torres, que lo fue muchos años en esta isla y en la de Santo Domingo de la Española, y sirvió a Vuestra Majestad en España y Flandes con el valor y satisfacción que le es notorio en sus Reales Consejos de Guerra y Indias. Murió en el sitio que puso el enemigo holandés el año de veinte y cinco a esta fuerza de un mosquetazo.*

---

[5] Cited in Medrano, *op. cit.,* 150.
[6] Cited in Medrano, *op. cit.,* 131 #6.

He is the son of the Captain and Sergeant-Major, García de Torres, who spent many years on this island and that of Santo Domingo de la Española, and who served Your Majesty in Spain and in Flanders with the bravery and competence noted in the Royal Councils of War and of the Indies. He died from the impact of a musket shot during the siege laid to this fortress by the enemy Dutch in [16]25.[7]

Shortly after this account, we know that one of his soldier brothers, García, was killed in 1640, and he tells us (#72) that his other brother Alonso died while in the military at twenty years of age. Both of these deaths may have occurred while Torres y Vargas was still in Spain. They may also explain while he held out for a salaried post that would allow him to return to Puerto Rico. He explains that he declined appointment to other cathedrals because he had to financially support two sisters. The connection between the death of his two brothers and his responsibility to provide for two sisters are linked, but other details, including the names of the women, are not explained.

Appointment as a canon of the San Juan Cathedral came in 1641 at the age of 26 while Torres y Vargas was still in Spain where such decisions were made. He was probably ordained that same year, since the Council of Trent required all priests to be at least twenty-five years old. Sailing from Seville, he arrived in Puerto Rico before the September 12th hurricane in 1642. We can trust this date for his voyage home because he describes this storm in his history (#68). The diocesan see was vacant at the time because the family's friend, Bishop Juan Alonso de Solís, had died in 1641. While waiting for a new bishop, ordinary business went on. In one case, Canon Diego was named to a panel of judges deciding between Pedro Montañés Salinas and Canon Luis Ponce de León (who was one of Torres y Vargas' many cousins). Torres y Vargas cast his vote in favor of Montañés Salinas. We cannot be sure, but there might have been considerable family "fall out" over this decision for having decided against a relative. We can see that in later moments of his career, Torres y Vargas showed considerable caution when making decisions involving relatives.

---

[7] Medrano, *op. cit.*, 130–131.

Puerto Rico had changed while the canon had been studying at the university in Spain. A new town, Loiza Aldea, had been founded and its church dedicated to St. Patrick on account of deliverance from a scourge of ants as recounted in his history (#28). Moreover, the Franciscan Order had been reestablished in Puerto Rico, with an important foundation in San Juan (#16). No longer did the Dominicans have a monopoly upon the piety of the city or exclusive claim to the sons of criollos. The friars were housed on a street named appropriately, "San Francisco" and are still in the same place.

The next bishop, Fray Damián López de Haro, was clearly a post-Tridentine reformer. Former provincial head of the Trinitarian Order in Spain, he entered Puerto Rico in 1644 with an intention to attack laxity. For that task, he convoked a Diocesan Synod in 1645 that enacted many of the Tridentine reforms for Puerto Rico (#42) It should be remembered that the territory for the Diocese of Puerto Rico included the Lesser Antilles as far south as the coast of Venezuela, and thus fell under bishop López de Haro's jurisdiction. As a result, the bishop set out to visit each of these possessions where a parish had been established. Such trips were arduous, even for a young man, and the bishop was already over seventy years old. Moreover, sailing on the seas was dangerous since Spain was at war, even if Puerto Rico had been declared the winter port for the Spanish navy's Windward fleet.

Events on the island of St. Martin (now Sint Maarten) are explained in a section of the history about these outlying islands (#99–100). As mentioned in the second essay, a military expedition had been sent from Puerto Rico in 1633 to drive out the Dutch, which had set up their own settlement in 1631. Spaniards, with help from Puerto Rican workers, built a fort on a bluff called "Punta Blanca." The outpost was attacked by the Dutch in 1644 and an officer in the employ of the Dutch West India Company, Peter Stuyvesant, lost one of his legs, requiring the future ruler of New Amsterdam to walk on a peg leg for the rest of his life. Although this attack had been repulsed, St. Martin's governor, Diego Guajarado Fajardo, believed it would be impossible to resist future attacks. He turned to Puerto Rico to look for military reinforcements, because coordination of military action in the Caribbean was filtered through Puerto Rico. When the

French landed on Santa Cruz (Saint Croix) and Vieques, a military force was sent by Governor Fernando de la Riva Agüero from Puerto Rico to drive them out of both islands in 1647, although this happened the year that Torres y Vargas finished the first draft of his history and it is not narrated there. A year earlier in 1646, just such an expedition had been successful in expelling the Dutch from Tortola. Once again, the Spanish sent troops from Puerto Rico out into the Caribbean. But after nearly thirty years of constant war, the ranks of Spanish troops were thin.

The fate of St. Martin was decided when de la Riva Agüero received the orders from the king for the inevitable Spanish withdrawal. In January of 1648, five ships were sent from Puerto Rico to pick up the remaining settlers and a tiny garrison before abandoning the colony. They found an outbreak of the Bubonic Plague had already killed hundreds of settlers. Moreover, one of the ships ran aground, sending more than seventy persons to a watery grave. The expedition rescued everything of value from the settlement and burned the remains to prevent use by the invaders (#99–100). Adding still more to the woes, the island of Margarita that received survivors also underwent an outbreak of the plague. Among the eventual victims of the plague in Margarita was Bishop López de Haro who was on the pastoral visit to the island's parish as required by the Council of Trent. Torres y Vargas recounts symbolic moments that accompanied the death and funeral of the good bishop in 1648 (#101–102).

AN EMERGING PUERTO RICAN IDENTITY

The rise of a Puerto Rican identity traced in Torres y Vargas was not a literary mirage: decisions were made during those times that attest to a growing identity for Puerto Ricans in the awareness of officials. In 1648, Governor de la Riva Agüero gave a surprising order after sending army troops to St. Martin. He put native Puerto Rican militiamen into the ranks of Puerto Rico's defenders. Clearly, the war demanded Spanish soldiers being sent off the island to fight the Dutch, English and French, but there was need for troops to defend Puerto Rico itself. However, most of San Juan's garrison was composed of a Portuguese regiment. With Portugal in revolt against Spain, the governor did not want to rely only on these potential rebels and sent them on the off-island mission, trusting locals to man the city's fortress. For the audacity of placing the defense of Spanish interests with locals, de la Riva was rebuked by the king in 1649. But the fact remains that the governor's decision provided evidence that Puerto Ricans were capable soldiers loyal to Spain.

Outbreaks of the Bubonic Plague were not uncommon then: Amsterdam was struck in 1663 and London in 1665. However, it is noteworthy how Torres y Vargas casts blame for the plague upon the misconduct of St. Martin's governor, Diego Guajarado Fajardo, who had been excommunicated by the bishop on his pastoral visit to Margarita in 1647. On visitation to the island of Margarita, Bishop López de Haro based his decision on reports from the vicar of the parish in St. Martin. Since Guajarado Fajardo was in Puerto Rico at the time, Cathedral Canon Luis de Ponce de León (son of Juan III) was ordered to enforce the excommunication. Because this would have meant denial of the sacraments and implied the eternal damnation of his soul, the governor defended himself vigorously. Canon Ponce de León declined to enforce the bishop's decision. Torres y Vargas was the second clergyman from the cathedral ordered by Bishop López de Haro to implement the excommunication. But after conducting his own investigation in February of 1648, Torres y Vargas absolved the governor, preferring to wait until a higher civil court would decide the issue of Guajarado's administration at a tragic time of attack, withdrawal and plague.

Did this refusal to obey the order of excommunication establish some antagonism between Bishop López de Haro and Canon Torres y Vargas? The bishop might have been testing the loyalty of Torres y Vargas in contrast with the older canons, some of whom were family relations of the younger priest. Were the two San Juan born clergymen playing a game of favoritism to a member of their class? Or did they consider the governor to have undergone enough suffering in the disaster of St. Martin? We lack sufficient information to decide if this was a case with clearly defined sides or if the truth lay somewhere in the middle.

Moreover, even if we avoid speculating about personal motives, we need to remember that this bishop had been sent, as bishops sometimes are, to "clean up" a diocese. He came from outside Puerto Rico with few or no local ties to a complacent church society, whereas the local clergy often came from the city's wealthy families. The bishop would one day be replaced, but the local clergy would still have to deal with long-standing family rivalries. Waiting out a Spanish bishop may have been a delaying strategy to preserve the status quo and avoid later resentments from permanent residents.

Bishop López de Haro should not be judged negatively because of frictions with the local church. The diocesan synod he had convened in 1645 was the first in the history of Puerto Rico and a follow-up to a regional bishops' council in Santo Domingo attended by Bishop Balbuena (#39). Although Puerto Rico's Synod was convened some 80 years after the close of the Council of Trent, it clearly addressed basic issues of reform. It brought Puerto Rico's Catholic Church into conformity with conciliar decrees. The resolutions of the synod set policy for each parish in terms of services, fees, and regulations for the proper administration of parishes in Puerto Rico. At the same time that the Council of Trent had asked for reform, however, it obliged each bishop to take into account the particular needs of his diocese in order to best serve its pastoral needs. Bishop López de Haro's legacy has withstood the trials of history because his measures successfully balanced the Tridentine mandates. Far from antagonizing Torres y Vargas, the example of such a reforming prelate positively shaped the ecclesiastical career of the young Puerto Rican cleric.

Bishop López de Haro also contributed a document important to the history of Puerto Rico. The bishop wrote a long letter about the state of Catholicism on the island and sent it to Juan Diez de la Calle, a member of the Consejo de las Indias in Spain. The bishop's communication was not an official report, but rather a sort of personalized review of the obstacles he had faced in his episcopate and the contradictions he had encountered. It was not as comprehensive or historical as the work of Torres y Vargas, but comparison between the two demonstrates how Spaniards and criollos might have different perspectives about the same place. (See pp 27–29).

In 1648, this bishop was to pass away, as had many other prelates for Puerto Rico, while engaged in the strenuous apostolate of visiting the far away parishes in the Caribbean islands which were attached to the Puerto Rican diocese. The year 1648 was also when Diego Torres y Vargas completed the addendum to his history that was requested by Madrid. His testimony of respect to Bishop López de Haro helps to link the two church leaders in Puerto Rican history.

TORRES Y VARGAS AFTER WRITING HIS HISTORY

When he sent his description of Puerto Rico to Spain, Torres y Vargas was about 33 years old. As a diocesan priest without vows of poverty, Torres y Vargas maintained himself and his inheritance by investments and business transactions. For instance, he would send products like barrels of processed sugar to be sold in Spain. We should also note that the substantial family position of Torres y Vargas made him accustomed to the upper class customs, such as holding three black slaves to attend to his needs. Holding slaves should not be equated with cruelty towards blacks. Slaves working in the city supplied for the tasks performed to day by today's house servants like maid, janitor, gardener, and the like. In return, slaves were provided room and board. We cannot be sure in the case of Torres y Vargas, but at the death of their owner, many of these domestic slaves were given their freedom. Thus, while black slavery was an institution contrary to modern concepts of human dignity, during the seventeenth century it was not viewed in the same way. Torres y Vargas supported his two sisters (or perhaps sisters-in-law, the widows of his two deceased military brothers), so commercial income was not a selfish concern.

A new bishop, Fernando Lobo del Castillo arrived in 1650, but died scant months later in 1651. Torres y Vargas was named executor of the bishop's will and was asked by the other clerics to process the request for a replacement bishop. These tasks ordinarily were often the responsibility of the most senior canon, and it is a testimony to the respect Torres y Vargas had earned that at such a relatively young age, he would be assigned these duties. There is some ambiguity about his role in leadership. At this writing, there is no clear documentation to indicate whether he had

> Most clergy at the time of Torres y Vargas did not live in rectories, but with their family. A common arrangement for a priest was to live in his mother's house; she would clean and cook for him so no scandal would ensue for having a woman in the house. If the mother was deceased, a sister could fill this function. Sisters-in-law under the same roof, however, would have been less satisfying to propriety. If he lived with his sisters-in-law (*cuñadas*), calling them "sisters" (*hermanas*) may have been a choice of discretion. Without more precise information, this observation remains only speculation.

the canonical title as Vicar General of the Diocese. Nonetheless, it is evident that he had played a major role in administration of the diocesan affairs after 1651 and perhaps as early as 1649.[8]

Torres y Vargas was much respected for his knowledge of canon law and his prudence in adjudication. In 1652, two youths implicated in a case of fraud surrounding the Situado, attempted to assassinate Governor Diego de Aguilera. Don Diego was asked to resolve the issue of punishment, which he did with characteristic probity.

In 1653, he conducted the canonical inquiry of two novices of the Carmelite convent in San Juan which had been founded in 1646 through the generosity of a woman of high social standing (#17). It was left to his judgment whether these women were worthy to take vows. We many consider his choice for this and other important roles to be a measure of the esteem in which he was held. Moreover, it was not the last of special cases when he was selected as arbiter.

When Bishop Naranjo of Mexico declined nomination to the See of Puerto Rico in 1653, the administration of the diocese was formally given to Torres y Vargas with his election by the other canons as *Vicario Capitular* in April 17, 1654. This post officially replaces a bishop in all legal matters. It does not have the same sacramental power as a bishop in the faculty to ordain new priests,

---

The title of Vicar indicates that the person has power to act for the Ordinary, or bishop. Then, as today, a Vicar General is designated by the bishop to handle details of canonical authority for decisions or policies already determined. In the time of Torres y Vargas there was another route to becoming Vicar, namely to be elected as *Vicario Capitular* by the other canons when the office of bishop was vacant: *sede vacante*. In effect, this title invested all canonical powers as Ordinary of the Diocese in this Vicar, so as not to interrupt the good order of the diocese. As soon as a new bishop was named, however, canon law revoked the interim powers of the vicar. In many cases, such as with Torres y Vargas, the new bishop would name the previous *Vicario Capitular* his *Vicario General*. The difference in title is a legal matter, but the functions are virtually the same. Today, the Vicar General is often the head of the Chancery.

---

[8] Discrepancies in the official records and historical summaries are explored in Medrano, pp. 206–207. Torres y Vargas wrote in 1663 that he had exercised such administrative powers "for fourteen years" which would place the beginning of such functions as early as 1649.

but it entails business and policy decisions on a day to day basis with the full authority to represent the interests of the church in canonical matters. This document clearly indicates he was chosen to become the "acting" bishop at the age of thirty-eight, even though previously he had been exercising many of these functions on account of his leadership skills. In fact, he may have functioned as Vicar General under the bishop before assuming such powers during the interim.

Titles such as "Dean" carried more prestige and higher salary than Vicar, but not higher responsibilities. The Dean was the legal director of the civic corporation that administered the Cathedral's property. His responsibilities were separate from the pastoral powers of the bishop. Moreover, the title of Dean, as with other titles of the canons of the Cathedral, came through the King of Spain. Thus, as Vicar, Torres y Vargas administered the pastoral business of the diocese at the behest of the bishop (Vicar General) or by election of other canons when there was no bishop (Vicar Capitular). The Deanship, or the role of ecclesiastical governor, both of which he later achieved, were different responsibilities.

Another task that came with the absence of a prelate in San Juan was that of visitador. His responsibility was to be an impartial judge in legal matters of another jurisdiction. Thus, for instance, Torres y Vargas had been asked to hear an appeal in a 1653 case involving the Archbishop of Santo Domingo and a cleric accused of bad behavior by the king's civil judges (oidores). The confrontation was between the decisions of the Archbishop as head of the Church in Santo Domingo and the officials sent by the king. Pope Gregory XIII in 1573 had created the office of special investigators for clergy corruption as part of the Tridentine reforms. However, in 1606 King Philip III had reserved the right of the monarchy to name the investigators examining such conflicts. Thus, it remained ambiguous in both secular and ecclesiastical law as to who had the last word: the Church or the crown. In his report, dated February 7, 1653, Torres y Vargas declined to act in favor of the crown. He claimed that he had no clear jurisdiction and that he did not have enough evidence to make a clear judgment against the Archbishop's standing decision. Thus, he took no stand in the matter.

As a result of avoiding a decision, Torres y Vargas was reprimanded by the Consejo de las Indies on April 27, 1654 — just ten days after his election as

Vicar of the Chapter — and then by the King in May of the same year. The royal document is reproduced by Medrano and reads in part as follows:

> *Y así se ha extrañado mucho en el dicho mi Consejo que hubiésedes hecho semejante remisión, y aunque debiera hacerse con vos mayor demonstración, lo he suspendido por ahora esperando que en lo de adelante procederéis con más atención y menos ignorancia, como debéis y sois obligado. Y por la presente os encargo que resumiendo en vos la jurisdicción de dicha causa, pues en vuestro poder quedaron los autos originales, la determinéis en justicia sin hacer novedad en la observancia de dicho breve y cédula [de Gregorio XIII] y estilo recibido...*

And so it was very perplexing in my Council that you would have made a similar rendering [like the Archbishop's], which I have suspended for now, expecting that in the future you will proceed with greater care and less ignorance, as you should and are obliged to do. For now, since the original papers are in your possession, I charge you to deliver a just sentence when you resume your jurisdiction over this case, without striking any novelty in your abiding by the said brief and decree [of Pope Gregory XIII] that you have duly received.

Such harsh instruction from the highest authority in the Spanish Empire might have spelled the end of any ecclesiastical aspirations for Diego Torres y Vargas. If securing the bishop's miter had been his life's ambition, he probably would not have risked the action of offending the king by declining to decide the appeal in Española. Yet he chose his course of action with due deliberation, and doubtlessly was aware of the consequences. The censure from the King of Spain, which was predictable since he had sided with the Archbishop instead, appears not to have affected his election by his local peers. Much as discussed previously, it may be that there was advantage to clergy in paying attention to the desires of the local church rather than obeying distant higher-ups.

In 1654, Torres y Vargas was asked to judge in the case of Swedes living in Puerto Rico. These were survivors of a shipwreck in 1649 when enmity with Sweden had been inherited from the Thirty Years' War. By 1654, the Swedes had negotiated permission to leave Puerto Rico for any of the survivors who so wished. Torres y Vargas was asked to interview the Swedes and determine the freedom of their choice whether to stay in Puerto Rico or return to their homeland. His selection as judge in these cases reflects on the high regard he had earned within Puerto Rico.

Torres y Vargas received promotion to cathedral choirmaster (*chantre*) in 21 June 1655. (The post did not involve musical talents, but was a title that provided higher ranking within the Cathedral chapter.) Like other clerics, Torres y Vargas was promoted to a post that was being left vacant because the person holding it was also promoted. It was in this way that the same group of canons kept a closed circle with the same persons in power. Such promotion brought both prestige and a better salary. The text of the letter from King Philip IV in August of 1655 authorizing Torres y Vargas' promotion does not mention the problem of 1653–54, only that:

> ...*el dicho don Diego de Torres y Vargas es persona idónea y suficiente y en quien concurren las calidades que conforme a la erección de esa iglesia se requieren, le hagáis colación y canónica institución de la dicha chantría y le deis la posesión de ella, y hagáis acudir con los frutos y rentas, proventos y emolumentos a ellas anejo, debidos y pertenecientes, todo bien y cumplidamente sin que le falte cosa alguna...*

Don Diego de Torres y Vargas, whom I mentioned, is the ideally qualified person, possessing all the qualities that befit the necessary running of that church. You will reward him and install him canonically in the post of choirmaster and give him possession of it, attaching the fruits,

SWEDES IN PUERTO RICO

In the evening of August 27, 1649, the Swedish ship Kattan rammed a reef about 80 miles from Puerto Rico. In the struggle to alter course, the hull of the Kattan crashed into rocks, hopelessly grounding the vessel. The passengers were colonists destined for the settlement of Christina in New Sweden (Delaware). The men on board used lifeboats to transfer the women and children to the uninhabited Palominos Island, thirteen miles away from the wreck, and then brought over the provisions, fighting a storm.

With no fresh water on the island, the survivors would have perished except for the arrival a week later of two Spanish ships from Puerto Rico. Before committing themselves to the rescue, the sailors from Puerto Rico demanded the Swedes surrender, which under the circumstances was necessary because the sailors were outnumbered by the colonists. Moreover, Sweden's role in the Thirty Years' War as an enemy of Spain raised suspicions on both sides. The only way to transport the survivors to safety in Puerto Rico was to drag the Kattan off of the rocks, which the Puerto Rican sailors did, using ropes from their own ships to tow the Swedish vessel into San Juan harbor.

The narrative of the Swedish survivors expresses disbelief that the sailors from Puerto Rico said they "had never heard of Sweden," but sailors are usually from the common class and Sweden is a long way from Puerto Rico.

Although it had been rendered unseaworthy, the ship was a great prize. It carried 16 cannons, which were confiscated by the Spanish. Personal items such as jewelry and even the clothes of the survivors were taken, since the residents of Puerto Rico were suffering from shortages caused by the long war and did not think prisoners should possess more than they. The San Juan cabildo felt obliged to burn all heretical texts. However, it is unlikely that the Puerto Rican authorities knew enough Swedish to distinguish between religious books containing heresy and those of a secular content, so they burned them all.

Only the leader of the expedition, Commander Amundsson and his family, were permitted to leave in order to seek assistance, because safe passage could not be guaranteed for the many survivors when Spain was still at war with France. The survivors were offered a choice: they could renounce Lutheranism, profess Catholicism and live a normal life in Puerto Rico or they would be imprisoned until either ransomed or freed by decree. Some of those who refused to convert died in prison. Of the 70 original Swedish colonists only 19 chose to return to Sweden, the last of them in the fall of 1651. Thus, all of those interviewed by Torres y Vargas in 1654 chose to stay in Puerto Rico.

Cf: http://homepages.rootsweb.com/~roberts/COWAN/cowan013.htm

This incident demonstrates the bitterness between Catholics and Protestants that extended world-wide as one of the results of nearly a century of dynastic wars. There was no problem in rescuing the Swedes or in allowing them to live in Puerto Rico, but conversion was necessary. One of the sad characteristics of the age was how religion had erected barriers. Much of this antagonism from Catholics against Protestants formally ended with the decrees of the II Vatican Council.

rents, subsidies and pensions related, obligated and belonging to it, [to be done] in good order completely and without failing in any detail....[10]

On July 25, 1658 at the age of forty-three, Torres y Vargas was named Dean of the Cathedral upon the death of the former Dean, Juan Morcelo. Only the title of bishop was a higher appointment. Before he had died, Morcelo had written to the King on behalf of Torres y Vargas,[11] repeating the praise of the criollos who admired this Puerto Rican priest. However, being a public figure and a favorite of the bishop could have negative consequences. A sad incident involved Torres y Vargas a month later, during the recitation of the rosary in San Juan's hospital chapel. A priest named Francisco Daza barged into the church with a knife in his hand, screaming that he was going to kill Torres y Vargas. To use modern lingo, Dean Torres y Vargas "talked him down," until the police came. Once arrested, Father Daza was scheduled for trial. But when the day in court dawned, the priest, who had come to Puerto Rico from Venezuela, was nowhere to be found. And although Torres y Vargas recused himself from the case, he had already invoked his authority as Dean to order Fr. Daza to leave the island on account of having publicly spoken ill of leading figures on the island.[12] This incident suggests that Torres y Vargas understood both the demands of reform for clergy and also the need for compassion. Avoiding a public trial most likely also spared the diocese considerable embarrassment.

With Torres y Vargas installed as Dean, the new Bishop Francisco Arnaldo de Isasí arrived in 1659. He had a low opinion of local clergy, including Torres y Vargas and in a letter he calls them "*interesados*," which might be translated as "money-grubbing."[13] The year 1659 also occasioned the signing of the treaty that confirmed that the war with France had been lost. By this time, Spain was bankrupt. King Philip IV asked that a collection be taken up to help the monarchy settle its debts. Called the Donativo, it was decreed in July 1659 and

---

[10] Medrano, *op. cit.* 233.
[11] See Medrano, *op. cit.*,: 243–44.
[12] Perea, *op. cit.*, 204–205.
[13] Medrano, *op. cit*, 242.

entailed gifts from individuals, the voluntary suspension of salaries and the forfeiture of some expenses throughout the kingdom. Torres y Vargas organized the effort to raise money in Puerto Rico, probably asking relatives for contributions. Priests who raise significant sums of money for the church often gain ecclesiastical promotion. Hence, the characterization of *"interesado"* may indicate resentment at Torres y Vargas' social standing in Puerto Rico and the name-calling may reflect more negatively on the Bishop than on the Dean.

WHY WASN'T TORRES Y VARGAS NAMED BISHOP OF PUERTO RICO?

The process of naming bishops involves considerable scrutiny in addition to the need to have influential persons act on behalf of the candidate. The Council of Trent had reformed the process with the intention of eliminating noble birth or wealth as the main factors for selecting bishops. Secrecy in the proceedings was one of the means to get honest testimony about personal qualities, so that speaking the truth would carry no penalty or reprisal. Thus, any deliberations that might have been made about Torres y Vargas were kept secret and are unavailable to historians.

In general, Trent tried to avoid naming bishops in the place where they had family, so as to eliminate a conflict of interests. The bishop is supposed to have no other commitments than to the people in his diocese. The episcopal ring is treated more or less like a wedding band for the bishop with his diocese. Since Torres y Vargas had so many family members in Puerto Rico, it is unlikely that he would have been chosen to be bishop in San Juan. As demonstrated with other clerics in his family, advancement usually required leaving Puerto Rico for another diocese. As a young priest, he had already turned down such a path of advancement outside of Puerto Rico and he was unlikely to have abandoned the island once he had achieved prominence later in life. Finally, we need to recognize that clerics from Puerto Rico would not have enjoyed much visibility among authorities in Spain or Rome.

In fact, it was not until the nineteenth century when Juan Alejo Arizmendi (1803–1814) was named bishop that a Puerto Rican finally became ordinary in his homeland. Under the United States, it took more than fifty years before the second Puerto Rican would assume the episcopacy. Today, following the model of the II Vatican Council, we celebrate native bishops in their homelands.

When Bishop Isasí died in 1661, Torres y Vargas became Vicario Capitular again, a role that was prolonged when Manuel Molinero declined to accept the post as Bishop of Puerto Rico. While these refusals seem contentious to us today, it needs to be remembered that life in Puerto Rico involved traveling a great distance from Europe, taking up residence in a new climate fraught with tropical diseases and facing threats of assault from Spain's enemies. Because bishops were generally older men, these risks were truly life-threatening. Moreover, as described above, the Diocese of Puerto Rico then extended to the smaller islands of the Eastern Caribbean and travel to each of them for the required pastoral visitation was a daunting task that had taken its toll upon more than one prelate.

In 1664, a new bishop, Benito de Ribas, arrived in Puerto Rico. His pastoral care was marked by a royal decree that permitted all fugitive slaves arriving in Puerto Rico to become free. They were required to promise allegiance to Spain and practice the Catholic religion. In exchange, they were given parcels of land near a parish of San Mateo in an area called Santurce, after St. George ("*Turzi*" in the Basque language). Bishop de Ribas soon named Torres y Vargas ecclesiastical governor, a post that gave the Puerto Rican considerable power to settle legal matters of a civil nature for the diocese. The bishop also penned a comment about Torres y Vargas that both praises and criticizes don Diego.

> *Entre los prebendados, el deán es jurista; estudió en Salamanca y es bachiller por aquella escuela. Es gran eclesiástico y un sujeto muy digno de mayor puesto. Hállase mal de súbdito, porque con las vacantes largas de las Indias ha sido obispo mucho tiempo en Puerto Rico. Hoy le tengo nombrado provisor; no sé si se desdeña de ejercer hasta que falte yo. Propone para las prebendas de la iglesia sujetos que él los pueda traer a su mano. Sírvase Vuestra Excelencia de tenerlo advertido.*

Among the prebendaries, the dean is a jurist; he studied at Salamanca and has a bachelor's degree from that university. He is a great eccleiastic and a subject well worthy of a higher position [*Higher than dean would mean Bishop-ed.*]. He is not comfortable as a subordinate, because given the long vacancies of sees in the Indies, he has been [de facto] Bishop for many years in Puerto Rico. At the moment I have appointed him provisor; I do not know if he finds it beneath his dignity to act as such until I am gone. He nominates for the prebends such persons as he can control. Your Excellency should please take notice of this.[14]

The bishop's comments would have become part of the information offered to the new king, Charles II (1665–1700), who was only four years old when his father died. Physically deformed and mentally retarded, this Hapsburg never really ruled Spain, leaving decisions to contentious circles of advisors. As an adult, the king's tongue was so large, he could scarcely be understood when he spoke. He drooled often and was virtually incapable of grooming himself for dress or toilet. Yet, the royal court maintained the myth that his infirmities were the result of a witch's spell. The popular religiosity of the time entertained this fiction rather than confront the reality that the Spanish throne was occupied by an incompetent at a time when the nation had lost hegemony in Europe. Charles II would die without heirs and be the last of the Hapsburgs to rule Spain, providing an excuse for the French House of Bourbon to mount the Spanish throne in 1702. Torres y Vargas would not live to see this change in dynasty, however.

When Bishop Ribas died in 1668, Torres y Vargas once more became Vicario Capitular. His name can also be found in many pastoral tasks at the Cathedral, such as the priest administering baptisms and marriages. Apparently, many "high society" figures asked him to perform such ceremonies, no doubt because he was a good priest and in some instances, a relative. We do not know the exact date of his death, but Dr. Pío Medrano has offered evidence suggesting that he passed from this mortal life, probably on April 5, 1670 at the age of 55. The cause of death is unknown, but since he was signing official papers only weeks before, he seems not to have suffered from a long-standing and debilitating illness. Sudden death from a heart attack or stroke seems more likely. Considering that both of his brothers died before reaching 35 years of age, Don Diego Torres y Vargas can be considered to have lived a full life. The text he left behind

---

[14] Medrano, *op. cit.*, 269.

describing his homeland is part of his service to the Puerto Rican people and the Catholic Church.

NOTES ON THE TEXT AND TRANSLATION

The text of Torres y Vargas might have remained undiscovered, if not for a dedicated band of nineteenth-century Puerto Rican students in Spain. Alejandro Tapia y Rivera (1826–1882), although far from his island home, was committed to Puerto Rican history. This touch of nationalist sentiment near the midpoint of the nineteenth century led to an important discovery for the young university scholar. Tapia y Rivera explored the papers of Juan Bautista Muñoz (1745–1799), the principal organizer of the Archive of the Indies. Although the Archive was located in Seville, after Muñoz' death, his personal collection had been transferred to Madrid's Royal Historical Academy. Included in many folios were unpublished documents and reports that Muñoz had used in compiling his historical account of the Americas. The meticulous Enlightenment historian had identified the location of other relevant documents and his lists put Tapia y Rivera on alert for the report of Don Diego Torres y Vargas.

At the insistence of a fellow Puerto Rican student in Madrid, Ramón Baldorioty de Castro, Tapia y Rivera started the *Sociedad recolectora de documentos históricos de la isla de San Juan Bautista de Puerto Rico* [Collection Society for Historical Documents about the Island of San Juan Bautista of Puerto Rico]. It was intended to repeat and expand the effort of Juan Bautista Muñoz so the people of Puerto Rico would have access to their own history. Among the collaborators in this historical recovery project were future patriots like José Julián Acosta, Segundo Ruiz Belvis and Ramón Emeterio Betances. The eventual result far exceeded the initial documentary trove of Muñoz. Tapia y Rivera himself would later gain fame as a playwright and poet of the nineteenth century when he returned to Puerto Rico.

The report of Canon Torres y Vargas reproduced in this book was copied in 1851 from *Iglesias de Indias*, from the library of Don Domingo Del Monte. It is not clear if this was a codex, that is, a manuscript that was hand transcribed or one that had been printed. We know that the editors in Spain had received two installments of the report from Torres y Vargas, because the completed report published by Tapia y Rivera includes the note that at the request of Juan Díez de la Calle Torres y Vargas added some facts not in the first installment and corrected certain errors (#103). Thus, we can be certain that the first and largest part of the report (#1– #102) preceded the shorter segment (#103 – #130). Moreover, it appears from use of the word "*imprenta* / printed" (#130) that Torres y Vargas was given printed pages to review for accuracy, more or less as an author usually gets to review the copy editor's proofs before publishing. As discussed in (pp. 211–214), "Questions of Chronology," there remain unresolved issues about the dates of composition, revision and condition of the version of the report utilized by Tapia y Rivera.

Despite the ambiguities that persist about the original text, however, we can be certain that not every letter was clear in the two hundred year old document used by Tapia and his collaborators. When Torres y Vargas' report was finally printed in the nineteenth century, it appears that the typesetters did not recognize all of the stylistic devices that had been used in the seventeenth century, such as how "s", in the middle of a word was rendered as "ʃ". Not recognizing this form of a "s", the text of Tapia y Rivera substitutes an "f". Thus "*disce*," Latin for "learn" is printed as "*difce*," which is not a word (#107).

Tapia y Rivera and his colleagues were interested in many other documents besides that of Torres y Vargas, of course. The *Biblioteca Histórica de Puerto Rico que contiene varios documentos de los siglos XV, XVI, XVII, XVIII* [Historical Library of Puerto Rico that Contains Various Documents of the XV, XVI, XVII, XVIII Centuries] was published in Spain by the printing house of the Marquez in 1854. The Instituto de literatura puertorriqueña reprinted Tapia's *Biblioteca* in the twentieth century (1945), and in 1970 the text was again issued as *Obras Completas* by the Instituto de Cultura Puertorriqueña (San Juan). In this last cited version, the work by Torres y Vargas is found in Volume III, pp. 537–595.

Our text is taken from the reproduction and notes published in the second edition of 1976 of the *Crónicas de Puerto Rico*, (University of Puerto Rico Press: pp. 172–217) edited by Eugenio Fernández Méndez from the 1945 version of Tapia y Rivera's work. Unfortunately, the text in Fernández Méndez' collection omitted relevant sections of Torres y Vargas' work. For our volume, portions of what appears under "*Anexos*" had to be taken from that section in the Instituto de Cultura Puertorriqueña's 1970 edition of Tapia y Rivera's original work (1970: III, pp. 578–587). The reader will find that our text reproduces a pattern found in both of these versions: some illegible words are indicated by a series of dots, Latin phrases are put in italics as also other redactions by Tapia y Rivera. In order to avoid distraction from the text, we have confined most of our comments to side-bars and notes. In all of this, we were limited by lack of access to the manuscript used by Tapia y Rivera.

To show how Torres y Vargas utilized his sources, we have highlighted some passages by layout and type font. Where Torres y Vargas cites from an official list, we have left the text in the normal size: the comments of the canon on each of these persons in printed in a smaller type. Without claiming exactitude in each selection, we think that format helps the reader to see how Torres y Vargas composed his narrative. He took sure information from a published list of governors or bishops and then added facts from his own observation or from interviews with people who had further information of these personages.

In addition to the entries made within the text, several issues of translation style should be addressed. **First,** we made an editorial decision to divide the text into workable paragraphs, enumerating them so that specific passages can more easily be located and understood in translation. Although the Spanish original has only a few such breaks, we believe our innovation supplies greater clarity to the reader. We trust that our enumeration of the paragraphs will assist readers to more easily find selected passages and compare the original and translation, which are interfaced in the book for the convenience of the reader. The enumerations are printed in parentheses with the numerical sign (#).

Second, to render the translation in contemporary English, longer Spanish sentences have been broken into more terse English ones. At times, some nuance was sacrificed to readability but the intention was to provide a report in language similar to what a church official might use today. In this spirit, the translator has avoided archaic words like "vouchsafe," "forthwith," "beseech," etc.

Third, seventeenth century forms of spelling, accent marks and grammar are mostly preserved in the Spanish text. However, errors are corrected in the translation. **Fourth,** there are many religious terms about civic titles and ecclesiastical offices. Some of this terminology does not suffer easy translation into English, and to aid the reader, the original Spanish term was reproduced in brackets. Also, many of the posts or titles no longer exist in a post-Vatican II Catholic Church. The translator has made an effort to guide the reader with comments within the text and by a glossary.

A few terms deserve special attention here:

• *Vecino*, is not exactly the same as "resident" because it includes property and legal rights peculiar to the age. The translation leaves this term in Spanish throughout.

• The same decision was adopted for *hidalgo*, *criollo*, and *Audiencia*. (In the essays we have followed the general editorial practice of using Spanish words with italics only once. In the translation of the text, however, we have done so for every occurrence of a Spanish term, so as to facilitate citation of specific passages.)

• In most entries, we have translated the name of a place from the Spanish of Torres y Vargas into the term that is common in English. Thus, once mentioned in his original form, "San Martín" becomes "St. Martin" and "San Cristóbal" becomes "St. Kitts." However, San Juan remains San Juan and not "St. John" because "San Juan" is used for Puerto Rico's capitol. We also prefer the Spanish "Española" used by Torres y Vargas to the Latinized "Hispaniola" found in later writings.

• Manioc, which the Taínos called "*yuca*," a term still used by Spanish-speakers in Puerto Rico, is not translated at "yucca" — for in fact English usage refers to different plants.

• The Dutch general who attacked Puerto Rico in 1625 is referred to as "Bowdyn Hendrick" although the original Dutch is "Boudewijn Hendrieksz." (Many Spanish texts refer to him as "Enrico.")

• The City of San Juan is on a small island, *isleta*, in Spanish and in common usage distinguished the city from the larger island of Puerto Rico. Our translation uses "islet" throughout.

• Many Puerto Ricans tend to use a capital "I" for "Island," when referring to Puerto Rico or within the title of another place such as "the Island of Margarita." We have reproduced this style with the titles of "His Majesty," "Bishop" and "Governor" of a specific place as well as a capital "C" for the City of San Juan and the like, except where city is used as an adjective as in, "city walls."

•   The custom of citing saints as "my lord" has been repeated.

•   Perhaps the most difficult decision was how to translate the Spanish process of "*Residencia.*" The translation uses the English "evaluation" in most places and — for purely stylistic reasons — "audit" in another (see #74). It was an institution of Castilian law and required that the official remain in the place he had governed until a judge reviewed his administration. Complaints were heard, books were examined and a final evaluation was prepared for the crown. A good evaluation or *Residencia* would mean promotion; a bad one, dismissal or even criminal prosecution. The local residents and municipal officials played a major role in this process and it amounted to an instrument of the balance of powers in the Spanish government and a window for democratic input from the governed. It shares certain characteristics with the impeachment process of U.S. law, but would not be properly translated in this 17th century text as "impeachment."

Fifth, many of the Latin phrases are garbled and misspelled in the Spanish original, making them virtually unintelligible. Ignorance of the Latin language by either the compilers or the typesetters may be the cause in some instances. Most of these phrases in Latin are biblical passages because Trent obligated that citation from the scriptures ought to reference the Latin Vulgate. However, Torres y Vargas also cited classical sources in Latin. Where appropriate, we have identified these references and cross-checked the accuracy of Torres y Vargas' citation. All Latin phrases in the original Spanish text have been translated into English and placed in brackets within the translation so the reader will know to look to the Spanish text for the Latin phrases. In a few places, the Latin is also preserved in the translation because it better fits the meaning of the passage on account of word play (see #5 the theological citation from Fray Luis de León).

It appears that Torres y Vargas sometimes wrote these Latin passages from memory, perhaps recalling something he had been taught while a university student. Unfortunately, memories can be faulty. In one place (#30), he misquotes the Vulgate using the Latin "*timor*" where the Bible uses "*pavor*." While the words are nearly alike in meaning, the version of Torres y Vargas is not exact. In another place, he quotes Virgil's Æneid. He confuses the actual line with a phrase of similar meaning. This is noted in the translation. Instead of detracting from the effort of Torres y Vargas, these minor errors actually enhance the quality of his endeavor. In the absence of any extensive library to consult in San Juan and the paucity of university-trained scholars, the scholarly quality of Torres y Vargas' work is evident.

Special attention should be paid to a **sixth** and final issue. The historians of the period did not mark materials previously written or published as footnotes or citations. Authors were free to copy relevant information verbatim and include it in the text with only passing attribution, if at all. This was particularly true for well known sources, such as we today might label as "common domain." It appears all but certain that Torres y Vargas copied from different sources, including parts of the 1582 report written for Governor Juan López Melgarejo. Description of trade products of Puerto Rico and comparison of their quality to competing suppliers as well as information on the quantity of exports and sales appear to have been inserted from commercial reports, along with personal observations

Use of these sources does not mean, however, that the canon was guilty of plagiarism. Today's standards had not yet been invented. The use of so many other sources should be commended rather than condemned because Torres y Vargas worked hard to assemble all the written information as best he might in a city most of whose libraries and archives had been destroyed by the Dutch torching of the city some twenty years before.

In contrast to this style of incorporating local reports and documents for his text, there are other historical sources that are explicitly cited by Torres y Vargas. Principal among these is the seven volume work, *Historia General de los Hechos de los Castellanos en las Islas i Tierra Firme del Mar Océano* by Antonio de Herrera y Tordesillas, which had been published in Madrid over a period of years, 1601–1615. Even though it had been published thirty years before Torres y Vargas started to write his history, the work of Herrera was largely considered the most comprehensive and most authoritative of the time. Significant in its value to the compilation of historical works was the incorporation of as then unpublished sources from Bartolomé de las Casas and Bernal Díaz. The first volume dealt with the early history of the Spaniards in Puerto Rico and had been translated into Latin and French (1622) and also English and German (1624).

The frequent mention of Herrera leads to the supposition that Torres y Vargas had access to this work, perhaps even a personal copy of the very important first volume that he well might have brought from Spain after concluding his studies there. Other historical works were cited by Torres y Vargas, but it is unclear if he had actually read any of them. He may just be listing known works to either highlight Puerto Rico's importance in history or the inadequate information circulating in earlier written sources. Utilizing the comments provided by Fernández Méndez (1976), we have identified these sources and provided below a note about their relevance to Torres y Vargas' work.

> **Gierolamo Benzoni (ca. 1519–1572)** from Milán, had come to the Americas as a young man of 22 in 1541 or 1542. He lived in Santo Domingo from 1544 to 1555 and may have visited Puerto Rico. He published his *Historia del Mondo Nuovo* in Venice in 1565. It was very critical of Spanish behavior towards the natives. Later editions of the text were illustrated by the Flemish engraver Theodor de Bry (1528 – 1598), a Protestant who had fled his native land during the wars with Catholic Spain. By the time of the Thirty Years' War when Torres y Vargas wrote, de Bry's works including his illustration of Benzoni's history had become tools of Protestantism to disparage Catholic colonization. While the canon may have rejected the negative views in Benzoni's work as illustrated by de Bry, a competent rendering of the histories of the time would have not been able to escape mention of this work. In fact, Torres y Vargas asserts that his history is more accurate than Benzoni's.

> **Juan Paulo Galvera Salonense**. Next to no information has survived about this author, but the title of the work cited by Torres y Vargas, *Theatrum Orbis*, is virtually the same as that of Abraham Ortelius, *Theatrum Orbis Terrarum*, published in Antwerp in 1570 and cited

by Torres y Vargas in the opening paragraph of his text. Ortelius' publication became the indispensable atlas for the places named in the chronicles of discovery and colonization, especially among Protestants. The book of Galvera Salonense may have reproduced some of Ortelius' work, but been more accessible to a Catholic and Spanish reading public and therefore, more appropriate to be mentioned by Torres y Vargas.

Juan Solórzano y Pereira (1575–1654), a Spanish lawyer trained at Salamanca, published in Latin the volumes of *de Indianum Jure* between 1629 and 1639. He analyzed the principles of law relevant to Spanish colonization of the Americas. These volumes were replete with examples derived from actual historical accounts, including facts about Puerto Rico. The books would likely have been part of the general study of law for university students during Torres y Vargas's study at Salamanca.

Giovanni Botero (1544–1617) was an Italian clergyman, who joined the Jesuits for a time. He criticized the writings of Machiavelli about the nature of political power and the prerogatives of rulers in his treatise *Ragione di Stato* (*The Reason of State*), published in 1589. His *Relazioni universali* was published in four volumes, 1591–1598, and examined the nature of political authority around the world, including the Americas. Once again, it is not difficult to imagine why they would have been included in the study of law at Salamanca.

Johannes Laet (1593–1649) was a noted Flemish geographer and one of the Lord Directors of the Dutch West India Company. His book, published in Dutch in 1625 as *Nieuwe wereldt offe beschrijvinghe van West Indien*, is still regarded as one of the best sources on the Dutch colonies, as it was able to draw upon the files of the West India Company, including Adriaen Block's log books. The maps are some of the most significant to appear up to the time of its publication, and many of them were subsequently used in other seventeenth century works. It was translated into Latin by the author in an edition with improved maps and issued as *AMERICAE UTRIUSQUE DE-SCRIPTIO Novus Orbis seu Descriptionis Indiae Occidentalis Libri XVIII [Antwerp, 1633]*. This is the one cited by Torres y Vargas, although he gives 1632 as the date of printing: Segundo Ruiz Belvis is credited for having edited this work for its references to Puerto Rico and these were published as excerpts by Alejandro Tapia y Rivera in the *Biblioteca Histórica de Puerto Rico*.

Closer to the focus on Puerto Rico is the already mentioned report (pp. 8–9; 67) that was prepared in 1582 by Torres y Vargas' great uncle, Juan II (Troche) Ponce de León, at the request of Governor Juan López de Melgarejo. It lies beyond this work to make a detailed analysis of what sections are constructed the same and what vocabulary is repeated, but suffice it to say that information of the two reports is virtually identical on matters such as buildings and hospitals (Chapters 32-41) in the 1582 Report, (see *Crónicas* by Fernández Méndez, pp. 128–134; and #18–20 et passim in Torres y Vargas).

In this text and in the translation, we have respected the literary conventions of the baroque style in which Torres y Vargas was trained. While for some scholars, including Professor Fernández Méndez, this elaborated style was a distraction, we have considered it the backdrop for understanding this seventeenth century document. Moreover, as a religious age, the faith and the concern for the Catholic Church that shapes the narrative by Torres y Vargas cannot be ignored. This edition of the text and its first-time ever translation into English have been supplemented with notes and commentary to facilitate a theological appreciation of the work of the Puerto Rican canon, even if the reader does not happen to profess Catholicism.

In sum, Canon Torres y Vargas wrote a history of Puerto Rico that is thoroughly inserted into its own times. Its style echoes the literary, philosophical, theological and cultural norms of the Catholic Baroque era. In addition, this document reflects a unique Puerto Rican perspective on a changing world. The challenges provided by a Caribbean opened up to conflicts and competition with Protestant nations were to make Puerto Rico indispensable to the Spanish Empire until its rule was replaced by the United States in 1898. Perhaps most importantly, the narrative by this native Puerto Rican priest demonstrates a growing awareness of an identity shaped by unique forces. It is a sign of the achievements of Torres y Vargas that a band of Puerto Rican patriots like Tapia y Rivera in the nineteenth century included this narrative in their collection meant to awaken a Puerto Rican consciousness. It is with much the same intention, that this series has translated the work into English, giving the opportunity to readers in the twenty-first century to discover the importance of history to Puerto Rican identity.

AMSA
AMDS
JRV

SPANISH TEXT
AND
ENGLISH TRANSLATION

DESCRIPCIÓN DE LA ISLA Y CIUDAD DE
PUERTO-RICO,
Y DE SU VECINDAD Y POBLACIONES,
PRESIDIO, GOBERNADORES Y OBISPOS; FRUTOS Y MINERALES.
ENVIADA POR
EL LICENCIADO DON DIEGO DE TORRES VARGAS,
CANÓNIGO DE LA SANTA IGLESIA DE ESTA ISLA
EN EL AVISO QUE LLEGÓ A ESPAÑA
EN 23 DE ABRIL DE 1647

DESCRIPTION OF THE ISLAND AND CITY OF PUERTO-RICO,
AND OF ITS INHABITANTS AND TOWNS,
GARRISON, GOVERNORS AND BISHOPS;
AS WELL AS ITS FRUITS AND MINERALS.
SENT BY
DON DIEGO DE TORRES VARGAS,
LICENCIATE IN LAW,
CANON OF THIS ISLAND'S CATHEDRAL,
IN THE NEWS-PACKET WHICH ARRIVED AT SPAIN
ON APRIL 23, 1647.

Al Sr. Cronista Maestro Gil González Dávila

1.   La Isla de San Juan, cuyo puerto (por ser bueno) llamaron sus descubridores Rico comparada en la demarcación con las de la española y de Cuba, les cede sin duda en grandeza, porque no corre más de cuarenta leguas de este oeste, desde la cabeza de San Juan que es su primer promontorio, y toca el meridiano del Occidente hasta el cabo que se llama Rojo, y está situado al oeste de ella donde su fin termina. Boja en ámbito ciento y treinta y seis leguas (como parecerá de la medida, que por mandado de S. M., hizo el Gobernador Juan de Haro con cédula particular el año de 1629, que se llevó a Madrid, y se hallará en el oficio de Indias). Pero en el temperamento y calidades se adelanta mucho a todas las Islas de barlovento, porque goza de una perpetua primavera sin que calor ni el frío llegue a sentirse de manera que aflija ni descomponga la naturaleza, a cuya causa viven los naturales largos años, y los negros de los Ríos más que los de tierra de Angola, que deben de ser aquellos de más templados países, y assi se adaptan mejor con este.

> This appears to have been taken from a description already written with details for cartographers, travelers and sailors, etc. Note the use of "assi," an older form of the word "así", possibly an indication that this was copied from another source. The text in parentheses is likely added by Torres y Vargas as clarification.
>
> S.M. for "Su Magestad"

2.   Es toda ella fertilísima y verde a la vista de fuera por donde quiera que la miren los navegantes, y por los medios muy doblada, con que se hace áspera a los que la caminan por tierra, y útil a los esclavos que se huyen de sus dueños, que entrándose por las sierras, suelen no hallarse en diez y veinte años, y algunas veces se suelen quedar para siempre. La forma de la Isla es más angular que cuadrada, porque tiene en lo ancho de norte a sur veinte leguas donde más y diez y siete donde menos; con que viene a ser casi igual por lo ancho. En los estremos a las tres o cuatro leguas es más baja y se puede caminar casi toda por la playa, pasando las bocas de los ríos que salen a la mar que los más se vadean, principalmente los de la parte del Sur, que son más pequeños que los de la parte Norte.

> Torres y Vargas says runaway slaves are hard to capture once they get into the wilderness.
>
> Note that "s" is frequently used instead of "x" as in "estremos".

To the Historiographer Royal, Maestro Gil González Dávila

1.   The Island of San Juan, whose port was named Rich Port by those who discovered it (because of its goodness), yields to the Islands of Española and Cuba in size when you compare their extension. It stretches only forty leagues from east to west; from the Cabeza de San Juan, which is its first headland, and it touches the western meridian down to the cape which is called Red [Cabo Rojo], which is placed where its limits end at the west. Its circumference runs a hundred thirty-six leagues (as will appear from the measurements which Governor Juan de Haro made by command of His Majesty in a special warrant of 1629; this was taken to Madrid and will be found in the Office of the Indies). But in its temper and qualities it far surpasses all the Windward Islands, because it enjoys a perpetual springtime so that neither heat or cold are experienced in such a way as to afflict or discompose [human] nature. For this reason the natives of the Island live many years, and the blacks from the Rivers [Nigeria - Ed.] live there longer than those from the land of Angola, — the former must come from a more temperate land, and thus they adapt better to this one.

2.   The whole Island is extremely fertile, and is green when you look at it from outside, no matter from what angle the sailors gaze on it. In the middle, the terrain is very rippled, which makes it rough for those who travel by land. But it is very convenient for the slaves who run away from their masters; once they get into the sierras, they are often not found in ten or twenty years, and sometimes they remain there forever. The shape of the Island is more [rect]angular than square, for its width from north to south is twenty leagues at the widest and seventeen at the narrowest, so it is pretty much the same width all over. On the edges, for about three or four leagues, it is lower, and you can walk almost the whole circumference on the beach, passing through the mouths of the rivers which open to the sea. Most of these can be forded, especially those on the southern side of the Island, which are smaller than those on the north.

3.   This Island has not been so forgotten or dormant that its memory should be lacking in ancient annals, be it of cosmographers or of historians. Among others, its memory is found in Antonio de Herrera's *Crónica General de las Indias,* in Geronimo Benzoni's *History of America*, in Juan Paulo Galvera of Salona's

3.   No ha dormido tanto al olvido esta Isla, que falte su memoria en los ana
les antiguos assi de cosmógrafos, como de historiadores, y entre otros se halla la
suya en Antonio de Herrera, en su crónica general de las Indias, en Gerónimo Benzoni en su historia de América, en Juan Paulo Galvera Salonense en su libro *Theatrum orbis*, en Juan Solorsano Pereira, en el *Jure Indiarum*, en Juan Botero en sus *Relaciones universales*, y en Juan de Laet Auturpiense en el *Questiones de las W. Bestinas* que imprimió el año de 632 en Holanda (y siendo casi todos Juanes parece que quisieron pagarle la obligación adquirida en el nombre de la Isla.) Pero con todo, no la describieron tan en particular como yo lo pudiera hacer agora, donde se mostrara más hermosa que en común y general, por lo ameno de sus valles y arboledas, sino fuera por lo conciso que pide la historia donde no podrá gozar de tanto lugar. En el primero descubrimiento del Almirante Colón se nota en Antonio de Herrera, haberla conocido después de algunos años que se pobló la Española, que dice fue en 1508. Pero Juan de Laet y otros, tienen que el año siguiente del descubrimiento de las Indias que fue el 1493, y que el primer capitán que comenzó a conquistarla con orden del Almirante fue el adelantado Juan Ponce de León caballero noble

> Torres y Vargas lists historians who mentioned Puerto Rico in their texts. Note that the date given is "632" omitting the thousand (it was 1632). Both styles are found throughout the text, possibly reflecting usage in other sources as contrasted with Torres y Vargas' own preference. Torres y Vargas inserts Baroque era speculation about the coincidence of so many of these authors having the first name "Juan" like that of San Juan . Remember also, that Juan Ponce de León was Torres y Vargas' great-great-grandfather.
>
> The use of the first person singular suggests these words are his alone. He demonstrates great native pride in the beauty of the island.
>   *"Agora"* is for *"Ahora"*

de Sevilla, que lo era del Higüey en Isla de Santo Domingo, por tener la primera noticia de los indios que por aquella parte, que es la del Norte, se comunicaban. Navegando desde España a estas Indias hay otras islas antes de esta, como son la Dominica, San Estacio, Santa Lucia, la Granada, Marigalante, Matalino, Barbado y Barbada, San Martín, San Bartolomé, Santa Cruz, Las Virgenes y San Cristóbal, que en esta ledanía de escollos guarda igual proporción a su nombre, teniendo diez y ocho leguas de grandeza a que ninguna de las otras arriba. Habrá tiempo de 30 años poco más o menos que gobernando esta Isla D. Felipe de Biamonte y Navarra, se tuvo noticia de la población que tenían en estas de barlovento los ingleses, holandeses y franceses que rebelados de la

> The information about San Cristóbal, now St. Kitts Island, was relevant and controversial to Puerto Rico's role in the Thirty Years' War when Torres y Vargas composed this report (see essays). Note the use of the first person.

book *Theatrum Orbis*, in Juan Solorzano Pereira's *De Jure Indiarum*, in Juan Botero's *Universal Relations*, and in Jan van Laet of Antwerp's *Questiones de las W. Bestinas,* which he printed in Holland in the year [1]632. (Note that, since almost all of these authors are called John, it seems they wanted to fulfill the right this Island acquired by being named after Saint John.) But in spite of this, they did not describe it in as much detail as I could do now. Except that the brevity this history demands will not allow enough space, its pleasant valleys and woodlands could be shown more beautiful than perceived when describing it in common and general terms. In commenting on the first discovery of Admiral Columbus Antonio de Herrera said that it [Puerto Rico] became known in 1508, some years after La Española was settled. But Jan van Laet and others hold to 1493, the year following the discovery of the Indies. The first captain to begin its conquest by order of the Admiral was the Adelantado Juan Ponce de León, a noble gentleman of Seville, who was [Adelantado] of Higüey in the Island of Santo Domingo. He had the first news [about it] from the Indians who communicated with it on that side, which is the north. As you sail from Spain to the Indies, you meet other islands before this one, such as Dominica, San Estacio [St. Eustace], Santa Lucia, la Granada [Grenada], Marigalante, Matalino, Barbado y Barbada, San Martín [Sint Maarten/St. Martin], San Bartolomé, Santa Cruz [St. Croix], Las Virgenes [the Virgin Islands] and San Cristóbal [St. Kitts], which in this litany of islets keeps a proportion to its name, since it is eighteen leagues in size, which none of the others approaches. About 30 years ago, more or less, when Don Felipe de Biamonte y Navarra, was governor [1614–1620] of this Island, it came to his notice that the English, Dutch and French rebels from La Rochelle had settled almost all these Windward Islands, basing themselves, though wrongly, on the right of first occupation. According to the Spaniards who are leaving the Island of St. Kitts, they have more than 12,000 men, sugar mills, and other plantations such as tobacco, indigo, cotton and livestock, with many horses that they breed (of which they have great

---

The "Adelantado" was a royal emissary with the power to establish government in a newly conquered territory, which explains why many *adelantados* were military men like Ponce de León.

Torres y Vargas is wrong about the location: Higüey is in the southern side of Española, called here "Santo Domingo."

Torres y Vargas verbally plays on St. Christopher's image as a giant, so St. Kitts, being named after him, is a giant among smaller islands.

French Protestants or Huguenots rebelled against Louis XIII and Cardinal Richelieu, making them foes of Catholic Spain. Torres y Vargas disputes their claim that the islands, discovered by Spain, were open to colonization.

Rochela o ya fundados aunque mal en el derecho del primer ocupante, las han poblado casi todas, y en la Isla de San Cristóbal dicen los españoles que salen de ella, que tienen más de 12,000 hombres e ingenios de azúcar y otras grangerías de tabaco, añil, algodón y ganadas con muchos caballos que crían de que tienen grandes atajas, pero que ya cansada la tierra porque esta de las Indias no sufren más de tres frutos buenos no los da como a los principios, de que disgustado su Gobernador, se habla y discurre sobre desampararla y mudarse a otro sitio si bien el inglés está labrando una fuerza con fosos guarnecidos de artillería.

4.   y porque mi intento no es referir los de esta Isla digo que las de barlovento, las principales y que primero se descubrieron y poblaron fueron Santo Domingo, Cuba y Puerto-Rico y ésta la llamaban la Boriqueña sus naturales y las tuvieron par las Espérides, Plutarco, Plinio, Pomponio Mela, Tholomeo, S. Isidoro, Abraham, Ortelio y otros de los antiguos si bien el Abulense, Alerio, Vinegas, Mariana, Postello, Alegreti y otros las confunden con las de Canaria, que son las Afortunadas, y las de Cabo-verde que son las Gorgonias, por lo que Antonio de Lebrija llama a este cabo, Esperionceras.

> In his 1493 report to the crown, Columbus compared the Caribbean islands to the Canary Islands known in antiquity as the *Hesperides*. Torres y Vargas dwells on this often repeated comparison to link Puerto Rico to classical Greek and Roman history. Here he cites Augustinian Friar Luis de León (1528–1591) of Salamanca, who wrote poetry and theological commentaries that often were controversial for having avoided the Vulgate translation of the Bible mandated by the Council of Trent, among other things. The comparison of Puerto Rico to the beloved in the Song of Songs repeats the Baroque fascination with coincidence. In the style of Patristic writers, this theology explored a mystical or hidden application of every word of the bible to contemporary realities. The same style of theological reference can be found in *Imagen de la Virgen María*,* a 1648 treatise about Our Lady of Guadalupe by the Mexican priest, Miguel Sánchez (1594–1674)."
>
> *See: Timothy Matovina, (2003). "Guadalupe at Calvary: Patristic Theology in Miguel Sanchez's *Imagen De la Virgen Maria*". *Theological Studies* 64 (4): 795+.

5.   Siendo pues estas tres islas las que primero se descubrieran en este nuevo Mundo, dice fray Luis de León sobre el capitulo 8° de los Cantares, que se ha de entender y esplicar aquel lugar *Sorori nostre in die quando aloquenda est? Si murus est? edificemus super eum propugnacule argentea, si astium compingamus illud tabulis cedrinis*, de la gente de este descubrimiento, y siendo así, a quien le cuadra la explicación aun en el sentido literal con que habla la esposa sino a esta Isla de Puerto-Rico? que ella sola *"parvula est"* pues es de las tres la más pequeña, y ella *"ubera no habet"* porque habiéndose consumido sus naturales que

droves). But the soil of that Island is already exhausted, since this land of the Indies cannot bear more than three good crops, and so it does not produce as it did at first. And because their Governor is displeased at this, there are talks and discussions about abandoning it and moving to another place, although the English are building a fortress with moats protected by artillery.

4.   But, since it is not my intention to tell about this Island [St. Kitts], I say that the principal ones that were first discovered and settled were Santo Domingo, Cuba and Puerto-Rico, and that this last was called la Boriqueña [*rectè*: Boriquén] by its natives. Plutarch, Pliny, Pomponius Mela, Ptolemy, Saint Isidore [of Seville], Abraham Ortelius, and others among the ancients held these islands to be the Hesperides, but the Bishop of Avila, Alerio, Venegas, Mariana, Postello, Alegretti and others confuse them [the Hesperides] with the Canaries, which are really the Fortunate Islands, or the Cape Verde Islands, which are the Gorgonias, and, for this reason, Antonio de Lebrija calls this cape Esperionceras.

Alonso de Madrigal, called "Abulensis," or "El Tostado" was bishop of Avila in the XVth century. **Juan de Mariana** (1536–1624) was the Jesuit author of a history of Spain considered authoritative at the time Torres y Vargas wrote. The other works are obscure. — **Lebrija** was a codifer of Spanish grammar. (See #9 below).

"Hesperides" are mythological spirits dwelling near the setting sun in Greek mythology, and the islands furthest West inherited this name from sailors. Later discoveries, however, moved the label further west, confusing the issue.

---

5.   And, since these three Islands were the first to be discovered in this New World, Fray Luis de León says in his commentary on the eighth chapter of the Song of Songs that the passage *Sorori nostre in die quando aloquenda est? Si murus est? edificemus super eum propugnacule argentea, si astium compingamus illud tabulis cedrinis*, should be understood and explained as referring to the peoples of this discovery. And if this is so, whom does this explanation of the bride's words fit, even in a literal sense, except this Island of Puerto Rico? For she alone *"parvula est,"* [is little] since she is the smallest of the three, and *"ubera no habet,"* [she has no breasts] be-

This passage applies the Song of Songs to Puerto Rico. The translation in The New American Bible reads: **"Our sister is little and she has no breasts as yet. What shall we do for our sister when her courtship begins? If she is a wall, we will build upon it a silver parapet: If she is a door, we will reinforce it with a cedar plank."** (Song of Songs 8:8–9). Torres y Vargas plays on the Latin word *"ostium,"* (for "door") to its alternate meaning of "port."

beneficiaban sus ricas minas es la más pobre de todas, y ella *"si murus est"* es solo Ciudad de Muros cerrada entre las demás de las Indias, y ella si *"Ostium habet"* no solo tiene puerto sino que por ser tan bueno se llama San Juan de Puerto-Rico, y en él *"quid fatiemus sorori nostre en die quando aloquenda est,"* parece que la divina esposa previene a los Reyes de España, sus Señores y nuestros, que consideren la respuesta que han de dar a sus quejas cuando por dormido descuido llegare a peligrar: a la hostilidad de tan advertidos enemigos que se le han avecindado para lograr mejor sus ocasiones que Dios no permita. En algunas de las causas citadas se hallan tales disposiciones que las hacen aptas a predominar a otras de su especie, ejemplar sea el Sol de cuya luz como de mayor dignidad participan las estrellas y Luna, el hombre que es una semejanza del mundo, según Platón en su Thimeo, suele tener cierto imperio y señorío en otro hombre, como observo la curiosidad de Roma entre Marco Antonio y Julio César que aún en los juegos de burla le tenía César ganada la ventaja. Otras cosas hay que por la colocación de sus partes se hallan con disposiciones superiores, como la cabeza donde asiste la razón dominante a las partes del alma que respeto de las del cuerpo tiene el más eminente lugar.

The references to passages of scripture and classical history constitute a frequent literary device of the Baroque. Torres y Vargas linked Puerto Rico's importance to passages in the Bible and the philosophy of classical Greece and Rome, in support of Spain's King Phillip III's 1643 praise of Puerto Rico. That royal decree affirmed the strategic importance of the Island since the end the Thirty Years' War would permanently open the Caribbean to other European powers. As a native of Puerto Rico, Torres y Vargas was proud that his homeland had merited this attention from the monarch.

Fernando de la Riva Agüero is identified by Eugenio Fernández Méndez (1976: 177, ftn. 15) as a native of Puerto Rico, educated like Torres y Vargas at Salamanca. This is contradicted by Torres y Vargas in his text (see paragraph #81 below). It is hard not to prefer the accuracy of Torres y Vargas, a contemporary of Riva y Agüero, over the footnote inserted into the 1976 text.

---

6.   Pues de esta superioridad y eminencia viene a gozar en las Indias occidentales la Isla de Puerto-Rico como primera de las pobladas y principal custodia y llave de todas, como Su Magestad refiere en las cédulas que remitió el año de 1643. La fecha de una en Zaragoza a 20 de agosto y en ella inserta otra su fecha también en Zaragoza a 1° de mayo del año 1645 a Don Fernando de la Riva Agüero su Gobernador y capitán general, en razón de la situación de la Infantería de esta plaza cuyas formales palabras dicen hablando de ella. "Siendo frente y vanguardia de todas mis Indias occidentales y respecto de sus consecuencias la más importante de ellas y codiciada de los enemigos."

cause now that her natives, who benefited her rich mines, have died out, she is the poorest of all. "*Si murus est*" [If she is a wall] fits her, for only she is a walled City; enclosed among the others in the Indies, and "*Ostium habet*" [has a door] fits her because she not only has a port, but it is called "San Juan de Puerto Rico" because her port is so good. And in the words "*quid fatiemus sorori nostre in die quando aloquenda est*," it seems as if the Divine Bride warns the Kings of Spain, her [Puerto Rico's] sovereigns and ours, to consider what reply they should give to her complaints when from a sleepy carelessness she should come to be in danger on account of the hostility of such wide-awake enemies. They have moved into her neighborhood to seize their chances — may God forbid it! In some of the cases mentioned above we find conditions which make them likely to predominate over their own kind. For example, the Sun, in whose light (as being of a greater dignity) the stars and the Moon have a share, and man, who is as it

> The idea of the universe as analogous to the human body and vice-versa is frequently found in classical literature. It is also resonant with the Christian concept of the Church as the Body of Christ.

were a model of the universe as Plato says in his *Timæus*, and tends to have a certain rule and empire over other men, as the curious among the Romans noticed about Cæsar and Mark Antony, where Cæsar had the advantage of Antony even in trifling games. There are other things which are superior because of their placing, as is the head, which is the seat of reason, the ruler of the capacities of the soul, which is eminent with respect to the other parts of the body.

6.   Well, in the West Indies the Island of Puerto Rico enjoys this superiority and preeminence as being the first to be settled and the principal guard and key of them all, as his Majesty says in the royal letters which he sent out in the year 1643, of which one is dated in Zaragoza, August 20th, and it is inserted in another also dated from Zaragoza on May 1, 1645, sent

> In passage (#6), Torres y Vargas celebrates what was then a recent pronouncement of King Philip IV that praised Puerto Rico for its importance to the Spanish Empire. The reference to the West Indies was often used to refer to all of the Americas, much as "East Coast" or "West Coast," in common language refers to many of the several U.S. states.

to on Fernando de la Riva Agüero, its Governor and Captain-General, on the topic of the situation of the Infantry of this garrison, whose exact wording is, "[This City] is the front and vanguard of all my West Indies, and, with regard to its consequences, the most important among them, and the most coveted by our enemies."

7.   Esta Isla en general es fértil para cualesquier frutos que se quieran sembrar en ella y son de mejor calidad que las de las otras islas, porque el azúcar es más dulce (aun que el de la Havana sea más dura) y así con el de Puerto-Rico se refina en Sevilla, el de las otras partes de Indias y el gengibre tiene más valor dos ducados en cada quintal que el de Santo Domingo, pero él de Brasil es mejor que todos. Los principales frutos en que se funda el comercio de esta Isla son gengibre, cueros y azúcar de que hay siete ingenias. Cuatro en el río de Bayamón, dos en el río de Toa y uno de agua en el río de Canobana, que otros cuatro que había, dos en el río de Luysa, uno en el pueblo viejo y otro en el río de Toa arriba, se han desecho unos por las invasiones de los enemigos y otros por mayores conveniencias de sus dueños. También hay otros trapiches que hacen melado en la villa de San Germán y valle de Coamo, y las cañas se dan con tanta fertilidad que no necesitan de riego ni de sembrarlas más de una vez, que en cortándolas, vuelven al año a crecer de la mesma manera que de antes y dura un cañaveral sesenta y setenta años. El gengibre se da en gran cantidad habiendo año que se han cojido 14,000 quintales en toda la Isla, pero con la guerra o la abundancia se le ha minorado el precio, con que ha dejado de sembrarse, y este año de 1646 solo se han cojido 4,000 quintales, y se ha esforzado la siembra del cacao de que habrá dentro de cuatro años cantidad para poder cargarse bajeles, y se da con las ventajas que los demás frutos, y al presente se coje alguno más no obstante para poder hacerse comercio. Los cueros suelen llegar a 8 y 10,000 los que se cargan cada año para España y son de condición razonable y los morrudos buenos y todos bien beneficiados. El tabaco de diez años a esta parte se ha comenzado a sembrar y embarcarse para fuera de la Isla, dáse con gran de fertilidad y es mejor que el de la Havana, Santo Domingo y Margarita esceptuando el de Barinas, y vale la libra a dos reales.

8.   Hay escelentes maderas para fábricas de navíos y galeones, de que se han hecho algunos de porte de ochocientas y novecientas toneladas, y se pudiera poner fábrica Real en esta Isla; donde con mucha comodidad se labraran para las armadas de Su Magestad con solo traer jarcia y velamen. Así mismo hay en la Isla grandes minas de oro, cristal y cobre, que no se benefician por haber faltado los indios naturales, y en la villa de San Germán una salina de que se pudieran

---

The narrative turns from history to another source that describes products from Puerto Rico. The remark on Havana seems original with Torres y Vargas. Here as elsewhere, he selectively praises the goods from Puerto Rico, comparing them to those from other places.

"mesma" is an older form of *"misma"*

7.   Generally speaking, this Island is fertile for any fruit you might want to plant on it, and these are of better quality than those of other islands, for its sugar is sweeter (though that of Havana is harder). The sugar from Puerto Rico is refined in Seville, while that of other parts is refined locally. The [Puerto Rican] ginger sells for two ducats a hundred-weight more than that of Santo Domingo — but that of Brazil is best of all. The principal products on which the commerce of this Island is based are ginger, hides and sugar. There are seven sugar mills, four on the Bayamón River, two on the Toa River, and one water mill on the Canóvanas River. There were were four more: two on the Loíza

> Sugar was often shipped and sold in hard "loaves" and ground into crystals or powder by the buyer.
>
> The reference is not to Brazilian sugar, but to Brazilian ginger.
>
> Sugar mills were usually powered by oxen, so a water-powered mill was an exception.

River, one in the old town, and one on the upper Toa River, but these have been ruined — some because of the invasions of our enemies, and others because their owners found other investments more convenient. In the town of San Germán and in the valley of Coamo there are other mills which produce molasses, and the sugar canes grow with such fertility that they do not need to be watered, or planted more than once. When you cut them down, they grow again the following year just as they grew the year before, so that a canefield will last as much as sixty or seventy years. Ginger grows in great abundance and there have been years in which the yield for the whole Island has been 14,000 hundred-weights. But either because of the war or because of the large supply, the prices have fallen. As a result, the people have given up on planting it, so that on this year of 1646 only 4,000 hundred-weights have been harvested. The people have exerted themselves in planting cocoa, so that in four years there will be enough with which to load ships. It grows with the same abundance as the other kinds of fruit, and at this time some is being harvested, but not enough for commercial purposes. As for hides, as many as 8–10,000 are loaded for Spain each year; they are of reasonable quality, and the hides of big-snouted cattle are good; all of them yield good profits. Tobacco has begun to be planted and exported within the last ten years; it grows in abundance and is better than that of Havana, Santo Domingo and Margarita, excepting that of Barinas. It sells at two *reales* [*"two bits" or about 25 cents* — Tr.] a pound.

8.   There is excellent timber for building ships and galleons, and with it have been built ships of as many as 800 or 900 tons; a royal shipyard could be established on this Island, and ships could be built for His Majesty's Navy with

cargar cada año cien galeones de Sal, y en el valle de Coamo un baño de agua que de un risco arroja dos caños el uno más caliente que el otro, y es salutífero para humores gálicos y enfermedades de miembros tullidos, donde van muchos enfermos y quedan sanos. Las frutas de Indias son mejores y mayores que las de las otras islas; y las de España que se dan, son ubas, higos granadas y éstas tan buenas como las de Palma y Córdova de España; se dan tres y cuatro veces al año; y trigo, cevada y millo se ha sembrado y da muy bien. Pero la flojedad de los naturales no continua el sembrarle y así no se coje para el sustento ordinario, y por no dilatar la narración o descripción de la Isla que necesita de tratado copioso, vengo a la Península en la que la Ciudad esta fundada que es en la manera siguiente.

> Notice how the section above ends with a comparison between the Caribbean and Córdoba in Spain, which may have come from a travel narrative of a Spaniard or Torres y Vargas himself. He cuts short this description of physical features and commercial products to turn to history proper. The sentences in the first person are clearly his.

Península de Puerto-Rico (La ciudad)

> The history below has its own heading, and demonstrates how in the seventeenth century the chief city of a region was assumed to be repository of all intelligible historical events. The description of Torres y Vargas seems based on another source, but as a native of San Juan, he introduces various comments of his own. His comments exceeded the request by González Dávila, but were nonetheless appreciated.
>
> **Antonio de Lebrija** (1441–1522) had produced a grammar textbook, well known to all who could read. His classifications were considered authoritative. When Torres y Vargas refers to "the Spaniards," he probably includes himself and other criollos because of cultural rather than national identities. "*Naturales*" refers to the Taínos.

9.   La ciudad de Puerto-Rico al principio de su descubrimiento, se fundó en la banda del Sur, a la tierra firme de la Isla, una legua de la bahía que hay es el principal puerto, con nombre de la villa de Caparra; y de este nombre hallo en Antonio de Lebrija que hay una ciudad en Castilla junto a Ciudad Rodrigo, que se llama Caparra, y las ventas de Caparra; y como era costumbre de los españoles en los nuevos descubrimientos, poner los nombres de las tierras de donde eran naturales, pudo ser que en el principio de su fundación, algunos de los españoles principales le pusiesen este nombre porque no le habían de dejar el nombre de los indios fundándola con nombre de villa. En ella se labraron algunas casas de piedra de que hoy parecen cimientos y se hallan rastros aunque pocos, y porque

great convenience, merely importing the ropes and canvas for sails. There are also in the Island great mines of gold, rock-crystal and copper, which yield no profit because of the extinction of the native Indians. In the town of San Germán there is a salt-marsh from which a hundred galleons a year could be loaded with salt. In the valley of Coamo there is a hot spring which gushes from a cliff in two jets of water, one hotter than the other. It is health-giving for the

> The present municipality of San Germán is inland, but in the 17th century its municipal bounds included most of the south of the island; the salt-marsh in question may be in the modern coastal town of Salinas.
>
> The French disease is syphilis and the other reference may be to arthritis.

French disease and for paralyzed limbs; many sick go there and are healed. Fruits native to the Indies grow here better and larger than in other islands; among those native to Spain growing here are grapes, figs and pomegranates. The pomegranates are as good as those of Palma [de Mallorca] or Córdoba in Spain, and they bear fruit three or four times a year. Wheat, barley and millet have been planted and yielded good harvests, but the slackness of the local people has kept them from continuing the planting, so they are not harvested for daily sustenance. And now, so as not to overextend on the description of the Island (for which I would need a very long treatise) I come to the Peninsula on which this City is built, which is as follows:

Peninsula of Puerto-Rico (The City itself)

9.   At the beginning of its discovery, the City of Puerto Rico was founded on the southern side [of the bay], on the mainland of the Island, and the town was named Caparra. [It lay] a league from the bay which is [now] the Island's principal port. In Antonio de Lebrija's *Grammar* I find that there is a city [village — Tr.] in Castile, near Ciudad Rodrigo, which is called Caparra, or the Inns of Caparra. Since when making a discovery the Spaniards customarily named the new places after the lands from which they originated, it may have been that when the town [of Caparra] was created, some of the founders gave it that name. This was because they did not

> Note that by *peninsula* Torres y Vargas means what modern Spanish would call *islote*, or "*islet*" in English — a peninsula properly so called doesn't need bridges to connect it to the mainland.
>
> The word *mocezuelo* is not in the Dictionary of the Royal Academy, but in rural Puerto Rico the word is used for eye infections. —Ed.

see fit to leave the place with an Indian name when establishing it as an official [Spanish] town. Some stone houses were built there of which what seem to be

los que nacían en dicha villa no se lograban a causa del viento Sur, que corriendo sobre la tierra, era tan enfermo que ocasionaba mocezuelo en los niños; después de diez o doce años se mudaron a la Península en que hoy esta la Ciudad, que bañada del viento Este que es la brisa y corre de la mar, es saludable y alegre.

10.   Esta Península se abrocha a otra con un puente que llaman de los soldados, porque en ella se hacen guardias, y se tiene un fuerte para atalaya del enemigo si intentaren venir por la tierra, para que cortando el puente, den aviso a la Ciudad que esta media legua distante: de esta segunda Península, corre a la tierra firme de la Isla, otro puente mayor que llaman Martín Peña porque devió de ser su artífice, y así se quedó con el nombre. En la tierra firme del primer puente hay una fuente de agua dulce que en tiempo de seca, que falta el agua de los algibes de esta Ciudad, la socorre; y corre por dos caños poco menos gruesos que la muñeca y nunca, aunque se adelgazan a menos que un dedo, se ha visto faltar el agua; háse tratado de traer a la Ciudad y por estar más baja no se ha ejecutado.

> The notes on the Martín Peña Bridge and the water sources for the city read like information from a city native, which is what Torres y Vargas was.
>
> His family's military history influences his insight into the current state of the army garrisons and city fortifications.
>
> The seal of San Juan was used for notarial documents and the like.
>
> *"devió"* for *"debió"*

11.   Será población esta Ciudad de quinientos vecinos con razonable casería de piedra y alguna de tabla que llegan a 400; los materiales para fábrica de ellas son los mejores de las Indias, y tan cerca, que dentro de la Ciudad se halla todo el material necesario, y las maderas a menos de dos leguas. Consta de diez Regidores, Alférez mayor, Alguacil mayor, y Depositario general; con elección de Alcaldes ordinarios y otros dos de la Santa Hermandad, un procurador general, un fiel executor y un mayordomo de Ciudad con su portero, y a todos los Cabildos preside el Gobernador. Las armas que tiene le dió su Magestad, año 1511, siendo procurador un vecino llamado Pedro Moreno; son: un cordero (de San Juan que es su patrón) con su banderilla, y el cordero sobre un libro, y todo sobre una Isla verde que es la de Puerto-Rico, y por los lados una F. y una Y. que dicen Fernando e Isabel, los Reyes Católicos que se las dieron e hicieron igual en todos los privilegios y mercedes a la Isla Española; como lo dice Antonio de Herrera en su Crónica general de las Indias.

the foundations still remain, although the traces are few. But the babies born in that town did not grow to adulthood because the south wind which blew over the area was so unhealthy that it provoked eye infections in the children. So after about ten or twelve years the settlers moved to the peninsula where the City is now situated. It is healthy and pleasant, being refreshed by the east wind, which is called *the breeze*, and blows from the sea.

10.   This peninsula is connected to another by a bridge which they call "the Bridge of the Soldiers," [*Puente San Antonio*] because sentries are kept there, and there is a fort that serves as a watch-tower against the enemy should they attempt to invade by land. In that case, the bridge can be dismantled and they can warn the City, which is a half-league away from it. This second peninsula is connected to the Island's mainland by a larger bridge which they call Martin Peña's bridge; this must have been the name of its builder, and it stuck to the bridge. On the mainland end of the first bridge there is a fresh water spring which supplies the City in times of drought, when the water fails in the City's cisterns. This spring runs through two channels whose thickness is little less wide than a wrist, and its water has never been known to fail, even though [in times of drought] it can run as thin as a finger's breadth. Efforts have been made to bring this water into the City itself, but with no success, because the spring is at a lower level than the City.

11.   The population of this City should be about 500 *vecinos*, with a reasonable amount of stone houses, plus a few of wood, the total reaching about 400. The materials for building are the best in the Indies, and so conveniently placed that all the necessary materials can be found within city limits, and the timber within two leagues of it. The City Corporation is composed of ten aldermen [*Regidores*], a Bearer of the Royal Standard [*Alférez mayor*], a Bailiff [*Alguacil mayor*], and a Receiver General [*Depositario general*]; with elected Mayors-in-Ordinary and two sheriffs [*Alcaldes de la Santa Hermandad*], an Attorney General [*procurador general*], an alderman in charge of ensuring the accuracy of local weights and measures [*fiel executor*] and an Administrator of the City's finances with his gatekeeper. All meetings of the City Council are presided over by the Governor. The coat of arms it bears was granted by His Majesty in the year 1511, when a *vecino* named Pedro Moreno was the representative at court. It is a lamb as in the badge of St. John the Baptist (who is its patron saint) with its banner; the lamb is upon a book, and the whole thing on a green Island which is that of Puerto Rico, and on either side the letters F and Y which stand for Fer-

Alcaldes ordinarios (Mayors-in-Ordinary) were residents (*vecinos*) who enjoyed jurisdiction in their own names.

The "*Alcaldes*" were appointed yearly to investigate and punish crimes committed outside the city, while the *Santa Hermandad* has some similarities to the sheriff leading a "posse" (*posse comitatus*) in cowboy movies of the Wild West.

12.   La infantería es de cuatrocientos soldados con dos capitanes, un sargento mayor y un castellano en la fuerza de San Phelipe del Morro, que se hizo antes de la cerca de la Ciudad, y para su planta mandó Su Magestad al Maese de campo

"*Maese*" or "*Mastre*" *de campo*: for a superior officer over the Tercios* of an army, translated as "General."   *see glossary*

A *ducat* was a gold coin worth about 11 silver *reales* or about a dollar and a half.

Juan de Tegeda, cuando vino por Gobernador a la Havana, que pasase por este puerto y con Juan Heli su ingeniero mayor la designare, como la hizo el año 1584, y así esta planta y la del Morro de la Havana, me parecen una, con diferencia de que esta fuerza es mayor, porque tuvo más planicie por donde correr, y la de la Havana más fuerte, por ser por la mar y la tierra fundada sobre penas que hay; esta solo por la banda de la mar. Hase gastado en dicha fábrica del Morro aunque le falta la entrada cubierta y otros reparos, un millón y novecientos mil ducados, y si se acabare, llegará a dos millones sin lo que ha costado la cerca, que con lo que han dado los vecinos en veces, pasa de doscientos mil ducados; tiene dicha cerca de ambitu . . . . La fuerza del Morro dicho tiene ochenta y cuatro piezas de artillería, y algunas piezas que arrojan treinta libras de bala, las setenta son de bronce y las otras de hierro colado.

Torres y Vargas interrupts his description of secular and civic history to interject information on the cathedral, hospitals and convents for both men and women in Puerto Rico. However, there is a wealth of details about the funding of these institutions and the current number of posts in each, suggesting that Torres y Vargas used another source as an outline and filled in his current observations. Note how he emphasizes the achievements of San Juan natives who had risen to positions of authority, such as the Prior of the Dominican foundation.

The use of "*ansi*" in these portions contrasts with "*assi*" found elsewhere for "*así*," possibly indicating the styles of different sources or of different transcribers.

13.   En la Ciudad hay Iglesia Catedral, antiquísima, y que comenzó con gran

dinand and Isabella, the Catholic monarchs who granted the coat of arms, and who made the Island equal in all grants and privileges to the Island of Española, as is told by Antonio de Herrera in his *Chronicle of the Indies*.

> There is a some confusion here: the coats of arms of the city and of the island were both granted by Ferdinand in 1511, and are similar, but in the *island's* coat of arms the Lamb is **seated** on a book with seven seals, while on the coat of arms of the *city* it **stands** on an island on waves of the sea. Torres y Vargas seems to conflate the two coats of arms into one.

12.   The infantry [in the garrison] numbers four hundred soldiers with two Captains, one Sergeant-Major and the Castellan of the fortress of San Felipe del Morro, which was built before the city walls. His Majesty ordered General Juan de Tejeda, when he came as Governor of Havana, to stop at this port and design this fortress together with Juan de Heli, his chief engineer, as was done in 1584. And so the plan of this fortress and that of the Morro in Havana seem to me to be the same. The differences are that this fortress is the larger, because it had a wider plain on which to spread, while that of Havana is stronger, since it is built on rocky cliffs both on the land side and on the sea; this one is built on cliffs only on the side that faces the sea. So far a million and nine hundred thousand ducats have been spent on the building of Morro Castle, although it is still lacking its covered entryway and some other improvements. If it is ever finished, its cost will reach two million, not counting the cost of the city walls, which, including what the *vecinos* have contributed on occasion, amounts to more than two hundred thousand ducats. The circumference of these walls is. . . . The fortress of El Morro has eighty-four pieces of artillery, some of which fire thirty-pound balls — seventy of them are bronze and the rest cast iron.

13.   This City has a Cathedral Church, which is quite ancient and, if it had been finished according to the original plan, it would have been quite a large building. Its patron and titular is my lord Saint John the Baptist, and its coat of arms is a crowned Lamb standing on an islet. The Lamb is holding a cross diagonally, and is encircled by the motto "*Joannes est nomen eius.*" ["John is his name." (Luke 1:63)] Its diocese has a meager income, and its prebendaries are eight — there used to be nine, but some eight or nine years ago an order came to reserve the income of one canonry to subsidize the Inquisition, and so now there is a Dean (*Deán*), an Archdeacon (*Arcediano*) and a Precentor (*Chantre*), three Canons, two Prebendaries, a verger and a doorkeeper. The revenues the [Cathedral] Church receives from endowed masses, both sung and recited, amount to

fábrica, si se acabara. Es su patrón y titular Señor San Juan Bautista, y tiene por armas un cordero con diadema sobre unos islotes. El cordero atravesado con una cruz, metido dentro de un círculo que tiene estas letras *"Joannes est nomen eius."* Su obispado tiene corta-renta con sus prebendados, que son ocho, porque aunque eran nueve, se mandó consumir una canongía para la Inquisición, habrá ocho o nueve años, y así hay Déan, Arcediano y Chantre, tres Canónigos y dos Racioneros, pertiguero y portero. Los réditos de Misas de Capellanía, cantadas y rezadas, que tiene la Iglesia con veinte y seis mil y docientos reales de plata. Los diez y seis mil de misas cantadas, y los diez mil doscientos de Misas rezadas, y ésta la principal renta con que cortamente se sustentan, porque los diezmos valen muy poco, y así tienen suplicado a Su Magestad se la acreciente, y parece justo: en esta Santa Iglesia, aunque no hay canongía magistral, tiene dotación de cien ducados de renta cada año para un maestro de Gramática, que la lee de ordinario a los hijos de los vecinos de ella, y se paga la dicha renta con título de maestro de Gramática.

14.   El convento del Señor Santo Thomás del orden Dominico, también tiene muchas Capellanías que valdrán la mitad de lo que a la Iglesia; es convento grave y en tal asiento fundado, que mueve a devoción juntamente con las Imágenes que tiene, entre las cuales esta en el altar de Señor San Joseph, Nuestra Señora de Betlén, un cuadro pequeño como de tres cuartas y antiquísimo, pero tan lindo y lucido como si acabara de hacerse, haviendo más de cien años que está en el dicho convento; esta Santa imagen estuvo muchos años en el dormitorio del convento en Altar particular, y por tradición se tiene, que le cantaban algunas noches a Maitines los ángeles, y siempre los religiosos de aquel convento y vecinos la han tenido y tienen en suma veneración.

15.   También hay otra Imagen más nueva, de bulto, que se trajo ha treinta y cuatro años de Sevilla, que es de la advocación de Nuestra Señora de Candelaria; y estando el navío para que darse en aquella flota por la mucha agua que hacia, así como entró la Imagen Santísima estancó el agua e hizo el viage hasta esta Ciudad sin hacer ninguna, y en ella ha obrado muchos milagros y conmigo dos, que por la brevedad no refiero, pero es cierto que si no fuera ansi no

The painting of Our Lady of Bethlehem is a fifteenth century Flemish work, and has been attributed to Van der Weyden.

This plea to include a description of Marian devotions in Puerto Rico is specifically addressed to Gil González Dávila, and reflects the personal piety of Torres y Vargas, but his request was not respected in the published *Teatro Eclesiástico*.

six thousand two hundred silver *reales* [a year]. Sixteen thousand of these come from sung masses, and ten thousand two hundred from low Masses — and this is the principal revenue on which the cathedral clergy barely survive, because the tithes are very small, and so they have requested His Majesty to increase their revenue, which seems fair. Although there is no Magistral Canonry in this Cathedral Church, it does have an endowment of a hundred ducats a year for the salary of a teacher of grammar, who ordinarily instructs the children of the *vecinos* of the City, and this salary is paid to him under the title of Master of Grammar.

14.   The convent of my lord Saint Thomas [Aquinas], of the Dominican Order, also has many mass endowments, which must produce about half the income that the [Cathedral] Church receives from this source. It is an important convent, and built on such a location that it moves one to devotion, as do the images in it, among which is found (on the altar of St. Joseph) the image of Our Lady of Bethlehem, a small painting (about three open hand-spans in size). It is very ancient, but as pretty and splendid as if it had just been painted, although it has been in that convent for more than a hundred years. This blessed image was kept for many years in the convent's dormitory on its own altar, and it is believed by tradition that some nights the angels chanted Matins before it. The friars of this convent and the townspeople have held it, and still hold it, in the greatest veneration.

15.   There is also a newer image, a statue, brought from Seville some thirty-four years ago, under the title of Our Lady of Candlemas. The ship [that was to bring it] seemed about to stay in port because it was leaking so much, but as soon as that most holy image was brought on board, the water stopped leaking in, and the ship made the voyage to this City without leaking any more water. In this City it has worked many miracles, and two of them in my own favor, which I do not relate so as not to unduly lengthen the narrative, but you can be sure that if it were not so I would not bring it up, and I should be witness to them under oath if it were necessary. And I beg that [in the book that is to be printed] these two worshipful Madonnas in the convent of my lord Saint Thomas, Our Lady of Bethlehem and Our Lady of Candlemas, be not left unmentioned. The friars are normally thirty, because it is a Novitiate by a disposition in 1645 from the Provincial of this Order, Fray Jorge Cambero, a native of this City. The Novitiate had earlier been here, but had been brought back to Santo Domingo. Similarly he set up a house of studies for Arts [Philosophy] and Grammar for the benefit of the novices and of the *vecinos* of the City who might want to study them. At this point they

lo dijera, y siendo necesario, lo juro, y suplico no se deje de hacer memoria de estas dos devotas Señoras, la de Betlen y Candelaria, del convento de Señor Santo Thomás. Los religiosos ordinarios son treinta, porque hay casa de noviciado que alcanzó el Provincial de esta orden, fray Jorge Cambero, como natural de esta Ciudad, el año de 1645, que aunque la hubo antiguamente, se había reducido a Santo Domingo, y ansi mismo puso casa de estudio de artes y de Gramática para los novicios y vecinos de la Ciudad que quisieren estudiarlos y hoy se está fabricando nueva casa de noviciado, para que en ella se hagan generales los estudios.

16.   El convento de Señor San Francisco, es nuevo, que la licencia se alcanzó el año de 1642, aunque los Religiosos vinieron antes ocho años, con intento de fundarle a instancia de Don Francisco de Villanueva y Lugo, Depositario general de esta Ciudad, que se halló el año de 1633 en la de Santo Domingo, y por devoción de nombre y del Santo, pidió a los Religiosos que iban a hacer su capitulo a la ciudad de Caracas, tratasen de fundar en esta Ciudad; y así le hicieron a que ayudó el Obispo Don Juan López Agurto de la Mata que se halló entonces en la visita de la isla Margarita.

Houses of *mendicant friars* are convents, while those of *monks* are monasteries, unlike the common U.S. usage, where houses of women are convents and houses of men are monasteries.

When Torres y Vargas wrote, there were two new religious foundations in San Juan that likely were not included in any older report he could have used. The comments on the Franciscans, therefore, would seem to be original with Torres y Vargas.

Margarita is on the coast of Venezuela, but was part of the diocese of Puerto Rico.

---

17.   La licencia para el convento de Monjas que se suplicó a Su Majestad se fundase en esta Ciudad, se alcanzó el año pasado de 1646. La fecha de la Cédula, en Zaragoza a 19 de julio: concedió tres Monjas de Sevilla del órden del Carmen calzado, que así lo quiso Doña Ana de Lanzós natural de esta Ciudad, que es la persona que con su hacienda se ha ofrecido a ser su fundadora; tiene fabricada la casa para el dicho convento junto a la Iglesia Catedral, en casa particular suya y que antes fue colegio de estudiantes donde se leía gramática con vocación antigua de Señor San Idelfonso, y por ser de la Iglesia se vendió con otras que tenia por parecer al Obispo Don Juan López Agurto de la Mata que era de más útil a la Santa Iglesia de esta Ciudad;

are building a new house for the Novitiate, where the studies may become a *Studium Generalis*.

> The headquarters of the Antillean Province of the Order of Preachers was in Santo Domingo, the city named after their founder. A *Studium Generalis* was authorized by the General of the Order, and could bestow degrees that would be recognized throughout the whole Order, in various disciplines: it was analogous to what we now call a university. This plan did not come to fruition. See glossary.

16.   The convent of my lord Saint Francis is new, since permission for it was only obtained in 1642. The friars had come with the intention of founding it eight years before, at the request of Don Francisco de Villanueva y Lugo, Receiver General of this City, who happened to be in Santo Domingo in 1633 when these friars were leaving for Caracas to attend their [Provincial] Chapter. Out of devotion to the saint after whom he was named, he asked the friars to try to found [a convent] in this City, as they did, with the help of Bishop Don Juan López Agurto de la Mata, who happened at the time to be holding the visitation in the Island of Margarita.

17.   The license to found a convent of [cloistered] nuns in this City, which was requested from His Majesty, was obtained last year, 1646. The decree, dated in Zaragoza on July 19th, granted three nuns from the Seville convent of the Calced Carmelite order, as was the wish of Doña Ana de Lanzós, a native of this City, who has offered herself and her property for the founding of the convent. She has built a house for this convent near the Cathedral Church in a house of her personal property, which had earlier been a school where Grammar was taught under the patronage of my lord Saint Ildefonso. This was the property of the [Cathedral] Church and had been sold together with others that belonged to it since it seemed to Bishop Don Juan López Agurto de la Mata that selling it was to the advantage of the Church in this City.

> Doña Ana de Lanzós was the widow of Captain Pedro Villante de Escobedo and owner of a sugar mill in Canóbanas. She promised a yearly pension of 50,000 pesos to support the convent of Carmelites (not the strict branch of St. Teresa of Avila), which was founded by three Spanish nuns from a Dominican convent in Santo Domingo. Six of the first Puerto Rican nuns were related to Doña Ana. Her property in San Juan across the street from the Cathedral, previously used as a grammar school, became the first convent. Today it is an elite hotel named *El Convento*.

The description of the founding of a convent for women is of high importance. It shows that women in colonial Puerto Rico acquired great wealth, knew how to administer it and had concern for other women of less fortunate financial status. As indicated in the essays of introduction, such convents offered a secure life for widows or women with little likelihood of marriage. Scholarly research on women's history has noted that convents represented institutions controlled by women alone and permitted the education and practice of the arts that otherwise would have been restricted to males.

This was the original grammar school for the city, founded in the sixteenth century; Saint Ildefonso / Alfonso, a Visigothic archbishop of Toledo and the patron saint of the first bishop of the island (Don Alonso Manso) is still the patron of the island's minor seminary.

18.   y en ella hay dos Hospitales, el uno de la vocación de Nuestra Señora de la Concepción, fundación de un vecino de los antiguos y ricos llamado Francisco Juancho, Vizcayno de nación, pero no se hallan papeles de la antigüedad aunque tiene descendientes legítimos en esta Ciudad. Las elecciones de diputados y mayordomos, se hacen por los Cabildos eclesiástico y secular, alternando cada un año. Tiene este hospital, capellán con cien ducados de renta y casa y servicio y renta de tributos con que se sustenta, e indulgencias a los que murieren, lo que no se sabe más que por tradición, por haberse perdido los papeles, y que algunas personas principales, por gozar de dichas indulgencias, se hacían traer a morir en el dicho hospital. Otro hospital hay más nuevo con vocación de Santiago; que es de la Infantería del presidio; la casa es de Su Magestad, y la renta de la misma Infantería, que de sus sueldos le sustentan y también algunos tributos, que a los principios pusieron sus fundadores, aunque pocos.

19.   Hermitas hay, la de Señora Santa Ana, Señora Santa Bárbara, Señor San Sebastián, y había la de Señora Santa Catalina, y por que cayó fuera de la muralla, la deshizo Don Iñigo de la Mota Sarmiento, Gobernador que fue de esta Ciudad, y sobre la misma muralla, le hizo otra capilla y altar donde se celebra su fiesta en su día.

"Hermitas" (are here translated as "chapels") were not parish churches, but more like shrines, that is, places where devotion suggested that passers-by stop and pray.

The chapel of St Ann still exists on Tetuán Street, and is the size of a small church; the chapel of St. Barbara is now incorporated into the Castle of San Cristobal, and the chapel of St. Catherine is incorporated into La Fortaleza (the Governor's residence) and serves as a private chapel for the Governor's family. All that remains of St. Sebastian chapel is the name of the street.

18.   In the City there are two hospitals, one of them dedicated to Our Lady of the Conception, founded by one of the early settlers, a rich man called Francisco Juancho, a Basque by nationality. There are no documents to attest its antiquity, although Juancho has legitimate descendants in this City. Its trustees and directors [*Mayordomos*] are elected for one-year terms, alternately by the Cathedral Chapter and the City Council. This hospital has a chaplain with a hundred ducats [a year] income and it has its own building and servants, as well as an income from supporting annuities. There are indulgences for those who die in it, although this is only known by tradition, since the documents have been lost and by the fact that some important persons have themselves been carried to this hospital when they are dying so as to gain the indulgences. There is another, more recent[ly constructed] hospital under the patronage of my lord Saint James, which is for the Infantry of the garrison. The building belongs to His Majesty, and its income comes from the Infantry itself, which supports it out of the [soldiers'] salaries. There are also some encumbrances on property with which its founders endowed it with in the beginning, although this income does not amount to much.

Hospitals in the 17th century were not as much places for healing as hospices for those about to die who had limited financial resources and could not be attended to at home, which was always preferred. The church aspired to provide a setting for a holy death and afforded the consolation of indulgences to those who passed on within the hospital walls.

---

19.   There are some chapels, dedicated to my lady Saint Anne, my lady Saint Barbara, my lord Saint Sebastián, and there was one to my lady Saint Catherine, but, since its location lay outside the city walls [when they were built,] Don Iñigo de la Mota Sarmiento, who was [at the time] Governor of this City, tore it down and built her another chapel and altar right upon the wall, where a feast is held for her on her day.

Torres y Vargas now returns to the source he used on Puerto Rico's geography. Having interjected information on the religious institutions in San Juan, he describes the rivers in the rest of the Island of Puerto Rico. Since he was particularly eager to include religious attributes, he focuses upon the curative powers attributed to river waters in the 17th century. He emphasizes acts of martyrdom, since the teaching of the Church says that any martyr for the faith is also a saint. Martyrs, therefore, is the same as saints in Puerto Rico, a quality that makes the Island more important to Catholicism.

---

20.   In the whole islet on which this City is built — which would be about half a league in length — there is no spring water, and so cisterns for rain water

20.   En la isleta en que esta fundada la Ciudad, que será de media legua de largo, no se halla agua manantial y así se han hecho en las casas, algibes, y cuando falta, se acude a la fuente que esta media legua, y por mar y tierra se trae a la Ciudad; y también del río que se llama Bayamón, que sale a la misma bahía de frente de las casas Reales del Gobernador, y otro que llaman Río-piedras que también sale a la misma bahía; y ambos son de escelente agua, porque todas las de la Isla, como son de oro, se tienen por bonísimas y muy digestivas, pero la más delgada, habiéndolas pesado todas, fue la del Aybonito, cerca del valle de Coamo, como dos leguas: y después de esta, la del río Guanajibo, que es donde esta fundada la villa de San Germán, y tiene este río, piedras salutíferas para mal de hijada, flujos de sangre, dolores de cabeza, y hacer venir la leche a las mugeres paridas que no la tienen, y otros males de estomago y diversas enfermedades, y así se llevan a todas-las partes de estas Indias y a España, por ser la virtud suya conocida en todas ellas. En dicha villa de San Germán hay tres cosas de grande estimación que son el río Guanajibo de agua muy saludable, una excelente campana, y una Imagen de la Concepción en lienzo de admirable maña y hermosura, que está en el hospital de la dicha villa donde hay también un convento del orden de Santo Domingo; y en la Aguada hubo en los principios de su fundación otro convento de Señor San Francisco, que es el que ahora se ha transferido a esta Ciudad con pretesto de reedificación por la contradicción que le hicieron los frayles Dominicos.

> Torres y Vargas mentions here the rivalry between the Dominicans and the Franciscans. As noted in the essays, two monasteries in the same city provided competition for contributions. The Franciscans then got around the objection by claiming that they were only refounding their old house at Aguada, for which permission had been granted in the sixteenth century. Issues of class were also at play, since the Dominicans, the older of the two foundations in the city, had attracted sons of the elite.
>
> "*pretesto*" for "*pretexto*"

21.   y deshizóse aquel convento porque los indios caribes, que entonces infestaban mucho la Isla, martirizaron cinco religiosos a flechazos de que no he podido saber los nombres por la antigüedad y falta de archivos y papeles, pero es cierto que fue la causa de su despoblación, el martirio de estos Santos religiosos, que como entonces había pocos y eran menester para obreros de esta nuestra viña del Señor, quisieron guardarse para confesores, los que quedaron, más que para mártires.

have been built in the houses. When there is little rain, one has recourse to the spring which is half a league away. Its water is brought to the City overland or by sea and also from the rivers called Bayamón, which flows into the bay across from the Governor's Residence, and another river called "Rocks River" [*Río Piedras*], which also flows into the same bay. Both of these have excellent water, and all the rivers of the Island, since they are gold-bearing, are held to have excellent water and good for digestion. But the lightest of all, when all were weighed, was that of Aibonito, near the valley of Coamo (about two leagues from it) and after this, that of the Guanajibo River, where the town of San Germán is built. This river also has stones which are good for kidney stones, bloody fluxes and headaches, as well as for making women who have no milk get milk in their breasts, and for other stomach ailments and other diseases. On this account, they are taken to all other parts of these Indies and to Spain, because their power is well known throughout these lands. In that town of San Germán there are three very wonderful things: the Guanajibo River, whose water is so healthy; an excellent bell; and an image of the Immaculate Conception painted on canvas, admirable for its art and its beauty, which is in that town's hospital. In that town there is also a convent of the Order of Saint Dominic [*Porta Cœli*] and in Aguada there once was — at the time the town was founded — another convent of my lord Saint Francis, which is the one that has now been transferred to this City under the pretext of re-founding it, because the Dominican friars had objected [to the foundation of a Franciscan house in the City].

21.   The convent [of Aguada] was abandoned because the Carib Indians, who at that time infested the Island, martyred five friars, shooting them with arrows. I have not been able to find out their names because this was quite long ago, and there are no archives or documents, but it is certain that the cause of that friary's abandonment was the martyrdom of these holy Friars. Since there were very few missionaries at the time, and they were needed as laborers in this our vineyard of the Lord, the survivors preferred to be known as Confessors [*practicing the faith*] rather than becoming Martyrs [*dying for it* — Tr.].

The following is perhaps the oldest written source on the unique Puerto Rican devotion to Our Lady of Monserrate in the town of Hormigueros. Giraldo, by this time a widower and ordained a priest, attended the Diocesan Synod called by Fray Damian Lopez de Haro in 1645, so Torres y Vargas could have got the story directly from him, or at least checked it for accuracy. Like the Mexican Guadalupe and the Cuban, Our Lady of Charity, the title, image and devotion had originated in Spain, but became localized by reason of events the *criollos* considered miraculous. In visiting the *hermita* even more miraculous favors were received, inviting pious pilgrimages. Eventually, the *hermita* became a church and remains such today.

"Confessors" in this context does not mean "priests who hear confessions," but saints who die in their beds and are not killed as martyrs.

22.   Tienen en dicha villa una Imagen en el sitio que llaman el Hormiguero, de la vocación de Nuestra Señora de Monserrate, es pintura del grandor de tres cuartas de largo, en hermita particular, y con tributos para su renta; de gran devoción y algunos milagros; y dejando de referir muchos, fue notorio que el mayordomo de dicha capilla, llamado Giraldo González, tuvo entre otras una hija que, de edad de ocho anos, se le perdió en los montes que en aquella parte son de

"Hermitage" here, since it was at that time "out in the middle of nowhere" unlike the *hermitas* in San Juan.—-Tr.

grandes sierras y alturas, y enviándola a buscar a muchas personas; al cabo de quince días hallaron la niña buena y contenta, y la ropa sana, como cuando se perdió: y preguntándola como había vivido sin sustentarse, dijo que una muger la había dado de comer todo aquel tiempo, alhagándola y acariciándola como madre: de que se entendió ser la de misericordia y Virgen de Monserrate, de quien el dicho su padre era devoto, y fundador de la hermita que hoy tiene, crecida su devoción con milagros que obra con la gente de aquella villa cada día.

23.   Es población la dicha villa de San Germán de doscientos vecinos, y está sugeta al Gobernador y capitán general de esta Ciudad, que pone teniente de su mano, pero tiene jurisdicción separada. Regidores y Alcaldes ordinarios, que como villa, elije cada año, con alférez mayor y alguacil mayor y escribano de Cabildo y público. El valle de San Blas de Coamo tiene otra hermita, demás de la Iglesia, con vocación de alta gracia, y también es de gran devoción, y su Imagen, pequeña, de bulto, de tamaño de una vara, y tiene tributos con

The detailed descriptions here of places outside San Juan and use of the first person suggests Torres y Vargas had visited these places.

que se sustenta la lámpara que es de plata, como la de la Iglesia del dicho valle, y está veinte leguas de esta Ciudad y será población de cien vecinos. La otra población; que esta doce leguas de está Ciudad, se llama San Felipe del Arecibo; tiene el mejor río con el mismo nombre de quien le tomó el pueblo, que yo creo que es el mejor que hay en la Isla; ancho, claro, bajo de buen agua y buen pescado y su ribera es de las mejores, para la labranza de gengibre y cacao, de cuantas hay en la Isla; el puerto es de costa brava, y así los bajeles paran poco en el porque cualquiera norte los echaría a la costa de fuera. Es tan hermosa la vista, que los enemigos le llaman jardín dorado, y el río donde está poblado el lugar, que será

22.   In that town they have an image in the place called El Hormiguero, representing Our Lady of Montserrat. It is a painting about three hand-spans in length, kept in its own hermitage and with endowments for its income. This image is held in great devotion by the people and has worked some miracles. Skipping over many of them, it is well-known that the keeper of the chapel, whose name is Giraldo González, had among other children a daughter who at the age of eight got lost among the mountains of that neighborhood, which are very jagged and high. Many persons went searching for her. After fifteen days, they found the girl in good health and good spirits, and her clothing in as good state as when she got lost. When they asked her how she had managed to live without sustenance, she said that a woman had fed her during that whole period, caring for her and cherishing her like a mother. They understood from this account that this woman was the Mother of Mercy and Virgin of Montserrat, to whom the child's father was devoted. He was the founder of the hermitage that is now dedicated to her, and the devotion to her increases by the miracles she works day by day for the people of that area.

23.   The said town of San Germán is a settlement of some two hundred *vecinos*, and is under the authority of the Governor and Captain-General of this City [San Juan]. He personally appoints his Lieutenant there, but it has its own separate jurisdiction [from San Juan] with its own aldermen and Mayors-in-Ordinary, which, as a formed town, it elects every year, along with a Bearer of the Royal Standard, a Bailiff, and a Secretary of the Town Council, who is also the public scrivener. The valley of San Blas de Coamo has another chapel aside from its parish church, dedicated to [Our Lady of] Altagracia, and the people are also quite devoted to it. Its image is small, carved in the round, about one yard in height, and it has an endowment to support its sanctuary lamp, which is made of silver, as is also the lamp of the parish church of that

> This image of Altagracia predates 1605 settlers from Española.

valley. This valley is twenty leagues from this City, and it must be a settlement of some hundred *vecinos*. The other settlement, which is about twelve leagues from this City, is called San Felipe del Arecibo. It has the best river [in the Island], bearing the same name [Arecibo], for which the settlement was named. In my opinion, this is the best river in the whole Island. It is wide, clear, low, with good water and good fishing, and its banks are among the best in the Island for the cultivation of ginger and cocoa. The port is rocky and thus few ships stop there, because any north wind would cast them on the rocks. The sight of it is so lovely that our enemies call it the Golden Garden, and the river where the village is set-

de cuarenta vecinos, por media legua corre tan a la orilla de la mar a donde sale, que no hay más de la mar al río, de como cuarenta pasos, que es de grande alegría a los que le miran; y es de manera, que podrán pescar con cordel, a un mismo tiempo, en la mar y en el río, más de media legua dentro de la boca, que no se podrá hacer en otro río de la Isla. Tiene este lugar, demás de la Iglesia, otra hermita de Nuestra Señora del Rosario donde van las proseciones, y con renta y capellanía de Misas que dejó un vecino y natural de aquel pueblo, llamado Juan Martín de Benavides.

24.   De este lugar hubo una muger llamada Gregoria Hernández que murió de más de ochenta años, y se enterró el de 1639, que murió en esta Ciudad, en el convento de Señor Santo Thomas de Aquino; de quien su confesor, que era un religioso del mismo convento, que es ya muerto, decía grandes cosas de su virtud y revelaciones; y de su vida dicen otras virtuosas mugeres, que vivían con ella, que era de gran Santidad y penitencia, y lo que vio toda la Ciudad, es, que era humilde; y pidiéndola su marido, que llevado de su valor natural se fue a Italia, donde fue capitán de Infantería y se llamaba Villodres, dos hijos que tenia solos y enviándoselos a España los cautivo un navío de Turcos a entrambos, y viniéndole la nueva de tan fuerte dolor jamás le mostró, ni impaciencia, sino una conformidad con la voluntad de Dios, que admiraban a los que la conocían, y su virtud era tan sólida y sufrida, que siendo pobrísima, jamás salía de casa sino era a Misa, ni pedía a nadie limosna, sino solo pasaba con la del convento de Santo Domingo, cerca de donde vivía, que imitaba a la beata Maria Raggi de Roma, y creo que no a de ser menos la gloria de esta buena muger por las virtudes de paciencia, humildad y pobreza, que toda esta Ciudad conocía en ella.

Gregoria Hernández of Arecibo is presented here by Torres y Vargas as a holy woman, similar to the mystics of Baroque Catholicism. As noted in the essay, a book about the life of Maria Raggi, a famous holy woman of Rome, had recently been translated into Spanish and similar traits in the life of the Puerto Rican Gregoria Hernández would be understood by readers throughout the Spanish Empire as testimony to the presence of extraordinary virtue on the island. Focus on miraculous events was typical of the age throughout the Catholic world.

25.   De milagros no hay mucho que decir de esta Ciudad como de todas las de Indias lo dice el Padre Maestro B[V]ictoria, si bien en su descubrimiento fue milagro la previa disposición con que movió Dios a los Reyes Católicos y a Cristóbal Colón su primero descubridor, para una empresa tan de esperanzas fáciles y así se pudo decir en la conversión de estos naturales *digitus dei est hic.*" y con

tled (by around forty *vecinos*) runs for half a league so close to the shore of the sea into which it flows that there is no more than forty paces separating the shore from the riverbank, which is a glad sight for those who look on it. Its location is such that you could fish with lines at the same time in the river and in the sea more than a half league in from the river's mouth — something that could not be done in any other river in the Island. This village has, aside from its parish church, a chapel to Our Lady of the Rosary to which processions are directed. It has its own income and an endowed chaplaincy for Masses, which was left to it by Juan Martín de Benavides, a *vecino* and native of that village, in his will.

24.   From this village came a woman named Gregoria Hernández who died in this City at over the age of 80 years old and was buried in 1639, in the convent of my lord Saint Thomas Aquinas. Her confessor (now deceased), was a friar of that same convent. He used to tell great things about her virtues and revelations. Some virtuous women who lived in community with her say that her life was marked by great holiness and penance. What the whole City witnessed is her humility. Her husband, Villodres by name, was led by his natural bravery to go off to Italy, where he was a captain of Infantry, and asked her to send him their only two sons. On their way to Spain, both were captured by Turkish pirates. When she received such tragic news, she never showed her sorrow, nor any bitterness, but conformity to the Will of God that left her acquaintances amazed. Indeed her virtue was so solid and long-suffering that, although she was extremely poor, she never left her home except to go to Mass. She never asked financial help from anyone, making do with only the help that the friars of St. Dominic gave her (for she lived near their convent). She imitated the Blessed Maria Raggi of Rome, and I believe that the glory of this good woman will be no less than hers on account of the virtues of patience, humility and poverty which this whole City witnessed in her.

> The Venerable Maria Raggi (1552–1600) went to Italy after the tragic death of her husband, an important man in the Genoese colony of Chios, overrun by Turks; she joined the Dominican Third Order Secular, lived in poverty, caring for the sick. In 1593 she received the stigmata. Her tomb, a landmark of Baroque art, was carved by Bernini at Santa Maria sopra Minerva, the principal Dominican church in Rome, in 1643.

25.   On the topic of miracles there is not much to say about this City, just as Father Master Victoria states about the Indies in general, although their discovery was a miracle for how God moved Ferdinand and Isabella, and their first discoverer, Christopher Columbus, for such an enterprise. About the conversion of the natives, we can say ["The Finger of God is here"] and with Balthasar Chanasio,

Balthasar Chanasio, *de nostra vere[a] Religionis*, en el capitulo último de su libro 4° *"Si aliquo est mihi quod volo: si nullo hoy ipsum magnum est miraculum potuise converti sine miraculo."* y si algunos naturales no se convirtieron de todo corazón, por su inocencia y simplicidad, menos se les podrá hacer el cargo que dice San Juan, capitulo 12. *"Cum tanta signa fecisset coram eis, non crediderunt in eum."*

> Francisco de Vitoria, OP, died 1546, professor at Salamanca, was a pioneer in the theory of International Law.
>
> "B" and "V" are virtually identical in pronounciation.

> The Latin of this title is garbled, probably by Tapia or the printer, because Torres y Vargas would have known better. It should be *De nostra vera Religione*.

26.   Un milagro hallo comprobado en el libro de Nuestra Señora de Guadalupe, que fue cuando en la tormenta rigorosa de San Bartolomé, que hubo en esta Ciudad, ha más de 70 años, se llevó el aire una criatura, que pasaba de una casa a otra, y encomendándose a la Virgen de Guadalupe, de allí a tres días se halló viva y sana debajo de una teja. La Virgen de la Candelaria, ha hecho aquí algunos milagros, y Señor Santo Domingo Soriano, que tiene altar y cuadro particular en el convento de Señor Santo Thomas de esta Ciudad. Pero como no están comprobados no me atrevo a ponerlos por verdaderos y no es la menor alabanza de la fe de estos vecinos y naturales, que creyesen, como dice San Gregorio en el libro 9, epístola 58, y el venerable Beda en el libro primero de la "historia anglicana" que fue menesteres Inglaterra al principio de su conversión, y el Cardenal Baronio en los anales de la Iglesia, año de 632, que fue menester en Holanda.

> In this section on the bishops of Puerto Rice (#27–42), Torres y Vargas lists essential biographical facts for each prelate, apparently taken from trustworthy sources. Torres y Vargas, however, made a mistake in the order. To give a better account for each bishop, Torres y Vargas added comments from whatever sources he could, and seems to have depended on considerable oral testimony and even inscriptions on tombs of bishops in the cathedral crypt. He shows respect for oral history, although not without some inaccuracies.
>
> His commentaries are indented below.

27.   En bien dilatados discursos se pudieran esplayar las noticias de esta Isla, pero en historia general, que ha de tener concisas las relaciones, no podrá gozar de tanto lugar, y así lo hago de los Obispos que ha tenido desde su principio y descubrimiento admitiendo con Antonio de Herrera en su historia general de las Indias, que el primero que pasó a ellas desde España fue el licenciado Don Alfonso Manso, clérigo canónigo, y *natural de Salamanca, que con retención de

in the last chapter of his fourth book of *De Nostra Vere Religionis*, ["If (there was) some (miracle), that's what I wanted; if none, that (such a multitude) could be converted without any miracles is itself a great miracle."] And if because of their innocence and simplicity, some of the natives perhaps did not wholeheartedly convert, they [the missionaries] cannot be charged with the accusation of John, Chapter 12: ["Although he made so many miracles in their presence, they did not believe in him"].

26.   I do find one miracle attested in the book of [The Miracles of] Our Lady of Guadalupe, which happened during the terrible hurricane of Saint Bartholomew's Day [August 24th] which hit this City more than 70 years ago [1568]. The wind carried away a child who was running from one house to another, and the child cried for help to Our Lady of Guadalupe, and was found alive and well three days later under a tile. Our Lady of Candlemas has worked some miracles here, and also my lord Saint Dominic's icon of Soriano, who has an altar and painting in the convent of Saint Thomas Aquinas in this City. But, since these are not certified, I do not dare write them down here as true. It is no small praise of the faith of these *vecinos* and natives that they should have believed [without miracles] when Saint Gregory [the Great] says in the 58th letter of Book IX [of his *Letters*] and the Venerable Bede in the first book of his *Ecclesiastical History of the English People,* that these were needed in England at the beginning of its conversion, and Cardinal Baronius says in his *Annals of the Church* in AD 632 that this was also necessary in Holland.

> Cesare de Barono (1538–1607) was a saintly post-Reformation church historian and Cardinal. The date given here is likely for the publication of his collected works.

> See accompanying note for #27–42.

27.   We could well stretch out the information about this Island into quite lengthy discourses, but in a general history [of the Indies], where the narratives must be concise, this Island can not take up so much space, so I must make mention for the bishops it has had since its beginning and discovery. Along with Antonio de Herrera in his *General History of the Indies*, I note that the first [bishop] to cross to the Indies from Spain was the Licenciate Don Alfonso Manso, a secular cleric and a canon, a *native of Salamanca, who accepted this bishopric with permission to retain his canonry. Thus, this Island was the first to receive an episcopal blessing on the face of its land, out of the whole West Indies and the New-discovered World.

la canongía, aceptó el dicho Obispado, y así fue esta Isla la primera que recibió bendición episcopal sobre la haz de su tierra, en todas estas Indias Occidentales y Nuevo Mundo descubierto.

El dicho Obispo sobre diferencias de los diezmos personales que pedía, volvió a España; y mandándole Su Magestad venir a su Obispado le hizo merced de título de Inquisidor, que siendo el primero que hubo en estas partes, podemos decir que lo fue general en estas Indias, y así de todas ellas se traían los delincuentes y se castigaban, quemando y penitenciando, a cuya causa hasta hoy está en pie la ¤cárcel de Inquisición, y en la Iglesia Cathedral hasta la venida del enemigo Holandés Boduyno Enrico, el año de 1625, se veían muchos† Sambenitos colgados detrás del Coro. Murió dicho Obispo en esta Ciudad y se enterró en su Catedral; donde hasta la venida del dicho Boduyno Enrico, se conservó al lado derecho del Evangelio un nicho con figura de Obispo de alabastro y un **cordero a los pies, la cual figura deshizo dicho enemigo.

¤ Once known as *"Charco de las Brujas"* it was outside what was known as Saint James' gate, or as the Land Gate (*Puerta de Tierra*) — it is approximately at the site of the present Plaza de Colón at the entrance of Old San Juan.

---

28.   En tiempo de este Obispo destruían las hormigas la yuca, que es de lo que se hace el pan ordinario que llaman cazabe, sacóse por suerte por abogado a Señor San Saturnino y cesó luego la plaga; después hubo otro gusano que se comía la dicha yuca, y echando nueva suerte, salió Señor San Patricio, más pareciendo al Obispo y Cabildo Eclesiástico que este Santo era poco conocido y estraordinario, se volvió a reiterar la suerte tres veces, y siempre salió el mismo, con que teniéndolo por notorio milagro, se tomó por abogado del dicho cazabe y se le votó fiesta en ambos Cabildos, haciéndola de Ciudad, con Misa, sermón y procesión, con que hasta hoy se celebra y guarda, sin que haya habido falta notable (sino en las tormentas) del dicho cazabe, y porque se ha enfriado algo el afecto de los ánimos en su celebración, aunque siempre se ha continuado, este año de 1641 comenzó otra vez el gusano a comer la yuca, y haciéndole mucha fiesta con tres procesiones, cesó luego y ha vuelto a reverdecer la yuca, que son los panes de estas partes, con admiración de los labradores, dándoles a entender que los Santos no se enojan pero que se obligan.

This was a common practice in the Mediterranean at the time; all the saints in the calendar were written on slips of paper, and whichever was drawn was believed to be intended by God as patron for the given situation.

The aforementioned Bishop returned to Spain over arguments about the personal tithes he was demanding [from the settlers] and, when His Majesty commanded him to go back to his diocese, he granted him the title of Inquisitor. Since he was the first Inquisitor in this part of the world, we can say that he was Inquisitor General of the Indies, which was the reason delinquents from all over the Indies were brought here and were punished here by burning at the stake or by being given penances. This is why the ¤jail of the Inquisition still stands [in this City]. Until the coming of the Dutch enemy Bowdoyn Hendrick in 1625 you could see many †*sambenitos* hanging behind the choir of the Cathedral. This Bishop died in the City and was buried in the Cathedral, where (until the coming of the aforementioned Bowdoyn Hendrick) his niche tomb survived on the Gospel side with the statue of a Bishop in alabaster, and a **Lamb at his feet, but the enemy destroyed it.

---

* Research shows Manso came from the village of Becerril de Campos in the Diocese of Palencia and not a native of Salamanca, although he had been Rector of its university and retained title as canon, perhaps to secure income supplementing the doubtful finances of a frontier discese. The Licentiate is roughly equivalent to a Master's degree.

†The *sambenito* was a special garment with badges to be worn over their clothes by persons comdemned by the Inquisition, either to the stake or even to lesser crimes. If the convicted confessed and repented, the *sambenito* was worn for the duration of their penance. Afterwords it would be hung in the Cathedral as a witness that the person had been condemned by the Inquisition. These were destroyed when the Dutch invaders gutted the Cathedral and burned San Juan. The presence of the Inquisition in Puerto Rico was a motive of civic pride, just as a US town might be proud of housing a regional headquarters of the FBI.

**The Lamb was the charge on the arms of Puerto Rico, and also on the family arms of Manso, suggesting the name of the bearer. This pictorial representation of the actual name was called "canting arms." *See below (#30) for the same trait with the arms of Bishop Bastidas.*

---

28.   In the days of this Bishop a plague of ants was destroying the *yuca*, which is the plant out of which they make the common bread of this land, which they call *casabe*. They drew lots for a patron saint against this plague and the lot fell on my lord Saint Saturnin, and the plague ceased at once. After that there was another worm that also ate up the *yuca*, and casting lots again, the lot fell on my lord Saint Patrick, but since the Bishop and Chapter thought that this saint was little known and unusual, his name was thrown back and lots were cast again. The same saint still came out three times in a row, so it was taken as a clear sign of God's will, and he was made the patron saint of the *casabe* crop. Both the Cathedral Chapter and the City Council vowed to celebrate his feast, which is kept as a city holy day, with a Mass, sermon, and procession, as is kept

29.   Sucedió en la silla episcopal al dicho licenciado D. Alonso Manso Clérigo y Canónigo de Salamanca, el Maestro Don Fray Manuel de Mercado del orden de San Gerónimo.

No murió en esta Ciudad, pero no se sabe donde fue promovido ni se tiene noticia de sus obras, por la falta de papeles que tienen los archivos, con los sacos y invasiones de los enemigos, que han robado dos veces la Ciudad. Su Crónica de San Gerónimo dirá su promoción y cosas particulares a quien me remito.

> This is an error; Manso was succeeded by Rodrigo de Bastidas, and Mercado was the third bishop, not the second.

30.   Al dicho Maestro Don Fray Manuel de Mercado, sucedió Don Rodrigo de la Bastida, clérigo y Deán de la Catedral de la Isla de Santo Domingo de la Española, y natural de ella, de donde fue promovido por Obispo de Caracas, provincia de Venezuela, de quien escribe Antonio de Herrera, en su general historia, que tuvo una vacada que en veinte años le valió 800 ducados de plata;

en tiempo de dicho Obispo se debía de hacer, o por lo menos comenzar, la capilla mayor de la Iglesia Catedral, porque en el principal testero de ella, están labradas de piedras, las armas del Señor Emperador Carlos 5°, y debajo las del dicho Obispo Don Rodrigo de la Bastida, que son; un escudo en cuarteles, en los dos una estrella, y en los otros dos una torre con una bastida a grúa que sale de una ventana de ella, y a la puerta un león atado con una cadena. La fábrica de esta dicha Iglesia se deja a las dos primeras capillas colaterales que siguen a la mayor, creo que porque faltando los indios, se dejaron de labrar las minas de oro, que es el que levanta los ánimos, y es torre que da fortaleza según lo de el Eclesiástico, *"substantia divitum urbs fortidudinis eius, *timor pauperum egestas eorum."* y si como se comenzó dicha Iglesia, se ejecutara hasta el fin, fuera, según parecía en la planta que yo vi de ella hecha en pergamino, tan grande como lo es hoy la de Sevilla.

> Most of the *Capilla Mayor* (translated here as "sanctuary") had already been built by Manso, until Bastidas, as Bishop of Coro and Royal Visitor of Puerto Rico, forced him to stop the work. After becoming Bishop of Puerto Rico himself, Bastidas finished the little that was left to be done, and put his own arms on it as if he had done the whole work.
>
> See: Murga / Huerga, II:56–57
>
> *The Latin is garbled. — Tr.*
>
> An exaggeration, because the cathedral of Seville is even now the fifth largest church in Christendom in cubic feet, and second only to St. Peter's in Rome in square feet.

and celebrated to this day. Since that time there has been no noticeable scarcity of *casabe* except after a hurricane. But because the enthusiasm for this celebration has grown lukewarm (although it has been held without interruption), in the year 1641 the worms began once again to eat up the *yuca* plants. However, once a major celebration with three processions was done in [St. Patrick's] honor the plague ceased right away, and the *yuca* has grown green once again to the wonder of the farmers. Thus, they came to understand that the saints are not resentful, but that they must be obliged.

29.   The said Licenciate Don Alonso Manso, a secular cleric and canon of Salamanca, was succeeded by Master Don Fray Manuel de Mercado, of the order of Saint Jerome.

He did not die in this City, but we do not know to what diocese he was promoted, nor do we have any notice of his works, because of the lack of documents in the archives, due to the attacks and invasions of our enemies who have twice sacked the City. The chronicle of his Order of Saint Jerome must tell where he was promoted to, and other particulars about him; I remit myself to it.

30.   The said Master Don Fray Manuel de Mercado was succeeded by Don Rodrigo de la Bastida, a secular cleric and Dean of the Cathedral of the Island of Santo Domingo de La Española, and a native of that Island, from which deanery he was promoted to be Bishop of Caracas, in the province of Venezuela. About him Antonio de Herrera writes in his *General History* that he owned a herd of cows which earned for him 800 silver ducats in twenty years.

Actually, he was born in Triana, near Seville; from there he came as dean to Santo Domingo, where his father had been a conquistador and had lands. His subsequent transfer was to Coro in Venezuela before coming to Puerto Rico.

*Torres y Vargas uses the Latin word, "*timor*" (destructive fear); the Vulgate says "*pavor*" (ruinous fear).

It seems that the sanctuary of the Cathedral Church was built, or at least begun, in this Bishop's time, because the arms of my lord the Emperor Charles V are carved in stone on the principal wall of this chapel. Underneath them are those of the said Bishop Rodrigo de la Bastida, which are, quarterly, on the first and fourth quarters, [black,]a [gold] star, and on the second and third [red,] a [silver] tower with a *bastida* or crane issuing from a window of it, and at the door a lion bound by a chain. The building of this church was given up after the two side [the transept] chapels that follow the *Capilla Mayor*. I think this was because

31.   Dicho Obispo Don Rodrigo de la Bastida, fue promovido a la silla arzobispal de su patria, Santo Domingo, donde murió, dejando en ella un mayorazgo
de casas y otras haciendas, que gozan hoy en la dicha Ciudad sus herederos y
descendientes. Al dicho Arzobispo Don Rodrigo, sucedió en esta silla Obispal
de Puerto-Rico, D. Fray Diego de Salamanca, del orden de San Agustín,

> que fue el que hizo, a su costa y espensas, las gradas de fuera de la Iglesia Ca-
> tedral de esta Ciudad; obtuvo licencia de Su Magestad para volverse a España,
> como lo hizo y murió, dejando
> casada una sobrina que trujo
> consigo, en esta Ciudad, de que
> hay sucesora en la de Santo Do-

Rather, he returned to Santo Domingo under the scent of scandal for having sought a more prestigious appointment to a see in Mexico.

> mingo; quedó por su Provisor y Gobernador del obispado, Gaspar de Santa
> Olaya, Canónigo de esta Catedral.

32.   Al Obispo Don Fray Diego de Salamanca del orden de San Agustín, sucedió en el Obispado Don Fray Nicolás Ramos, del orden de Señor San Francisco, y natural de Carrión de los Condes, en Castilla;

> hombre tan virtuoso, que no se entendió solicitase el Obispado, porque se le dió
> sin pretenderle, dicen que el decía ser de humilde linage e hijo de un carbonero,
> y así era de condición llana y afable; era gran letrado y escrivió mucho, pero
> por ser muy viejo no se pudieron leer sus cuadernos, por lo temblado de la letra,
> con que fue más arcano y misterioso en lo escrito que en lo razonado. En el ofi-
> cio de Inquisidor, que hasta entonces le tenían los Obispos de esta Isla, desde
> que se concedió al licenciado Don Alonso Manso en su primero principio, se
> mostró severo y riguroso, como lo pide su recta administración, quemando y
> penitenciando en los autos que hacia, algunas personas, y hasta hoy se conserva
> el lugar del quemadero que cae fuera
> de la puerta de San Cristóbal. Fue
> promovido dicho Obispo a la silla ar-
> zobispal de Santo Domingo, donde
> murió con opinión de Virgen, guar-
> dando siempre el instituto de su

See sidebar on *Charco*: paragraph #27 above.

Franciscans who became bishops were not technically bound by this rule, or by the vow of poverty.

> orden en no tomar dinero, y una vez que de su renta le llevaron trescientos pesos,
> los mando poner debajo de su cama, y a media noche hizo que los sacasen y re-
> partiesen a pobres, testificando que no había podido dormir hasta aquella hora,
> por el cuidado y escrúpulo que le ocasionaba el dinero; y con ser tan gran letrado
> no conocía el valor de cada moneda, como no la había tratado por toda su vida,
> que creo fue bien aventurada conforme su buena fama.

once the Indians became extinct the gold mines ceased to be worked, and gold is what raises up men's spirits and is a tower of strength to them; as the Book of Sirach says, ["The rich man's wealth is his fortress, the *ruin of the poor is their poverty" Proverbs 10:15]. And if this church had been brought to completion according to the way it was begun, it would have been (as appears by a parchment plan of it which I saw) as big as the Cathedral of Seville.

31.   This Bishop Don Rodrigo de la Bastida was promoted to the archiepiscopal see of his homeland, Santo Domingo, where he died, leaving there an entailed estate of houses and other real estate, which to this day is enjoyed in that City by his heirs and descendants. The said Archbishop Don Rodrigo was succeeded in the see of Puerto Rico by Don Fray Diego de Salamanca, of the Order of Saint Augustine,

> who at his own expense built the outside steps of the Cathedral Church of this City. He obtained a license from His Majesty to return to Spain, as he did, and died there, leaving a niece whom he had brought with him married in this City [to Juan III Ponce de León — Ed.], who has descendants in Santo Domingo. Gaspar de Santa Olaya, a canon of this Cathedral, remained as his Provisor and Vicar in this bishopric.

32.   Bishop Don Fray Diego de Salamanca of the Order of Saint Augustine was succeeded in the See by Don Fray Nicolás Ramos, of the Order of my lord Saint Francis, born at Carrión de los Condes in Castile.

> He was a man of such virtue that there was no suspicion of his having solicited the rank of bishop, which was given to him without any efforts on his part. They say that he always would state he was of a poor family and the son of a charcoal burner, and was therefore of a plain and affable disposition. He was a great scholar and wrote much, but since he was so old, his notebooks turned out to be illegible because of his shaky handwriting. It was more difficult to understand what he wrote than what he meant. In his office as Inquisitor (which the bishops of this Island held until that time, as had been initially granted to the Licenciate Don Alonso Manso) he showed himself severe and strict, as the right management of that office demands, burning and imposing penances on some persons in the autos da fe that he held. To this day the site of the stakes for burning is pointed out just outside the gate of Saint Christopher. This Bishop was promoted to the archiepiscopal See of Santo Domingo, where he died with the reputation of being still a virgin, and having always kept the rule of his order about not touching money — indeed one time that he was brought three hundred pesos

33.   Al Arzobispo Don Fray Nicolás Ramos sucedió en este Obispado, el Doctor Don Antonio Calderón, clérigo y Arcediano que fue de la Catedral de Santa Fe, en el Nuevo Reino. Era natural de Baeza

> y viniendo a este Obispado, en una Isla, 24 leguas de este puerto, que se llama Santa Cruz, le tomó un enemigo inglés llamado Santa Cruz, día de la Cruz, y el bajel en que venia embarcado se llamaba Santa Cruz. Lo más estimable que le quitó, fue una cruz que traía por pectoral al pecho, y se le pudiera acomodar los del Evangelio "*tollat crucem suam.*"

This description of the repeatedly occurring Holy Cross plays on Baroque theology's fascination with "coincidence" as evidence of God's presence in all things.

The English captain's name was Juan de la Cruz, according to Huerga, who gets the information from documents in the Archive of the Indies. Mercenary service often led to switching sides during war.

---

34.   Fue promovido al Obispado de Panamá, y por su promoción, hubo una larga Sede vacante de trece o catorce años en esta Catedral, y murió en Santa Cruz de la Sierra, siendo de allí Obispo. Fue proveído en el Obispado, por promoción del dicho Obispo Don Antonio Calderón, Don Fray Martín Vázquez de Arce, fraile del orden de Santo Domingo, colegial de Santo Thomas de Sevilla, Colegio de su Orden, y Rector que era en el, cuando le proveyeron.

> Era natural del Cuzco en el Reyno del Perú y sobrino de Rodrigo Vázquez de Arce, Presidente de Castilla, hijo natural de su hermano. Vino a su Obispado por la Isla Margarita, que se incluye en el, donde estuvo tres años, y desde allí a esta Catedral por el año de 1603, y murió el de 1609 por principio de Henero: dejó su hacienda a esta Iglesia, que era de veinte mil ducados, porque faltaron algunos días desde que hizo testamento hasta que murió, los Oficiales Reales pusieron pleyto por falta de tiempo, como el derecho dispone, pero Su Magestad mandó con piedad Católica, se diese a la Iglesia, por ser pobre, aunque la lució poco por estar ya convertida en los prebendados de ella. Mandóse enterrar en su Iglesia, como se hizo al lado de la epístola en bóveda particular, donde estuvo hasta que el año de 1641 se quitó con la otra del Obispo Manso, para acrecentar las gradas del Altar mayor, y se pusieron los huesos en el mismo Altar mayor al lado de la epístola.

from his rents as bishop, he had them placed under his bed. At midnight he had the money taken away and given out among the poor, claiming that he had been unable to sleep up to that hour because of the worry and scruple which that money caused him. Although he was such a learned man, he did not really know the value of the different coins, since he had not handled them in his whole life — a life which I believe was truly blessed, according to his good reputation.

33.   Archbishop Don Fray Nicolás Ramos was succeeded in this diocese by Doctor Don Antonio Calderón, a secular cleric and Archdeacon [*actually Dean* — Tr.] of the Cathedral of Santa Fe [de Bogotá] in the New Kingdom of Granada [*modern Colombia* —Tr.]. He was originally from Baeza [in Andalusia].

> On his way to this diocese, and being on an island called Santa Cruz [Saint-Croix], which is about 24 leagues from this port, he was captured by an English enemy captain called Santa Cruz on the feast of the Holy Cross [May 3, 1594], and the ship on which he had been traveling was also called Santa Cruz. And the most valuable thing he was robbed of was a pectoral cross he wore on his breast, so we could apply to him the words of the Gospel, ["Let him take up his cross." Mt. 16:24.]

34.   He was promoted to the See of Panama, and because of this promotion there was a long vacancy of thirteen or fourteen years in this Cathedral. He died as Bishop of Santa Cruz de la Sierra [*in modern Bolivia* — Tr.]. By the promotion of this Bishop Don Antonio Calderón, the Diocese was given to Don Fray Martín Vázquez de Arce, a friar of the Order of Saint Dominic and a fellow of the College of Saint Thomas in Seville (which is a college of his Order). At the time of his promotion he was Rector of that college.

> He was a native of Cuzco in the Kingdom of Peru, and a nephew of Rodrigo Vázquez de Arce, President of the Council of Castile, being the illegitimate son of a brother of his. He came to his diocese by way of the Island of Margarita, which is part of the diocese, and where he spent three years. He came to this Cathedral around the year 1603, and died in early January of 1609. He left his property to this Church — it was worth about 20,000 ducats — but because there were only a few days between the signing of his will and his death, the royal Officers challenged the testament as being a last-minute will, as the law commands them to do. But His Majesty (with Catholic piety) commanded that the money be given to the local Church, since it was so poor. It did not help much, since it was already distributed among the prebendaries of the Cathedral. He stipulated that his body be buried in his Cathedral Church, and in fact he

35.   Por muerte del dicho Don Fray Martín Vázquez de Arce, se hizo merced de este Obispado al Maestro Don Fray Alonso de Monroy, del orden de Nuestra Señora de la Merced, Provincial en su orden;

acéptalo y consagrose, mas no quiso venir a su Obispado, por lo que el Real Consejo de las Indias, (como está advertido al principio de la Curia Ecca) mandó que los Obispos de las Indias no se consagrasen en España, mas ya se comienza a dispensar, como se ha hecho este año pasado de 1644, que vino consagrado de Madrid el Obispo Don Fray Damián López de Haro a este Obispado, y otros lo vienen por el gasto y riesgo que se ocasiona de irse a consagrar a otras

> Huerga has shown from documentary evidence that Monroy resigned the Royal nomination without having obtained the Papal bulls that were necessary before a bishop could be consecrated. The convent where he was buried has been turned into a museum, and Monroy's tombstone is not in public view. The claim to have personally read its claim of Monroy's consecration is therefore unexplained.

partes. El dicho Obispo Don Fray Alonso de Monroy murió en Sevilla, donde está enterrado en su convento de la Merced, con losa en su sepultura, que dice haber sido electo y consagrado Obispo de este Obispado, la cual yo vi en la Ciudad de Sevilla.

36.   Al Obispo Don Fray Alonso de Monroy, y que no quiso venir a su Obispado, sucedió el Maestro Don Fray Francisco de Cabrera y Córdova natural de la misma Ciudad y del Orden de Santo Domingo, del convento de Santa Maria del Monte de su orden, que esta fuera de dicha Ciudad de Córdova,

era hermano de Don Alonso de Cabrera, del Consejo Real y de la Cámara de Su Magestad y vino el año de 1610 y fue promovido el de 1613 al Obispado de Truxillo, en el Perú, porque el año de 1612, se dividió dicho Obispado, como el de Guamanga, de el de Cuzco que lo tenia todo antes, como dice Solorzano Pereira en su libro de "*Jure indiarum*".

37.   Por promoción de dicho Maestro Don Fray Francisco de Cabrera y Córdova, se proveyó este Obispado en el Maestro Don Fray Pedro de Solier, del orden de San Agustín; hombre mozo y gran predicador, del lugar de Barajas, cerca de Madrid.

Vino a su Obispado el año, de 1615, y en el fue la rigorosa tormenta que sucedió en esta Isla, después de mas de 40 años que había pasado la de San Mateo, que llaman, y esta fue a *12 de Setiembre. Hizo tanto daño a la Iglesia Catedral, que fue necesario por una parte cubrirla de paja, y avisar a Su Magestad, supli-

was buried in a private vault on the Epistle side where his body was until the year 1641. This vault and that of Bishop Manso were destroyed to enlarge the steps of the High Altar, and then his bones were laid under the High Altar itself, on the Epistle side.

35.   On the death of the aforementioned Don Fray Martín Vázquez de Arce, this Bishopric was granted to Master Don Fray Alonso de Monroy, of the Order of Our Lady of Ransom, and Provincial of that Order.

He accepted and was consecrated Bishop, but did not choose to come to his diocese, for which reason the Royal Council of the Indies made a ruling (as is stated at the beginning of the Ecclesiastical Curia) that bishops appointed for the Indies should not receive their consecration in Spain. However, they are already beginning to grant dispensations from this rule, as happened this last year of 1644, when Bishop Don Fray Damián López de Haro came to this diocese already consecrated in Madrid. Others also come already consecrated because of the expense and risk entailed by going to be consecrated in other parts [of the New World.]. The aforementioned Bishop Don Fray Alonso de Monroy died in Seville, where he was buried in his convent of the Order of Ransom, with a tombstone, which I saw in the City of Seville, that says he was elected and consecrated Bishop of this See.

36.   Bishop Don Fray Alonso de Monroy, who did not choose to come to his diocese, was succeeded by Master Don Fray Francisco de Cabrera y Córdova, a native of that same city and a member of the Order of Saint Dominic, of the convent of Santa Mariá del Monte of that Order, which is on the outskirts of the City of Córdova.

He was a brother of Don Alonso de Cabrera, a member of the Royal Council and of His Majesty's Chamber. He came over in the year 1610 and was promoted in 1613 to the See of Trujillo in Peru, because in 1612 that bishopric as well as that of Huamanga was separated from that of Cuzco, which used to cover that whole territory, as Solorzano Pereira says in his book *De Iure Indiarum*.

37.   Because of the promotion of the said Master Don Fray Francisco de Cabrera y Córdova, this bishopric was granted to Master Don Fray Pedro de Solier, of the Order of Saint Augustine, a young man and a great preacher, from the village of Barajas, near Madrid.

He came over to his See in the year 1615, on which occurred a terrible hurricane, more than 49 years after the hurricane which they call Saint Matthew's, which

cando la hiciese una limosna para su fábrica; y concedió cuatro mil ducados con su acostumbrada grandeza; y con ellos, y lo que debían los prebendados, desde el tiempo del almoneda de la hacienda del Obispo Don Fray Martín Vázquez de Arce, se hizo un arco y dos pilares, con que se reparó el Crucero de la dicha Iglesia, y sobre ellos se fundó el nuevo, que el año de 1641 se hizo, a solicitud de Don Iñigo de la Mota Sarmiento, Gobernador de esta Ciudad, como también la mitad del convento del Santo Thomas de Aquino del orden de Santo Domingo a espensas de la infantería del presidio, con precepto de capilla y entierro suyo. El dicho Don Fray Pedro de Solier

*Actually on the 21st, which is Saint Matthew's day; the digits must have been transposed here. "*Setiembre*" for "*Septiembre*."

fue promovido el año 1615, a la silla arzobispal de Santo Domingo, que aceptó con mucho disgusto, y como con espíritu profético adivinó su temprana muerte, que fue a los dos o tres años de su arzobispado, de edad de 46 años.

38.   Al dicho Don Fray Pedro de Solier, sucedió el Doctor Don Bernardo de Balbuena, natural de Valdepeñas, en la Mancha, clérigo Abad de la Isla de Jamaica, de donde vino rico.

For more on the writings and the fame of Balbuena, which reflected favorably on Puerto Rico, see the second essay, pp. 54–55.

Pretendió hacer un convento de monjas Bernardas en el lugar del Visa, en Extremadura, y aunque envió muchos frutos y dineros en los navíos que salieron aquellos años de este puerto, los más se perdieron, con que conociendo que Dios Nuestro Señor quería que se gastase la renta en utilidad de la parte donde se ganaba; mudó de parecer, y muriendo el año de 1625, mandó su hacienda a la Iglesia, con cargo de que se labrase una capilla al Señor San Bernardo para Sagrario, y en ella se colocasen sus huesos, dotando la lámpara del aceite que pudiera gastar cada año, y en cada primer domingo de mes, se le dijese una Misa cantada, y el día de Señor San Bernardo otra con sermón y vísperas como todo se hace. También los oficiales de la Real Hacienda pusieron pleyto al testamento de dicho Obispo, por decir no era valido su otorgamiento; y Su Magestad mandó, se diese la hacienda a la Santa Iglesia.

occurred on *September 12th. This hurricane did so much damage to the Cathedral Church that parts of it had to be re-roofed in thatch, and a letter had to be sent to His Majesty begging him to send a contribution for the rebuilding. With his accustomed generosity, the King granted four thousand ducats, with which money, along with the money owed by the prebendaries from the time of the auction of the goods of Bishop Don Fray Martín Vázquez de Arce, an arch and two pillars were built thus repairing the transept of the church. On this arch and pillars the new transept was built in 1641 by the care of Don Iñigo de la Mota Sarmiento, Governor of this City, as well as half the convent of Saint Thomas Aquinas of the Order of Saint Dominic, which was done at the expense of the Infantry of the garrison with the stipulation that they should have a chapel and burial vault assigned to the Infantry. The aforementioned Don Fray Pedro de Solier was promoted in 1615 to the Archiepiscopal See of Santo Domingo, which he accepted with great displeasure, as if he had with a prophetic spirit discerned his early death, which occurred only two or three years after his promotion to that archdiocese when he was 46 years old.

38.   This Don Fray Pedro de Solier was succeeded by Doctor Don Bernardo de Balbuena, a native of Valdepeñas in la Mancha, a secular cleric and Abbot of the Island of Jamaica, from which he arrived a rich man.

He attempted to build a convent of Bernardine [Cistercian] nuns in the village of El Viso in Extremadura. Although he sent much of his income and money in the ships that set out in those years, most of them were wrecked, which led him to figure out that God our Lord wanted his income to be spent for use in the part of the world where he was gaining it. He changed his mind, and when he died in 1625 he left his property to the Church [of Puerto Rico] on the stipulation that a chapel should be built [in the Cathedral] in honor of my lord Saint Bernard for the reservation of the Blessed Sacrament, and that his bones should be buried in that chapel, endowing the sanctuary lamp with the income for the oil that might be burned in it each year, along with an endowment for a high Mass for his soul on the first Sunday of each month, and for another high Mass on the day of my lord Saint

> If the will had been broken, the money would have gone to the Royal Treasury.

Bernard [August 20th] with a sermon and vespers in his honor, all of which is done accordingly. The officers of the Royal Treasury challenged the will of this bishop too, claiming that it was not done validly, but His Majesty commanded that the property should be given to the Church.

39.   Vino a su Obispado el año de 1623, y el de 1621 mandó Su Santidad y Su Magestad celebrar Concilio Provincial en la Metrópoli de Santo Domingo, y que acudiesen los Obispos sufráganos, y así fue a el, Don Fray Gonzalo de Angulo, Obispo de Caracas, por su Iglesia, y por esta, que estaba Sede vacante, el Racionero Bernardino Riberol de Castilla, y por la de Cuba el Deán Don Agustín Serrano, con poderes de D. Fray Alonso Enríquez de Toledo su Obispo, que se escusó por su vejez y poca salud. Este Concilio se llevó a España y le presidio Don Fray Pedro de Oviedo, Arzobispo de la Metrópoli de Santo Domingo, grande letrado y catedrático de Alcalá. Pero hasta ahora no se ha confirmado.

40.   Al Doctor Don Bernardo de Balbuena, sucedió en el Obispado el Doctor Don Juan López Agurto de la Mata, clérigo natural de Tenerife, en las Canarias.
Fue primero Deán de Mérida en la provincia de Yucatán. Pero antes de venir a su Iglesia le hizo merced Su Magestad de una ración en la de Tlaxcala, y estando en ella vacó la canongía Doctoral de aquella Iglesia y por oposición se la llevó. Hizole Su Magestad merced del Obispado, y cuando tuvo la nueva, dio seis mil ducados de limosna al gran Santuario de Nuestra Señora de Candelaria de su tierra, y aquí hizo muchas a la Iglesia y a personas necesitadas. Era hombre entero, ajustado de vida, y como dicen los Italianos de *Testa,* y tenía otras muchas partes de las que pide San Pablo para los Obispos, con que no contento a algunos pareciéndoles muy severo para lo relajado e infeliz de estos tiempos. Visitando su Obispado en la Margarita pasaron los frayles Franciscos de su capítulo, con intento de fundar en esta Ciudad un convento, como desde Santo Domingo llevaron acordado, y para la obra de la Casa dió mil ducados de limosna en la Real Caja, cumpliendo con la obligación de su oficio. Fue promovido a la Catedral de Caracas, donde murió a pocos años, y era de los mejores predicadores que tenía este Obispado.

> It seems the diocese of Yucatán was significantly poorer than that of Tlaxcala/Puebla, so that a plain canon in the latter had better income than the Dean of the former; hence, although the transition from Dean to canon was technically a step down, in terms of finances and cultural environment, this one amounted to a promotion.

41.   Al Doctor Don Juan López Agurto de la Mata, sucedió el Maestro Don Fray Juan Alonso de Solís de la Orden de Nuestra Señora del Carmen, y natural de Salamanca.

39.   He arrived in his diocese in the year 1623, and in 1621 His Holiness and His Majesty had commanded that a Provincial Council be held in the Metropolitan See of Santo Domingo, and that all the suffragan bishops should attend. And so Don Fray Gonzalo de Angulo, Bishop of Caracas, attended to represent his diocese, and this diocese, whose See was vacant, was represented by the Prebendary Bernardino Riberol de Castilla, while the diocese of Cuba was represented by its Dean, Don Agustín Serrano, with powers of attorney from its Bishop, Don Fray Alonso Enríquez de Toledo, who excused himself from attendance because of his old age and poor health. The minutes of this council were taken to Spain [for Royal approval], but it still has not been confirmed. It was presided over by Don Fray Pedro de Oviedo, Metropolitan Archbishop of Santo Domingo, a great scholar who had been a professor at [the University of] Alcalá.

40.   Doctor Don Bernardo de Balbuena was succeeded in the bishopric by Doctor Don Juan López Agurto de la Mata, a secular cleric born in Tenerife in the Canary Islands.

First, he was Dean of Mérida in the province of Yucatán. But before he came to his Church, His Majesty had granted him a prebend in the Church of Tlaxcala. While he was there, the Doctoral canonry of that Cathedral became vacant, and he won it by competitive examination. His Majesty then granted him this bishopric, and upon receiving the news, he gave six thousand ducats as an offering to the great shrine of Our Lady of Candlemas in his native Island. Here [in the Indies] he made many donations to churches and to needy individuals. He was a man of integrity, very exact in his lifestyle, and a man of *Testa* [*literally," head"; colloquially, "of sound good sense"*— Tr.], as the Italians say, and he had many of the qualities that Saint Paul wants in a Bishop [cf. I Timothy 3:1–7, Titus 1:7–11, I2:1–8], which discontented some, who felt that he was too severe for our unhappy and permissive times. When he was holding the visitation of his diocese and was at the Island of Margarita, the Franciscan friars came from their Chapter with the intention of founding a convent in this City, as they had already planned when they went to the Chapter from Santo Domingo. For the building of that friary, the Bishop made a contribution of a thousand ducats from the Royal Treasury as was his duty as Bishop. He was promoted to the Cathedral of Caracas, where he died a few years later. He had been one of the best preachers this diocese ever had.

41.   Doctor Don Juan López Agurto de la Mata was succeeded by Master

Fue antes que religioso, caballero seglar y casado, de cuyo matrimonio tuvo dos hijos. Entróse clérigo en siendo viudo de donde pasó a ser religioso del Carmen. Decía que había dado y recibido todos los Sacramentos de la Iglesia Católica, y como tal y virtuosísimo religioso, murió en esta Ciudad después de haber venido de la visita de Cumaná, Margarita y demás anexos a su Obispado, en donde bautizó más de diez mil indios; dejando su hacienda a la Iglesia, que le valió tan poco, que no llegó a dos mil pesos, y a sus hijos sólo en Salamanca en el lugar de Retortillo, y la granja que ha había renunciado en ellos cuando se metió a fraile. Está enterrado en el Altar mayor de la Catedral de esta ciudad, y tiene una losa al lado derecho del Evangelio donde fue su sepultura, con el epitafio siguiente: *"Doctor Don Joannes Ildefonsus de Solis, faeliciore saeculo vigil toto virtu turn cumulo nitidisissimum exemplar, Huius urbis presul sine exemplo. Die XIX Aprilis anno 1641. Obist plorandus, cuius in memoriam lapiden hunc duraturum minus. Sobrinus Dominus Ignacens de la Mota Sarmiento dicavit"*.

Since Roman-rite priests normally have not received the sacrament of Matrimony, and only bishops confer the sacraments of Confirmation and Holy Orders, receiving all three sacraments is unusual. Solis distinction was earned because he was a widower who became a priest and then a bishop. Torres y Vargas notes how strictly he kept his vow of poverty. Technically, friars who become bishops are dispensed from this vow, but Solís kept it anyway.

This presumably means that the Bishop, while in Margarita, gave the friars a bill payable in San Juan out of the money which the Royal Treasury was supposed to pay him.

---

42.   Al maestro Don Fray Juan Alonso Solís, sucedió el Maestro Don Fray Damián López de Haro natural de Toledo y fraile de la orden de la Santísima Trinidad, Provincial que estaba siendo en ella, de la provincia de Castilla, cuando se le hizo merced del Obispado.

Vino a esta Ciudad el año de 1644, y luego trató de celebrar Sínodo Diocesano, como lo hizo, el cual remitió a Su Magestad y le confirmó y está mandado imprimir. En el se reforman muchos abusos y da asiento a muchas cosas que necesitaban de tenerle fijo, y en particular puso precio a las Misas de capellanías perpetuas,* que hasta ahora era de ocho reales la limosna de la Misa, y la subió hasta quince, para que mejor puedan sustentarse los capellanes. Así mismo escribió carta a Su Santidad** el año de 1646 sobre el aprieto que se hace a los

Don Fray Juan Alonso de Solís, of the Order of Our Lady of Mount Carmel, and a native of Salamanca.

> Before taking his vows he had been a lay gentleman and a married man, with two sons from his marriage. As a widower he became a cleric, and then became a Carmelite friar. He used to say that he had conferred and received all seven sacraments of the Catholic Church. He died in this City as a most virtuous friar after returning from holding the Episcopal Visitation of Cumaná, Margarita and the other territories annexed to his diocese, where he baptized more than ten thousand Indians. He left all his property to the Diocese, but it gained little by this inheritance, for his property did not add up to two thousand pesos. His sons received nothing but the manor in the village of Retortillo in Salamanca, which he had signed over to them when he became a friar [*and also income to maintain it.* — Ed.]. He is buried by the High Altar of the Cathedral of this City, and has a tombstone on the Gospel side of it, where he was buried, with the following epitaph: ["Doctor Don Juan Alfonso de Solís, who looked forward to a happier world than this, was a shining example of all the virtues, and a peerless bishop of this City. He died on the 19th day of April of the year 1641, deserving our tears. This stone, which will not last as long as his memory, was dedicated to him by †his nephew Don Iñigo de la Mota Sarmiento."]

† It appears that the reference to Mota Sarmiento as a "nephew" is an adoptive title, rather than a familial or blood relation.

42.   Master Don Fray Juan Alonso Solís was succeeded by Master Don Fray Damián López de Haro, a native of Toledo and a friar of the Order of the Most Holy Trinity. He was Provincial of Castile in that Order when he was granted the Bishopric.

The original edition of this synod's Acts (Madrid, 1647) was thought to be completely lost, but Fr. Alvaro Huerga, OP, was fortunate enough to discover a copy of it, which he edited in 1989 in the second volume of his Episcopologio de Puerto Rico, and later as a separate volume. The diocese of Puerto Rico was run by the Synodal Constitutions of 1645 until the Synod of 1918, when Bishop William Ambrose Jones adapted the regulations of the diocese to the modus operandi of American dioceses.

> He came to this City in the year 1644, and at once endeavored to hold a Diocesan Synod, as he did succeed in doing [in 1645] He sent the decrees to His Majesty, who confirmed them, and ordered their printing. In this Synod's decrees many abuses are reformed and many issues in need of fixing are set up with a firm policy. In particular, he set a fee for the Masses in perpetual endow-

indios de la Margarita y provincia de Cumaná que es anexo a este Obispado, y hasta ahora se esta haciendo aquella visita*** de que se esperan grandes frutos en bien de las almas, y reverencia del Culto divino y estimación de sus prelados.

See accompanying note for #43–81.

43.   Como Juan Ponce de León, capitán de *Higüey* en la Isla Española, fue el primero que tuvo noticia de esta Isla, según Antonio de Herrera en su general Historia, parece que de derecho se le debía su primero gobierno, y así fue, el primero Gobernador de esta Isla,

y era de casa de ayo del †príncipe, Pedro Núñez de Guzmán, hermano de Ramiro Núñez, Señor de Toral. En su tiempo, se fundó el primer pueblo llamado Caparra, a la banda del Norte, año 1509, y después de 12 años se despobló por malsano. Gobernó hasta el año 1512. Sucediéronle Juan Cerón y Miguel Díaz, por elección del Almirante Diego Colon, y luego nombró al comendador Moscoso, como dice el mismo Herrera y creo que natural de la villa de Sanervaez. Y como en aquellos tiempos la mayor ansia de los españoles, eran los nuevos descubrimientos, pidió el de la Florida, y Su Magestad le dió titulo de Adelantado de ella, y ansí mismo quiso fundar en la *Trinidad, pero comenzando la población en verano, con las avenidas del invierno, se inundaron las casas, con que se le frustro el intento y murió en esta Ciudad donde tienen sus descendientes su casa cercada de almenas, y su sepultura en el altar y capilla mayor del convento de Santo Thomas del orden de Santo Domingo, y en una losa se sella. "Aquí yace el muy ilustre Señor Juan Ponce de León primero Adelantado de la Florida, primer conquistador y Gobernador de esta Isla de San Juan." Este entierro y capilla es de sus herederos y el padronazgo de ella, de Juan Ponce de León su nieto, y de sus hijos y de Doña Isabel de Loaysa su mujer.

44.   El segundo Gobernador, que sucedió al dicho Juan Ponce, fue el capitán Cristóbal Mendoza, como dice Antonio de Herrera, en su general historia, tuvo guerra con los Caribes, que hasta entonces no habían pasado ingleses ni holandeses a estas partes, y se mostró valeroso, buscándolos fuera de la Isla hasta la de B[V]ieque.

ments,* whose stipend until now had been eight *reales*, and he raised it up to fifteen, so the chaplains could have better support. Along the same lines he wrote a letter to His Holiness** in the year 1646 about the oppression that is suffered by the Indians of the Island of Margarita and the province of Cumaná, which are annexed to this diocese. At this moment he is making that Visitation,*** from which we expect great fruit for the good of souls and the reverence of divine worship, as well as the respect due to our prelates.

---

* In modern parlance, he adjusted their income for inflation — in the case of old endowments, the obligations would have remained the same, but the buying power of the income attached to them would have become significantly less.

**This may be an error for "to His Majesty," since he must have known that the crown would have resented a bishop going over its head to Rome, and would have taken measures to impede the Pope from meddling in its colonies.

***Torres y Vargas wrote this while Bishop López de Haro was away from the Island, on Visitation of the regions annexed to the diocese of Puerto Rico. The Bishop died of plague in Margarita on August 24, 1648, and was buried there. See #101–102 and consult the Appendix on the question of dates for composition.

Torrer y Vargas returns to secular history, describing the governors of Puerto Rice (#43–81). As he had done for the list of bishops, the basic information is supplemented with commentary and opinion of his own, inscriptions from monuments and tombs, and most especially from oral history.

These sections are indented.

43.   Since Juan Ponce de León, captain of *Higüey* in the Island of Española, was the first to have knowledge of this Island [of Puerto Rico] — according to Antonio de Herrera in his *General History [of the Indies]* — it would seem that by rights he was owed its governorship in the first place, and thus indeed he was the first Governor of this Island.

He had been in the household of the Tutor to the †Prince, Pedro Núñez de Guzmán, the brother of Ramiro Núñez, Lord of Toral. In his days was founded the first town in the Island, which was called Caparra, on the north side of the Island. Founded in 1509, twelve years later it was abandoned as unhealthy. Governor until 1512, he was succeeded by Juan Cerón and Miguel Díaz, who were chosen by Admiral Diego Columbus, who then named Commander Moscoso as the aforementioned Herrera says. I believe he [Ponce de León] was from the town of Sanervaez. And since in those days the greatest eagerness of Spaniards

The home of Ponce de León still exists, and is known as the *Casa Blanca*; it is now a historical museum.

Ponce de León actually died in Cuba but his body was transferred to San Juan by his grandson, Juan II Troche Ponce de León. The tombstone is no longer extant, but a carving of the arms of the Ponce de León family can still be seen on the left wall of the *Capilla Mayor* of the church. Displaying one's coat of arms in a prominent place in a church or chapel was one of the rights of a patron.

* *Trinidad's colonization was actually assigned to Juan II Troche, who suffered from its failure (see pp. 72–73). —Ed.*

45.   El tercer Gobernador fue el Comendador Moscoso,
que no se sabe su naturaleza, ni de que hábito fuese, por la antigüedad; y solo Herrera en su historia, dice, que fue Gobernador de la Isla. El dicho Comendador Moscoso, estuvo poco tiempo en el cargo y el Almirante nombró por su sucesor a Cristóbal de Mendoza &c. (año 1547).

Comendador is not of the army (*comandante*), but a Knight Commander in a Military Order.

46.   El cuarto Gobernador fue Francisco Manuel de Obando; caballero gallego
y por ser deudo de Doña Teresa de Rivera, la envió a llamar a Sevilla para casarse con ella, de donde vino de la casa del Señor Duque de Alalá, donde como a deuda suya la tenía; con ella paso Alonso Pérez Martel su hermano que es uno de los caballeros de que hace mención Antonio de Herrera, que pasaron al principio de su descubrimiento a las Indias. La dicha Doña Teresa de Rivera dejó sucesión en esta Ciudad, pero no Alonso Pérez Martel porque nunca fue casado y murió en la Ciudad, de Santo Domingo, como el Gobernador Francisco Manuel de Obando [sic] en esta de Puerto Rico, por ser muy viejo y con opinión de gran virtud y Santidad.

was to make new discoveries, he asked for that of Florida. His Majesty named him Adelantado of that land. He also wanted to found a settlement in *Trinidad, but they began the settlement in summer, and when the heavy rains of winter flooded the houses, the attempt was frustrated. He died in this City, where his descendants have a house walled with battlements. There is also a family burial vault in the High Altar and Capilla Mayor of the convent of Saint Thomas [Aquinas] of the Order of Saint Dominic, sealed by a tombstone that says: "Here lies the very illustrious Señor Juan Ponce de León, first Adelantado of La Florida, and first conqueror and Governor of this Island of San Juan." This burial vault and chapel belongs to his heirs, and its patronage belongs to Juan Ponce de León, his grandson, and to his children by his wife Doña Isabel de Loaysa.

†The prince referred to is Juan, Prince of Asturias, son and heir of Ferdinand and Isabella, who predeceased his parents.

The abundance of details on persons related to the Ponce de León family may have come to Torres y Vargas from the memories of his relatives. The details include highly personal incidents.

44.   The second governor to succeed Juan Ponce de León was Captain Cristóbal Mendoza, according to Antonio de Herrera in his *General History*. He waged war against the Carib Indians (the English and Dutch [*Spanish allies at the time* — Tr.] had not yet come over to this part of the world) and he showed himself a man of valor, pursuing them beyond the Island as far as the Island of Vieques.

45.   The third Governor was Commander Moscoso;
        we do not know where he was born, or of what Military Order he was a Knight-
        Commander, because it was so long ago — only Herrera's *History* mentions
        that he was Governor of this Island. Commander Moscoso was governor for
        only a short time, and the Admiral appointed Cristóbal de Mendoza &c. to suc-
        ceed him (1547).

46.   The fourth governor was Francisco Manuel de Obando; a knight from Galicia.
        He was related to Doña Teresa de Rivera, and had her summoned from Seville
        in order to marry her. She came here from the house of the Duke of Alcalá,
        where she lived as a kinswoman of the Duke. With her came a brother, Alonso
        Pérez Martel, one of the knights who were mentioned by Antonio de Herrera
        among those who came to the Indies in the early days of their discovery. This

47.   A Gobernador Francisco Manuel de Obando, [sic] sucedió el licenciado Caraza, montañés.

> Era letrado, porque entonces *como no habían pasado a las Indias, armadas de enemigos* sino cual o cual navío que solo trataba de su mercaduria o rescates, se atendía al buen gobierno de los vecinos y con estos parece que se entenderían mejor los letrados. A Caraza le prorrogó S. M. dos años, de los cuatro porque fue, por su buen proceder, por carta de 10 de enero de 1561.

Montañés indicates he was from a region of Castile in the present province of Santander, considered the source of many noble families.

The better preparation of this and subsequent governors shows Spain recognized the growing importance of Puerto Rico.

---

48.   Al dicho licenciado Caraza, sucedió el Doctor Antonio de la *Llama Vallejo, con título de Juez de residencia,

> que casó en esta Ciudad con Doña Leonor Ponce hija del primer Gobernador Juan Ponce, y llevando a España su residencia se ahogó, y con la pena y melancolía de su muerte, la dicha su muger cayó enferma, y estando un día en la cama, a medio día entro un hombre en forma de medico con cuello y guantes al modo que entonces se usaba, pero no conocido en esta Ciudad, y la visitó, y del temor que concibió con su visita, porque se le desapareció en la visita, comenzó a consolarse y mejoró, que Dios busca los medios que sabe que más importan para nuestro remedio.

49.   A este Gobernador, sucedió Francisco Bahamonde Lugo natural de Tenerife en las Canarias, (su título en 29 mayo 1564) capitán de caballos en Flandes,

> que fue a aquellos estados con el Adelantado de Canaria su tío, y como soldado, no traía vara sino la Semana Santa, que en esta entonces todos los gobernadores la traían como los Corregidores de España; y porque los Caribes infestaban la Isla por la banda de San Germán fue en persona a aquella guerra donde le dieron un flechazo en un muslo que estuvo de él, oleado, pero viviendo y acabando su gobierno fue a España, y tan pobre, que una vuelta de cadena que solo tenia, se la dio cuando se iba a

---

Vara, or "staff of justice," was a sign of office for aldermen and mayors. Persons holding such office were supposed to have standing among the nobility. See Glossary.

The incident with the gold chain is intended to praise him; it indicates he did not use his Governorship to feather his own nest — hence his final dramatic flourish as he was leaving the island.

Doña Teresa de Rivera has descendants in this City, but Alonso Pérez Martel left no descendants, because he never married. He died in the City of Santo Domingo (as Governor Francisco Manuel de Obando [sic] did in this City, Puerto Rico) as a very old man, and with a reputation for great virtue and holiness.

47.   Governor Francisco Manuel de Obando, [sic] was succeeded by Licenciate Caraza, a man from the Mountains of Castile.

He was a lawyer, because in those days (since enemy ships or fleets had not yet come over to the Indies, but only one or another ship that only came for merchandise or trade) attention was concentrated on giving the *vecinos* good government. It seemed that men with a legal education would be better at this. Because of his good governance, Caraza's term was extended by His Majesty two years beyond the four for which he had been sent, by a decree on January 10, 1561.

48.   He was succeeded by Doctor Antonio de la *Llama Vallejo, with the title of *Juez de Residencia*.

In this City he married Doña Leonor Ponce, a daughter of Juan Ponce, the first Governor. But when taking the report of his evaluation [*Residencia*] back to Spain, he drowned, and his wife was so upset and melancholy about his death that she became seriously ill. And one day when she was in bed, at midday, a man walked into her room dressed like a physician, wearing a collar and gloves as doctors did in those days, but no one knew him in this City. And from the fear that she got from this visit (because he disappeared while visiting her) she began to be comforted and got better, for God finds the means which he knows are best for our remedy.

*As reported in the essays, "Llama" is incorrect: this relative of Torres y Vargas was "Gama Vallejo," governor of Puerto Rico in 1520. Since the canon was a descendant of Ponce de León, this might have been a family remembrance delivered to him orally in the absence of written records: ("Gama" and "Llama" sound alike). A Juez de Residencia was a judge sent to conduct an inquiry about the way an outgoing official had exercised his position. "Audit" or "evaluation" both translate the concept "residencia." See Glossary.

49.   This Governor was succeeded by Francisco Bahamón de Lugo, a native of Tenerife in the Canary Islands, (his decree of appointment is dated May 29, 1564), who had been a cavalry captain in Flanders.

He had gone to those Estates with his uncle, the Adelantado of the Canaries,

embarcar, a la muger de un sobrino suyo, diciendo: Señora, no me agradezca el darle esta cadena, que no lo hago por servirla, sino por decir con verdad que no llevo nada de Puerto-Rico. Pero no le faltó el premio a sus buenos servicios, que dentro de cinco meses le dieron el gobierno de Cartagena de las Indias donde murió del trabajo que tuvo en defenderle a Francisco Draque la entrada, que en su tiempo pretendió hacer en aquella Ciudad, que por entonces no consiguió.

50.   Al dicho Francisco Bahamonde Lugo, sucedió Francisco de Obando: por título de 12 de . . . de 1575 con 375,000 maravedís en lugar de Francisco Solís por cuatro años con 775,000 maravedís de salario.

Haciendo viaje a la Isla de Santo Domingo, a curarse de una enfermedad grave, a la vuelta, le cautivó un corsario inglés, que pidió por el, rescate, que se le dió y fueron 4,000 ducados, que . . . en la villa de San Germán de donde volvió hasta aquí y murió en ella. Era natural de Cáceres en Estremadura. Por muerte del dicho Francisco de Obando gobernó el interin, por nombramiento de la Real Audiencia de Santo Domingo, Gerónimo de Aguero Campuzano, caballero vecino de ella.

It took 34 *maravedís* to make one silver real, which itself was only an eighth of a dollar or about 12 cents. Grants and salaries were usually reckoned in hundred-thousands of *maravedís*, which sounded impressive, but 300 *maravedís* amounted to about a dollar.

---

51.   A este sucedió Juan de Solís, caballero de Salamanca,

tuvo pesadísima residencia intentando agraviarle en ella ciertos vecinos de la Ciudad, que en habito de penitentes, le salieron al camino del convento de Santo Thomas, donde acostumbraba ir a Misa, pero no lo consiguieron, y aunque no se pudo probar plenamente su delito, les costó haciendas y destierros por solo la presunción; que en los gobernadores aun en la residencia resplandece la escelencia de su dignidad y oficio por tiempo de un año, como disponen las leyes.

Apparently, these *vecinos* intended to humiliate him publicly by demanding justice for some actions he had taken against them, while wearing the garb of *Penitentes*, which included a hood that covered the face, so that the penitent not be identified. (See Glossary) Such a public humiliation of a magistrate, even while he was being called to account by a *Juez de Residencia*, would be a *desacato*, or an act of contempt of the Royal Majesty he represented in the city, analogous to "contempt of court" in United States' law.

and as a military man he did not [while he was Governor of Puerto Rico] carry a staff of office except during [the processions and ceremonies of] Holy Week, during which all Governors bore such a staff, as do *Corregidores* in Spain. Since the Carib Indians were infesting the Island on the side of San Germán, he went in person to that war, where he got an arrow wound in his thigh. It was serious enough that he was given the Last Rites over it, but he lived and finished his term of office, after which he returned to Spain in such poverty that he only owned a strand of [gold] chain. As he was about to take ship he gave it to the wife of a nephew of his, saying: "My lady, do not thank me for the gift of this chain; I do not do it to give you pleasure, but so I can truthfully say that I am not taking anything from Puerto Rico." But he did not miss out on a reward for his good service [to the Crown,] for within five months he was granted the Governorship of Cartagena of the Indies, where he died from the efforts he made to bar Sir Francis Drake from taking the City when he tried to do so during his term as Governor — but Drake's attempt was unsuccessful.

50.   The said Francisco Bahamón de Lugo was succeeded by Francisco de Obando [Messía]; his appointment was dated on . . . 12, 1575, and he was appointed with a salary of 375,000 *maravedís* while Francisco Solís had been appointed for four years with 775,000 *maravedís* for his salary.

As he was returning from the Island of Santo Domingo, where he had gone to be treated for a serious illness, he was captured by an English corsair [*actually French* — Tr.] who held him for ransom. He was ransomed for 4,000 ducats. . . . in the town of San Germán, from which he returned here [to San Juan] where he died. He was a native of Cáceres in Extremadura. Because of the death of the said Francisco de Obando the Royal Audiencia of Santo Domingo appointed as interim Governor Gerónimo de Agüero Campuzano, a gentleman and *vecino* of that City.

51.   He was succeeded by Juan de Solís, a gentleman of Salamanca.

He had a very rough evaluation during which certain *vecinos* of this City attempted to insult him by coming out to meet him in the garb of *Penitentes* on his way to the convent of Saint Thomas, where it was his custom to go to Mass. They did not succeed in meeting him. But, although their misdeed could not be completely proven, the mere presumption cost them exile and confiscations, for a Governor, even when he is being subjected to an evaluation [*Residencia*], still keeps the excellence of his dignity and office for the length of a year, as the laws command.

52.   Sucedió a este Gobernador, Juan López Melgarejo, natural de Sevilla, alguacil mayor por Su Magestad de la Audiencia de Santo Domingo, y Gobernador por ella, en el interin, de esta Ciudad.

53.   A este Juan López Melgarejo, sucedió Juan de Céspedes con título de Gobernador en 24 de abril de 1580 en lugar de Francisco de Obando con 375,000 maravedís.

> Murió en esta Ciudad con opinión de Santo, y cuando murió, toda la gente della, acudió a verle porque tuvo la cruz. . . en la mano derecha, hasta que le enterraron, que siendo tan admirable en vida, se puede entender haber, nuestro Señor, querídola mostrar en esta maravilla. Su hacienda la dejó a pobres porque ansi lo había hecho en su vida. Su entierro y sepultura está en el convento de Santo Thomas de la orden de Santo Domingo, junto al del Gobernador Juan Ponce, con losa y un epitafio que dice de esta manera. "Aquí está sepultado el muy ilustre Señor Juan de Céspedes, Gobernador y capitán general que fue por Su Magestad, en esta Isla, y murió el 2 de agosto de 1581; dejó toda su hacienda a pobres."

54.   A este Gobernador Juan de Céspedes, sucedió Menéndez de Valdés, asturiano de nación, la cédula en 18 de junio de 1582 con 1,000 ducados, capitán que fue de la fuerza de esta Ciudad, con 50 soldados de guarnición, que entonces no eran menester muchos.

> Ni la fuerza se hizo sino para defenderse de los indios, y después ha quedado como se hizo la de San Felipe del Morro, por casa de morada de los Gobernadores, y es de las mejores que hay en las Indias, aunque entren los palacios de los Virreyes del Perú y México, porque aunque en fabrica y aposentos puedan escederle, en el sitio nunca podían igualarsele por estar en la bahía y entrada del puerto, en un brazo de mar, en la eminencia de unas peñas, colocada con tal disposición, que se compiten lo agradable y lo fuerte, porque también tiene debajo de unos corredores que caen en el brazo de mar, plataforma con artilleda, y puertas de un lado y otro, con vista de arboledas y isletas como se podía pintar en el país más vistoso de Flandes. Este Gobernador Diego Menéndez, gobernó tiempo de 11 años, y se quedó para vecino de ella. Constancia de. . . que entonces tenía mucho valor y casas propias en la plaza que después han gozado sus hijos y sucesores. Intitulábase Gobernador y capitán General, pero en su tiempo, vino Pedro de Salazar por capitán de infantería y título de capitán a guerra que dio a entender una vez tocando de noche a rebato sin avisar a dicho gobernador ni al Obispo, de que se mostraron ambos quejosos.

52.   This Governor was succeeded by Juan López Melgarejo, a native of Seville and His Majesty's High Sheriff in the Audiencia of Santo Domingo, who was interim Governor of this City by that Audiencia's appointment.

53.   This Juan López Melgarejo was succeeded by Juan de Céspedes, whose decree of appointment as Governor was dated April 24, 1580, in the place of Francisco de Obando, with a salary of 375,000 *maravedís*.

> He died in this City with a reputation for being a saint, and at his death all the people of the City rushed in to see his body, because he had the Cross [*imprinted*?—Tr.] on his right hand up to the point when they buried him. Since he was so admirable in his life, we can well understand that our Lord wanted to witness to it by working this marvel. He left all his property to the poor, as he had given all he had to them while he was alive. His burial and tomb are in the convent of Saint Thomas, of the Order of Saint Dominic, next to that of Governor Juan Ponce, with a tombstone and epitaph that say as follows: "Here is buried the very illustrious Señor Juan de Céspedes, Governor and Captain General of this Island in the name of His Majesty, who died August 2, 1581; he left all his property to the poor."

Statements made on one's deathbed and epitaphs on one's grave carried great weight as truthful testimony. Afterall, if a person is dying, why lie?

---

54.   Governor Juan de Céspedes was succeeded by [Diego] Menéndez de Valdés, an Asturian by origin. His decree of appointment was dated June 18, 1582, with 1,000 ducats for his salary. He had earlier been Captain of the Fortress [*La Fortaleza* — Tr.] of this City with 50 soldiers for its garrison, for in those days not too many were needed.

> This fortress was only built for defense against the Indians, and later, after the building of the castle of San Felipe del Morro, it has become the residence of the Governors. It is one of the best in the Indies, even if you include the palaces of the Viceroys of Peru and Mexico, because, although these may be better in their building and rooms, they will never be equal to it in their placement. It is on the bay, at the entry of the port, built upon some outstanding rocks on an arm of the sea. It is placed in such a location that it is hard to decide whether it is stronger more than it is pleasant, or the other way around. For it also has, underneath some corridors which face the arm of the sea, a platform with artillery, and gates on either side, with a view of groves and islets such as might be painted in the finest Flemish landscape. This Governor Diego Menéndez ruled

55.   Al Gobernador Diego Menéndez de Valdés, sucedió Pedro *Xuarez, Coronel, Gobernador y capitán general en esta Isla, natural de Piedrahita en Castilla, (su título en 11 de marzo 1593).

En su tiempo vino Francisco Draque, el año 1595 a expugnar esta Ciudad y robar la plata de la Capitán a de Nueva España, que llamaban Santa María de Cabogeña, su general Sancho Pardo Osorio, y no entró en el puerto, sino que echó 30 lanchas de noche con 1,000 hombres, y como Su Magestad Don Felipe II nuestro Señor, había prevenido este intento enviando las cinco fragatas con Don Pedro Tello, caballero de Sevilla, que vino por cabo de ellas, no hizo más efecto que quemar una de las fragatas que fue su mayor perdición, porque alum-

---

The 1595 defeat of Sir Francis Drake's attack on Puerto Rico by the island's residents was not only a military victory over a famous marauder, but also proof that Catholics could vanquish English Protestants. Doubtlessly, Torres y Vargas took information from persons who had lived through the attack. We may consider some details the reflections by eye witnesses, an important factor in compiling history.

"*Xuarez*" for "*Suarez*" as also "*truxo*" for "*trujo*" and "*Roxas*" for "*Rojas*" below.

---

brando la bahía, vieron las lanchas de que se les defendió la entrada por el dicho Gobernador Pedro Xuarez, coronel, y Francisco Gómez Cid que era gran soldado y capitán y Sargento mayor por Su Magestad, en aquella ocasión, de aqueste presidio; y como el Draque se quedó con la armada, fuera, media legua del puerto, aquella noche fue, cuando a la lumbre que mostraba una ventanilla de su Capitana, hizo el tiro aquel artillero que refiere Lope de Vega en su *Dragontea* y le dió mala herida a Juan Asle su sobrino y otras diez personas, por cuya causa, se levó la Capitana y armada, y en el puerto de la Aguada, 24 leguas de este, dejó una carta en que refiere lo dicho. Al artillero le dio el Gobernador una sortija con un diamante, y merecía mayores premios su acierto.

Drake was called the "Dragon" for his raids on Spanish colonies. Lope de la Vega composed an epic poem, *La Dragontea*, in 1597 shortly after Drake's defeat in Puerto Rico. It would have been a source of local pride to be mentioned by this famous Spanish writer. Among other praises it said: "*ninguna ardiente bala de las de Puerto Rico se perdía*," [no burning bullet of Puerto Rico was wasted] and "*al fin de Puerto Rico sale en vano, vació y lleno de dolor y heridas*" [at the end he fruitlessly left Puerto Rico empty-handed, but full of painful wounds]. See pp. 48–50.

---

56.   Sucedió a Pedro Suárez c[C]oronel, Antonio de Mosquera gallego gran soldado capitán en Flandes,

the Island for 11 years, and stayed there afterward as a *vecino* of the City. [There is] evidence that he then had a lot of valuable things, and his own house in the plaza, which his children and descendants later enjoyed. His title was Governor and Captain General, but during his tenure, Pedro de Salazar arrived as Captain of the Infantry, and with the title of Captain-at-War, a rank which he acted upon on one occasion by ringing the tocsin at night without first informing the Governor or the Bishop, which gave them both grounds for resentment.

55.   Governor Diego Menéndez de Valdés was succeeded by Pedro *Xuarez Coronel, Governor and Captain-General of this Island, a native of Piedrahita in Castile (his decree of appointment was dated March 11, 1593).

*The comma gives the impression that it means "Pedro Xuarez, a Colonel," but this may be a printer's mistake. Other sources (e.g., Bishop Nicolás Ramos) call him Governor Coronel, as if it was a surname, and it indeed is a surname which appears as early as the 16th century, when Alonso Fernández Coronel is mentioned in the Chronicle of Pedro the Cruel, while the military title of Colonel only arises in the 16th century. Translated here as "Pedro X[S]uarez Coronel" with no comma.

During his term, Sir Francis Drake came in 1595 to take this City by storm and steal the silver borne in the Flagship of New Spain, which was called Santa María de Cabogeña, and whose general was Sancho Pardo Osorio. Drake did not enter the harbor, but sent out 30 launches with 1,000 men in a night attack. But since His Majesty our lord Don Philip II had foreseen this attack by sending five frigates under Don Pedro Tello, a gentleman of Seville who came as their commander, the launches had no effect except setting fire to one of the frigates. This was the worst thing that could have happened to them, because when the fire lit up the whole bay, the launches were seen, and their entry was prevented by the said Governor Pedro Xuarez Coronel, and by Francisco Gómez Cid, who was a great soldier and at that time [served as] Captain and Sergeant-Major of this garrison in His Majesty's name. Drake and his ships remained outside the harbor, about half a league away from it. It was on that night that one of the artillerymen (by the light that came from a window in Drake's flagship) fired the shot that Lope de Vega relates in his *Dragontea*, which badly wounded John Asle [*Ashley?*—Tr.], Drake's nephew, and ten other persons. Because of this the flagship and the rest of the fleet weighed anchors, and Drake left a letter which tells what happened in the harbor of Aguada, which is 24 leagues from this City. The Governor gave the artilleryman a diamond ring, and his marksmanship deserved even greater rewards.

de quien se dice, que tuvo la mejor compañía que ha tenido capitán en aquellos estados, porque habiendo un motín casi general, solo su compañía quedó firme en la obediencia, y todos los Señores Maeses de campo, capitanes y personas de puesto, se agregaron a su compañía que gobernó como su capitán y estuvieron a su orden, hasta que se sosegó el motín. El año 1596 fue promovido y llevó 200 soldados para el presidio, 18 de diciembre.

> The threat of mutiny was particularly acute when the army had not been paid. Moreover, some regiments were recruited from conquered regions such as Portugal, and the loyalty of the troops would be in doubt. This passage also notes mutiny once reached the famous Army of Flanders.

57.   Su título en 20 de junio de 1596, de Gobernador capitán general y alcayde de la fortaleza de ella, con 1,000 ducados de salario al año. Era más buen soldado para obedecer que para mandar, y así le sucedió 1a desgracia de tomar la Ciudad a pocos días de su gobierno el conde Jorge Cumberland, Inglés de nación, y del hábito de la Jarretiera de Inglaterra, que por mandado de su Reina Isabel, vino a solo esta facción, corrida del desaire de Francisco Draque, y aunque no había fuerza entonces, ni cerca en esta Ciudad, fue mayor su perdida que su ganancia, y habiendo entrado a los primeros de agosto, salió día del Señor San Clemente a 23 de noviembre con sólo media de los órganos y campanas de la Santa Iglesia, que en la Ciudad, no hizo más daño que *llevar un mármol de una ventana de un vecino, por parecerle admirable como lo era.* Hallóse también el Gobernador Pedro Suárez, c[C]oronel en esta Ciudad, cuando vino el Conde, pero como ya no la gobernaba no corría por su cuenta la pérdida y así le dieron el gobierno de Cumaná que tuvo más de diez y ocho años.

58.   Al Gobernador Antonio de Mosquera, sucedió Alonso de Mercado, natural de Ecija en Andalucía, se título en 26 de diciembre de 1598,
persona que por su valor y servicios, alcanzó ser capitán en Flandes, y cierto que viendo sus papeles en poder de un hijo suyo que dejó en esta Ciudad, me parecían aventuras de caballería o las relaciones de Fernández Pinto, según eran de prodigiosos. Vino enviado por la Magestad de Felipe 29 nuestro Señor, el año de 1599, como tan gran soldado, a recuperar la Ciudad, del conde de Cumberland, con los galeones de Don Francisco Coloma, y orden que si estuviese el enemigo en la tierra, saltase Mercado con tres mil hombres de que había de ser general, para con ellos desalojar al dicho conde, y si se hubiese ido, quedase por Gobernador y capitán general con cuatrocientos soldados de presidio, como se hizo.

56.   Pedro Suárez Coronel was succeeded by Antonio de Mosquera, a Galician and a great soldier who had been a captain in Flanders,

> about whom it was said that he had the best Company of any captain in those States, because at the time when there was an almost general mutiny in the army, his Company was the only one to remain firm in its obedience, so that all the Generals, Captains and other persons of position in the army attached themselves to his Company, which he ruled as its captain. They were under his orders until the mutiny was calmed. In the year 1596, he was promoted to Governor of Puerto Rico, and brought 200 soldiers for the garrison, arriving on December 18th.

> 57. His decree of promotion was dated June 20, 1596, and his title was Governor, Captain-General and Castellan of the City's Fortress, with a salary of 1,000 ducats a year. As a soldier he was better at obeying that at commanding, and so he had the misfortune of losing the City only a few days after taking office, to George, Earl of Cumberland, an Englishman and a knight of the Order of the Garter. He came just for this action, at the command of Elizabeth, his Queen, who was chagrined at the rebuff Sir Francis Drake had received here. Although there was no castle at the time in the City, and it was not yet walled, his loss was greater than his gain, for having entered in the early days of August, he left on the feast my lord Saint Clement, which is November 23rd, with only half the organ and the bells of the Cathedral Church. In the City itself he did no more harm than to take away a marble window from the house of a *vecino*, because he found it an admirable piece of art, as indeed it was. Governor Pedro Suárez Coronel was also in this City when the Earl came, but since he was no longer in charge, the loss of the City was not his responsibility, and so they granted him the governorship of Cumaná, which he held for more than eighteen years.

58.   Governor Antonio de Mosquera was succeeded by Alonso de Mercado, a native of Ecija in Andalusia. His decree of appointment was dated December 26, 1598.

> By his bravery and services to the Crown he came to be made a captain in Flanders, and truly, when I saw his papers which are now in the hands of a son of his who lives in this City, they were so marvelous that they seemed to me like adventures in a romance of chivalry or in the stories of Fernández Pinto. He came here in 1599, sent by His Majesty Philip II, with the galleons of Don Francisco Coloma, with the mission of recovering the City from the Earl of Cumberland, since he was such a great soldier. His orders said that if the enemy was

59.   y dando aliento *a la fábrica del Morro,* hizo un caballero que hasta hoy conserva su nombre, y el algibe que esta dentro en la fuerza donde puso las *armas que le dio Felipe* II *nuestro Señor;* que fue, un revellín de que sale un brazo con una espada, por el que ganó en Flandes con tanto valor y riesgo volándole una mina que tenia el enemigo, pero sin embargo le ganó y el general en aquella ocasión que llegó a su presencia sin espada y una gran herida en el rostro, le ciñó la suya y la truxo a esta Ciudad como testigo de aquella hazaña. Gobernó tres años y envióse a despedir, y dándole Su Magestad licencia, por no hallar embarcación para España, la fue a buscar a Santo Domingo y en una nao que llamaban la Pava, se embarcó en aquella Ciudad y hasta hoy no se supo más nuevas de ella, acabando infelizmente en el agua, quien tantas veces se había librado en Flandes del fuego.

"Caballero" translated as "cavalier." It was an inner fortification in a fortress, which is higher than the others, to cover them with its fire, either to protect them when attacked, or to harass the enemy if it has taken them. Revellín was a triangular embanked salient outside the main moat of a fortress. See Glossary.

---

60.   Al Gobernador Alonso de Mercado, sucedió *Sancho Ochoa de Castro,* vizcaino, (año 1602),

gran repúblico y como tal, *hizo las Casas de Cabildo en la plaza de esta Ciudad.* Fue capitán de galeones y en sus bandos se intitula Señor de la Casa y Solar de los condes de Salvatierra en Viscaya. También hizo una fuente que esta junta a la casa y fuerza de los Gobernadores que hasta hoy conserva su nombre, y tiene en una piedra el título del Señor de la Casa y Solar de los condes de Salvatierra. En este tiempo se introdujeron los créditos que se dan a los soldados de este presidio, destrucción general de ellos y de la tierra, y aun a lo que se puede entender de todos los Gobernadores que le han imitado, pues desde su antecedente ninguno de los que siguen hasta hoy ha gozado otro gobierno, que todos han muerto en el siguiente o antes de tenerle aunque no veo que les escarmienta.

The word "*se intitula*" is translated as "used" since in Spain it is possible for a man to be the head of a noble family while holding no title of nobility, while heads of younger branches of that same clan are counts or dukes.

61.   Fue dicho Gobernador a España con su residencia y habiéndole hecho merced de un hábito y General de la flota de Nueva España, murió en la Corte el año 1609. Y volvió a proseguir la fábrica del Morro el año de 1600 a 8 de enero. En tiempo de este gobernador Sancho Ochoa año de 1602, hizo Su Ma-

in the land, Mercado should land with three thousand men whose General he was to be, to dislodge the Earl. If the Earl had left, he should remain with a garrison of four hundred soldiers, as was done.

59.   He encouraged *the building of El Morro,* and built a cavalier [*caballero*] which to this day is named after him, and the cistern which is within the castle, where he placed the coat of arms that our lord Philip II granted him, which is a ravelin out of which issues an arm bearing a sword. It commemorates the ravelin which he took from the enemy in Flanders with much bravery and risk to himself. In spite of everything, he captured it, although a mine, which the enemy had placed there, exploded. And on that occasion he presented himself before his General swordless and with a great wound on his face. The General girded him with his own sword, which he brought to this City in witness of that feat. He governed the Island for three years, and requested his discharge. When His Majesty granted it to him, he found no ship ready to sail for Spain, so he went to Santo Domingo to see if he would find one there. He set sail for that City in a ship called *La Pava,* and to this day no news has been had of it, so that a man who had so often been saved from fire in Flanders came to end miserably on the water.

60.   Governor Alonso de Mercado was succeeded in 1602 by *Sancho Ochoa de Castro,* a Basque.

He was very civic minded and as such *he built the House for the City Council in the plaza of this City.* He had been Captain of the Galleons, and in his proclamations he used the title of Lord of the House and Lineage of the Counts of Salvatierra in Biscay. He also installed a fountain next to the house and fortress of the Governors, which to this day is named after him, and which has carved on a stone the title of Lord of the House and Lineage of the Counts of Salvatierra At this time were introduced the "Credits" which are given [*as loans on their salaries* — Tr.] to the soldiers of this garrison. This has proved the general ruin of both the soldiers and the Island — and even, as far as one can figure it — of all the governors who have imitated him in this [practice]. His precedent continues until today, and none of his successors have enjoyed another governorship; rather all have died in their next governorship or even before getting a new post, although I do not see that this has been a lesson to them.

61.   This Governor went to Spain with the papers of his evaluation, and was granted the habit of one of the Military Orders. Made General of the Fleet

gestad merced de la Sargentía mayor de la plaza, al capitán García de Torres; con 60 escudos al mes, soldado antiguo de Flandes, de gran opinión en tiempo

Captain García de Torres was the father of Don Diego Torres y Vargas. He praises his father in the third person, without emphasizing the family relationship.

del conde de Fuentes. Era muy padre de sus soldados y tuvo muchos encuentros con el Gobernador por contradecirle los créditos, de que dio cuenta a Su Magestad, y por sus Reales cédulas, lo prohibió y es de advertir que la esperiencia ha enseñado que por estas plazas de las Indias, importa mucho sean los Gobernadores soldados de Flandes, porque como allá no aprenden a mercadear se contentan con poco, con que enriquecen la tierra con el buen pasage y contratación común de sus vecinos. Créditos, es anticipar la paga a los soldados, dándola en drogar a más de su justa valor.

62.   A dicho Gobernador Sancho Ochoa de Castro, sucedió Gabriel de Roxas. . . natural de Illescas seis leguas de Madrid capitán de galeones y Sargento mayor de Sevilla, por título de 29 de abril de 1608, por 5 años; vino el año de 1608, a 22 de julio entro en esta Ciudad, y truxo infantería para rehacer las dos compañías de presidio, que había en esta.

63.   Fue el Gobernador más asistente que ha tenido la fuerza del Morro y hizo el caballero de Austria, que es el mejor de la dicha fuerza, las casas matas, y sus algibes y se entró una de las dos compañías, con que parecía la fuerza un razonable pueblo. Y aquí advierto, que desde que Juan Ponce de León que era Alcaide perpetuo de la fuerza vieja, que es hoy Castillo de morada de los Gobernadores, siempre se intitularon los de esta

The word "*casas matas*" has been translated as "casemates," for artillery within a fortress. See Glossary.

Ciudad, Alcaide de la fuerza, cuyo título pasaron a la del Morro, y ponían subteniente aunque sin particular sueldo, por serlo, sin con el que tenían de alférez o soldado sencillo, como gustaban los Gobernadores de nombrarle.

64.   El dicho Gabriel de Roxas, hizo el fuerte del Boquerón con vocación del Señor Santiago, de quien era muy devoto, y con esto obligó a esta Ciudad que con particular voto se le hiciese fiesta con Misa, sermón, toros y cañas como muchos anos se ha hecho, así mismo hizo el puente con fuerte de piedra, que hasta entonces solo tenía de tabla, y así fue fácil al conde Jorge Cumberland el ganarla aunque se le hizo fuerte resistencia, y en el mataron a un capitán de mi-

of New Spain, he died at court in 1609. The building of *El Morro* was taken up again in 1600, on January 8th. In the days of this Governor Sancho Ochoa, in the year 1602, His Majesty granted the rank of Sergeant-Major of this City to Captain García de Torres, with a salary of 60 *escudos* a month. He was a veteran of Flanders, with a great reputation from the days of the Count of Fuentes. He was a real father to his soldiers, and had many run-ins with the Governor because he opposed payment by credits. He notified His Majesty of this abuse, and the King, by his Royal decrees has forbidden it. It should be noted that this experience has taught us it is very important that the Governors of these fortified cities in the Indies should be veterans of Flanders. Since over there they do not learn how to engage in commerce, they are content with little remuneration; thus the land is enriched with the efficacious traffic and common trade of its inhabitants.

62.   This Governor Sancho Ochoa de Castro was succeeded by Gabriel de Roxas . . . a native of Illescas, which is six leagues away from Madrid. [He was] a Captain of the Galleons and Sergeant-Major of Seville. His decree of appointment (for 5 years) was dated April 29, 1608. He came over in 1608, entering the City on July 22nd, and he brought infantry to renew the two companies of the garrison that was here.

63.   He was the most attentive Governor that the Fortress of El Morro has had, and he built the cavalier of Austria, which is the best cavalier in that fortress, as well as the casemates and water reservoirs, and he brought one of the two companies into it, so that the fortress seemed like a reasonably large town. And here I note that the Governors of this City always have borne the title of Castellan of the Fortress, since the days of Juan Ponce de León, who was the Castellan for life of the old fortress, which is now the fortified residence of the Governors. The title was transferred to the Castle of El Morro, and they would place in it a lieutenant, although such lieutenants did not get a special salary for their lieutenancy, aside from the one they enjoyed as Corporal or Private soldier, as they might when the Governor chose to appoint them.

64.   This Governor Gabriel de Roxas built the fort of El Boquerón and named it after the Apostle Saint James, to whom he was very devoted. Along with this he obliged the City Council to make a special vow to celebrate the Apostle's feast with

Bullfights and jousts were sport contests on horseback, not unlike today's rodeos.

licia llamado Bernabé de Serralta, que peleó con tan heróico esfuerzo, que ha merecido hasta hoy quedar muy vivo en su fama, que como dijo Ovidio, hablando de sí mismo: *"metamen extinto fama super est."*

The Spanish word *"subteniente,"* or "Lieutenant," was not a rank in the Spanish army [*teniente* was, #79], so the Lieutenant of the Governor at the Castle of El Morro kept whatever rank he already had in the army, with its salary. See Glossary for Alcaide.

65.   En tiempo del Gobernador Gabriel Roxas, se manifestó, que una negra tenía un espíritu que le hablaba en la barriga. Llevóse a la Iglesia y exorcísose, y dijo llamarse Pedro Lorenzo. Y cuanto le preguntaron decía de las cosas ausentes y ocultas . . . como Silico, que yo la oí algunas veces, y mandó el Comisario de la Inquisición no se le hablase con pena de escomunión, y luego se descubrió otro que si el primero hizo admirar, del segundo y de otros que después han salido no se hace mucho caso. Dicen las negras que le tienen, que en su tierra se les entra en el vientre en forma visible de animalejo, y que le heredan de unas a otras como mayorazgo.

This incident of spirit possession below apparently comes from an eyewitness (note the use of the first person). Torres y Vargas, who would not be born until 1614–15, could not have been present at this exorcism, but he may have added proof from his own experience in other cases. The Baroque period did not doubt the power of evil spirits, but considered an exorcism as proof of the greater power of God. The association with blacks and spirit possession is attributable to the relatively recent arrival of slaves directly from Africa where indigenous religions held sway.

66.   También hizo el fuerte del Cañuelo con vocación de San Gabriel, porque era su nombre. Y el año de 1625, el enemigo Boduino Enríquez, le quemó aunque bien a su costa, y hasta hoy no se ha reedificado si bien era muy necesario a la buena guarda del puerto. Escribió a Su Magestad que bastaba para esta plaza un capitán con trescientos infantes, y engañóse, y así Su Magestad mandó reformar uno de los que había, que aunque por más moderno, le tocaba a Juan de Amézquita Quixano el ser reformado, no quiso el otro capitán Martín Pérez Achetequi, por tenerle casado con su hija; y así fue dicho Martín Pérez reformado, y fue a España donde le hizo Su Magestad merced de la compañía de la fuerza vieja de la Havana.

The entrance to San Juan harbor has a small island (Isla de Cabras) in the middle. The main and easiest entrance is the channel (*caño*) of El Morro covered by the cannon of Morro Castle. On the other side of that small island is a smaller channel (*cañuelo*) which could serve invaders as a back door into the harbor if left unprotected by a fort. In 1625 the Dutch took this fort and controlled the cañuelo.

a Solemn Mass, a sermon, a bullfight and a joust with reed spears, as has now been done for many years. He also built the bridge with a stone fort — up to that time it had been only wooden, on which account the Earl of Cumberland had found it easy to take it despite bitter resistance. There they killed a captain of the militia named Bernabé de Serralta, who fought with such heroic courage that he has deserved to live to this day by his fame, as Ovid said about himself, ["My fame survives me when I am dead". *The text as printed garbles the Latin.* — Tr.]

65.   During the term of Governor Gabriel Roxas it became known that a black woman had a spirit that spoke within her belly. She was taken to the Church and exorcised, and the spirit said its name was Pedro Lorenzo. And it spoke about far-away and unknown things, whatever it was asked . . . (like Silico, as I heard it do more than once). The Commissary of the Inquisition forbade speaking with it under pain of excommunication. Afterwards another such spirit was discovered, and while the first one caused great wonder, not much attention has been paid to the second, or to others that have emerged later. The black women who have these spirits say that in their country they get into their bellies in the visible shape of a small animal, and they inherit them one from the other by primogeniture.

66.   He also built the fort of El Cañuelo under the name of Saint Gabriel, his name-saint, which the enemy Bowdoyn Hendrick burned in 1625 although it cost him dearly. To this day it has not been rebuilt, even thought it is necessary for protection of the port. He wrote to His Majesty that one captain with three hundred infantrymen would be sufficient for the needs of this garrison (he was mistaken). His Majesty, therefore, ordered that one of the two captains there be discharged. Although

> This passage (#66) contains observations that praises the Governor for his foresight in building the fort across the passage from El Morro and complains that it has not been rebuilt, exposing the city to further attack. Torres y Vargas comments on the Amézquita family probably result from personal friendship with the family.

Juan de Amézquita Quixano should have been the one discharged, since he was the more recently appointed of the two, the other captain, Martín Pérez Achetequi, did not accept because Amézquita was married to his daughter. Martín Pérez was thus the one discharged and went to Spain, where His Majesty granted him [the command of] a company in the old Fortress of Havana.

67.   Al dicho Gobernador Gabriel de Roxas Paramo, sucedió Don Felipe de Beaumont y Navarra, caballero navarro y deudo de los duques de Alba. Estuvo en esta Ciudad cuando vino Alonso Mercado a gobernarla, con plaza de soldado sencillo, y después gobernando Sancho Ochoa, arribó en el galeón San Ursula, donde venía por capitán, como lo fue de arcabuceros en la armada Real, y el año de 1614 vino por Gobernador y capitán general de esta Ciudad, con titulo de 14 de setiembre de 1613 por 5 años, y la gobernó 6 años.

The Beaumont-Navarra family produced the Count of Lerín and hereditary High Constable of Navarre. The heiress of the Counts of Lerín had married a Duke of Alba, a very powerful house. The family name is often Hispanicized into Beamonte or even Viamonte. This Governor is remembered as the founder of the town of Arecibo. Many Navarrese opposed Spanish rule, and had revolted at least twice. The governorship of rebellious Pamplona (#50) showed great trust, since the Beaumont-Navarras came from the former ruling family, and might have led a revolt.

68.   En su tiempo sucedió la gran tormenta de los 12 de setiembre, y acudió a la necesidad con admirable diligencia, enviando bajeles a todas las Islas vecinas, con que no se sintió el hambre, remediándola su providencia, y porque en los pulpitos le acomodaban el lugar del Evangelio, *"Philipe unde emenus panem"* señaló casa particular de depósito donde se diese el maíz y cazave que es el pan de las islas, a todos los pobres al mismo precio a que se había comprado de las otras de donde se truxo. Mostraba ser cristiano y devoto, dando buenas limosnas a personas necesitadas, y así Dios le dispuso de donde, porque en el tiempo de su Gobierno, entraron en este puerto once navíos de negros arribados, sin más de otros doscientos de islas, Portugal y Castilla. Fuese a España con su residencia el año de 1621, y Su Magestad le hizo merced del Castillo de Pamplona, cabeza del Reino de Navarra que hasta el no se había fiado a ningún natural de la tierra y murió dentro de pocos años.

The action of the governor is considered a demonstration of his virtue. Note also that part of the food was the local casabe (cazave) made from yuca since the time of the Taínos. See Glossary.

69.   En tiempo de este Gobernador, llovió en esta Ciudad el año de 1614 granizo que yo ví, y admiró la novedad, porque los antiguos jamás lo habían visto desde que se pudieron acordar, y luego a poco tiempo sobrevino la gran tormenta.

67.   Governor Gabriel de Roxas Paramo was succeeded by Don Felipe de Beaumont y Navarra, a Navarrese gentleman and a relative of the Dukes of Alba. He was in this City, with the rank of private soldier, at the time that Alonso Mercado came to be its Governor, and later, when Sancho Ochoa was Governor, he arrived here in the San [Santa] Úrsula galleon, of which he was captain, as he also had been captain of harquebusiers of the Royal Navy, and in the year 1614 he came as Governor and Captain-General of this City, with a decree of appointment for five years, dated September 14, 1613, but he governed it for six years.

68.   In his term occurred the great hurricane of September 12th, and he rushed to remedy the needs this occasioned with admirable diligence, sending ships to all the neighboring islands. As a result, there was no famine, since his providence had avoided it. And since from the pulpits the preachers applied to him the Gospel verse ["Philip, where shall we buy bread?" John 6:5], he assigned a specific house to be a warehouse where maize and casabe (which is the bread of these islands) should be distributed to all the poor at the same price that had been paid for it in the other islands from which it had been brought. He showed himself a devout Christian, giving copious alms to needy persons. Indeed, God granted him the means for these alms, when during his term of office eleven ships arrived in this harbor loaded with black slaves, not to mention another two hundred from the islands, Portugal and Castile [providing tax revenue]. He left for Spain with the documents of his evaluation in 1621, and His Majesty granted him the Governorship of the Castle of Pamplona, the capital of the Kingdom of Navarre, which up to that time had never been entrusted to a native of that land. He died a few years later.

69.   During the term of this Governor, in the year 1614, hail rained on this City, which I saw myself, and this novelty caused great wonderment, for the old people had never seen this here within living memory; shortly after that the great hurricane fell upon us.

Passage #69 is troublesome, since — at best — Diego Torres y Vargas was an infant the year of the hailstorm. Reference to having seen it with his own eyes may be an exaggerated way of saying that it occurred while he was alive. Whatever the explanation, his narrative suggests the custom in Puerto Rico of remembering years by the names of storms and hurricanes.

70.   Don Felipe de Beaumont y Navarra was succeeded in 1620 by Don Juan de Vargas, a general of the cavalry of Flanders who beheaded the Chief Justice

70.   Al dicho Don Felipe de Beaumont y Navarra, sucedió el año de 1620, Don Juan de Vargas, general de la caballería de Flandes que degolló al Justicia mayor de Aragón, y tan gran soldado como todas las historias refieren. Gobernó hasta el año de 1625 que vino por Gobernador Juan de Haro, y ambos se hallaron en la invasión de Boduino Enríquez, como en la otra invasión del Conde, Pedro Suárez c[C]oronel, y Antonio de Mosquera; retiraronse ambos al Morro, donde le defendieron, porque *la Ciudad no tenía cerca hasta entonces;*

y al Gobernador Juan de Haro le hizo merced Su Magestad de un hábito de Santiago y cuatrocientos ducados de renta en la pensión de un Obispado. Dicho Don Juan obtuvo merced del gobierno de Campeche y por un encuentro con los Oficiales Reales de aquella Ciudad, le llevaron a México, donde a pocos días murió pobre y desacreditado.

> Don Juan de Lanuza V, last hereditary Chief Justice of Aragon, was beheaded for rebellion against Philip II in 1591; the army that enforced the King's authority was led by don Alonso de Vargas, who executed the order to behead the Chief Justice. He may have been family of Governor Juan de Vargas.

71.   Al dicho Don Juan de Vargas, sucedió el capitán Juan de Haro, natural de Medina del Campo, con titulo de 6 de abril de 1625, capitán que fue de los galeones, Gobernador de Cumaná, y después Gobernador del tercio de galeones con propuesta de este gobierno.

Luego que llegó a esta Ciudad dentro de 26 días, apareció el enemigo holandés Boduino Enrico con 17 urcas, que no pudiendo hacer el socorro que en el Brasil intentaba por hallar la armada de Don Fadrique de Toledo en el, se deja descaer a este puerto. Hado infeliz de los desgraciados que aun de las venturas ajenas vienen a heredar desdichas propias. Retiróse la gente al Morro por no estar la Ciudad cercada y entró con viento favorable a 25 de setiembre, y a los 26 echó la gente en tierra y comenzó a batir la fuerza, donde el capitán y Sargento mayor de la plaza que era García de Torres, natural de la villa de Vélez en la Mancha, soldado de grande opinión en Flandes, fue herido en el pecho de una bala de mosquete y a pocos días murió de la herida.

> In May 1624, the Dutch had seized the city of Bahía in Brazil (Portugal and its colonies were then under the Spanish crown); but a Spanish expedition under Don Fadrique de Toledo, Marquess of Villafranca, had left for Brazil in February 1625, and expelled the Dutch from Brazil.

72.   Fue su muerte muy sentida por la falta que tan gran soldado hizo en aque-

of Aragon, and was as great a soldier as you can read in all the history books. He ruled until the year 1625, when Juan de Haro arrived as Governor, and both of them were present for the invasion of Bowdoyn Hendrick, just as both Pedro Suárez Coronel, and Antonio de Mosquera had been present for the Earl's attack. Both of them [Vargas and Haro] withdrew to Morro Castle, from which they defended the City, for it had no walls at that time.

> Governor Juan de Haro was granted the habit of the Military Order of Santiago by His Majesty, as well as a pension of four hundred ducats out of the income of a Bishopric. Don Juan [de Vargas] was granted the Governorship of Campeche [in Yucatán], and because of a clash he had with the Royal Officers of that City he was taken by them to Mexico City, where a few days later he died poor and discredited.

71.   This Don Juan de Vargas was succeeded by Captain Juan de Haro, a native of Medina del Campo, who had been Captain of the Galleons, Governor of Cumaná, and afterwards Governor of the regiment of Marines [*Tercio* of the Galleons], with the nomination for the Governorship of this City; his decree of appointment was dated April 6, 1625.

> As soon as he arrived in this City — within 26 days of his arrival — the Dutch enemy Bowdoyn Hendrick appeared before the City with 17 vessels. Hendrick had not been able to fulfill his aim of coming to the aid of the Dutch in Brazil, because he found the fleet of Don Fadrique de Toledo already there. He edged away towards this harbor — for it is the unhappy fate of the unlucky that even from the good fortune of others they come to reap misfortunes for themselves. The people took refuge in Morro Castle, since the City was not yet walled, and Hendrick entered the harbor with favorable winds on September 25th, and on the 26th his soldiers landed and he began to attack the castle. [That was] where the Captain and Sergeant-Major of the garrison, García de Torres, a native of the town of Vélez in La Mancha, and a soldier of high repute in Flanders, was wounded in his breast by a musket bullet, and died of this wound within a few days.

72.   His death was greatly mourned, because the absence of such a great soldier was a misfortune in such a situation. The Council [of the Indies] knew his worth, for when they were informed of the enemy's coming, Don Agustín Mexía (of whose *Tercio* Torres had been corporal in Flanders) said to the Council that they should be confident of success, because such a soldier as Sergeant-Major García de Torres was in the garrison. His Majesty rewarded the blood he

lla ocasión, que le tenia muy bien conocido el Consejo, pues cuando llegó el aviso del enemigo, dijo D. Agustín Mexía, de cuyo tercio había sido alférez en Flandes, al Consejo, que se confiase de buen suceso, por estar tan gran soldado como el Sargento mayor García de Torres, en esta plaza: Su Magestad remuneró su sangre vertida, en su hijo mayor Don García de Torres que se mostró allado de su padre, señalándose en particular, dando muestras del valor heredado de su padre; mandando que otra vez se presidiase la gente en dos compañías y se le diese la una como se hizo. Era el dicho Sargento mayor de tanta llaneza y tan padre y tan amigo de sus soldados, que se pudiera dudar como en Atenas de Epaminondas, si era mejor capitán que hombre, o mejor hombre que capitán. Los tres hijos varones que dejó, no solo imitaron a los Horacios que tuvo Roma, en el valor, sino que en la poca ventura también fueron los tres Horacios, muriendo Don García de Torres y Don Alonso de Torres, capitanes de este presidio, en los 33 y 26 años de su edad, y Don Diego de Torres que siguió las letras y se graduó en Salamanca, dejando mayores puestos que Su Magestad le hiciere merced en otras partes, por el remedio de dos hermanas solas y desamparadas, se contentó con una canogía de esta Catedral, del más limitado estipendio que hay en las Indias.

> This tribute to the heroism of his military father also notes the favors given to the family and his brothers by the king in gratitude for the father's ultimate sacrifice under fire. His two brothers also died when relatively young, and may have created family financial burdens. The comparison of his family to the Roman Horatii is a literary convention of Baroque writings. (*Compare with #81 below.*)

73.   Avisóse a Su Magestad la entrada del dicho Boduino y envió dos fragatas de socorro a la fuerza y por cabo de ellas a Pedro Pérez de Arecizabal, capitán de los galeones, ya Don Francisco de Villanueva y Lugo que en aquella ocasión había vuelto del socorro de Cádiz a la Corte, donde pretendía un hábito, con el pliego de Su Magestad a este de Puerto Rico, por más práctico en la tierra como natural de ella, y pasando a nado el río de Luisa, le puso en manos del Gobernador Juan de Haro con igual satisfacción de su persona y obligaciones. Luego el año de 1628 sucedió la quema del Morro ocasionada de una chispa que saltó, muriendo la guardia en la Casa mata donde había parte de la pólvora. Volola y los alojamientos con 43 personas, soldados y otros de la tierra, que fue espectáculo lastimoso, y de México y España se acudió con pólvora y municiones.

74.   Murió dicho Juan de Haro en esta Ciudad poco después de haber dado su residencia, y ocho días antes, su mujer de pesadumbre de la mala residencia,

shed in the person of his eldest son Don García de Torres, who had stood by his father's side and had distinguished himself, showing he had inherited [his father's] bravery. The King commanded that the garrison should once again be divided into two companies, and one of them should be put under his command, as was done. The late Sergeant-Major was such an unassuming man, and such a father and friend to his soldiers, that one could raise the doubt (as was raised in Athens with regard to Epaminondas) whether he was a better captain than he was a man, or a better man than he was a captain. The three sons he left not only imitated the three Roman Horatii in their bravery, but also in their ill fortune, for Don García de Torres and Don Alonso de Torres, both captains of this garrison, died at age 33 and age 26, respectively. Don Diego de Torres, who followed the career of letters and graduated from Salamanca, passing up better positions, which His Majesty would have granted him elsewhere, was content with a canonry of this Cathedral, the most limited income in these whole Indies, for the sake of helping two sisters of his who otherwise would have been alone and unprotected.

73.   His Majesty was informed of the coming of the said Bowdoyn, and he sent two frigates to reinforce the fortress, and as their chief officer he sent Pedro Pérez de Arecizabal, Captain of the Galleons. He also sent Don Francisco de Villanueva y Lugo (who at that time had returned from the raising of the siege of Cádiz to the court, where he was soliciting the grant of the habit of one of the Military Orders) with a letter from His Majesty to the Governor of Puerto Rico, because as a native of this land he would know the lay of it. Indeed, he swam across the River of Luisa [Río Grande de Loíza] and placed the letter in the hands of Governor Juan de Haro, satisfying equally the governor's person and his own obligation. Later, in the year 1628, Morro Castle was burned because of a flying spark, which caused the death of the guards in a casemate where some of the gunpowder was kept. The whole casemate was blown up, as well as the soldiers' lodgings, with 43 persons in them, both soldiers and other local inhabitants, which was a piteous spectacle; both Mexico and Spain sent gunpowder and ammunition [to make up for what was lost.]

74.   This Governor Juan de Haro died in this City shortly after his evaluation was rendered, and eight days before him, his wife died from her sorrow at the bad audit he received. He is buried in the convent of Saint Thomas of the Order of Saint Dominic. On the day of his funeral it was said that he was the most senior soldier in His Majesty's service, because from his papers it was

y está enterrado en el convento de Santo Thomás de la orden de Santo Domingo, y el día de sus honras se dijo que era el soldado más antiguo que tenía Su Magestad en su servicio porque de los de sus papeles, constaba haberle servido sesenta y ocho años, que murió de más de ochenta; por lo bien que procedió en esta le libro Su Magestad 2,000 ducados por haber ayuda de costa en lo procedido de la nao que se tomó en esta ocasión al enemigo holandés, y a los capitanes Juan de Amézquita y Andrés Botello 1,000 ducados a cada uno, por lo mismo.

He had sent his adjutant, and in-law, Luis de Castro, to Mexico to bring the Situado, but Castro absconded with the money, so de Haro was placed under house arrest, and blamed for having trusted the scoundrel.

75.   Al Gobernador Juan de Haro, sucedió Don Enríquez de Sotomayor, hijo 2° de aquella ilustre Casa de los Enríquez de Salamanca, que desciende de un infante de Castilla, su titulo de 24 de enero de 1631. Fue Gobernador y capitán general de Cumaná por 5 años con 2,000 ducados. Fue capitán en Flandes y Gobernador de Cumaná, y vino a gobernar, el interin, por 2 años, del Maestre de Campo Don Cristóbal de Bocanegra, a quien Su Magestad había hecho merced de este gobierno en propiedad: gobernó esta Ciudad de donde fue por Presidente a la de Panamá.

Bocanegra was officially Governor of Puerto Rico, but never came to the island, since he was on a special mission to Peru, and was soon appointed head of the armed forces there.

76.   Los dos años que tuvo el interin, gobernó escelentemente y en los otros dos, parece que le querían prevaricar malos Consejeros, pero al fin le sacó Dios, de este peligro y le llevó a su presidencia, año de 1635, y se puso un hábito de Santiago y le vino la nueva de la subversión del mayorazgo de su Casa, que son seis mil ducados de renta con el señorío de Villalva y Obera, lugares junto a Salamanca, y murió a dos años de su presidencia con gran de opinión y fama, dándole nombre de Presidente Santo. Lo que se afirma es que en esta Ciudad resplandeció en el con admiración de todos, la virtud de la continencia, que en años que no llegaban a 40 es digna de ponderación. Hicieronséle honras en esta Catedral y Conventos porque fue su muerte generalmente de todo el pueblo tiernamente sentida, correspondiendo al amor con que le gobernó. *En su tiempo mandó S. M. que se cercase esta Ciudad* por lo apretado de sus informes, y comenzó su cerca con tanto desvelo y trabajo que no reservaba ninguno, y *al fin*

clear that he had served him for sixty-eight years, dying at more than eighty years old. Because of how well he had acted in this Island, His Majesty granted him a gratuity of 2,000 ducats from the proceeds of the ship that was taken on that occasion from the Dutch enemies, and for the same reason he granted gratuities of 1,000 ducats each to Captains Juan de Amézquita and Andrés Botello.

75.   Governor Juan de Haro was succeeded by Don [Enrique] Enríquez de Sotomayor, 2nd son of that illustrious House of the Enríquez of Salamanca, descended from an Infante of Castile. His decree of appointment is dated January 24, 1631. He was Governor and Captain-General of Cumaná for five years, with a salary of 2,000 ducats. He was a Captain in Flanders and Governor of Cumaná, and came here as interim Governor for two years in place of the Maestre de Campo Don Cristóbal de Bocanegra, to whom His Majesty had properly granted the Governorship; he governed this City, from which he went to Panama as President [of the Audiencia].

The Enríquez are descendants of Don Fadrique, Master of the Order of Santiago, bastard son of Alfonso XI, murdered by his legitimate brother Pedro the Cruel. When Enrique II killed Pedro and became King, he took care of his nephew, and eventually made him hereditary Admiral of Castile. In the fifteenth century, after having acquired family links to converted Jews, an Enríquez married Juan II of Aragon, and became the mother of Ferdinand the Catholic.

76.   He ruled excellently during the two years that he was interim Governor, and during the next two [*when Bocanegra was promoted and Enriquez became Governor in his own right* — Tr.] it seems that evil counselors wanted to corrupt him in his duty, but in the end God snatched him from this danger and took him to his Presidency [of the Audiencia of Panama] in the year 1635. He received the habit of a Knight of Santiago and got the news that he had become the Head of his House, which brings an income of 6,000 ducats [a year] with the lordship of Villalba and Obera, villages that are near Salamanca. He died after being President for two years, with a great reputation and fame, for they called him the Saintly President. What is confirmed is that in this City the virtue of chastity shone forth in him, to the admiration of everyone, for in a man who had not reached the age of 40, this is worthy of high praise. Funeral rites were held for him in this Cathedral and the convents of this City, because the news of his death was felt sorely by the whole people. They returned the love with which he had governed them. During his term of office, His Majesty ordered that this City be walled, because of the seriousness of the information [*intelli-*

la dejó con una puerta y dos plata-formas. Hizo también las dos puertas que atrás quedan referidas.

77.   En tiempo de este Gobernador D. Enrique año de 1630, se dividióla alcaidía de la fuerza de San Felipe del Morro, del gobernador, en que hasta entonces había estado; S. M. le hizo merced de ella al capitán y Sargento mayor Agustín de Salduendo, por título de 30 de abril de 1630, con 600 ducados de sueldo al año, que le servía 30 años, natural de Dicastillo en Navarra. Murió a los 7 años de su oficio y por su muerte y servicios se le hizo merced a su hija Doña Constanza de Salduendo, de 3,000 ducados de ayuda de costa en vacante de Obispados de Indias.

78.   Sucedió a Don Enrique Enríquez de Sotomayor, Don Iñigo de la Mota Sarmiento, caballero del hábito de Santiago, del Consejo de de los Estados de Flandes, y primo hermano del conde de Salvatierra, natural de Burgos y capitán de caballos en Flandes, con título de 23 de febrero de 1635, por 5 años, con 1,600 ducados.

Siguió con tanto afecto la fabrica de las murallas que en los 6 años que gobernó *acabó la cerca con tres puertas escelentes* y así mismo hizo la mitad del convento de Señor Santo Thomás de Aquino de la orden de Santo Domingo, a expensas de la infantería, con pretesto de capilla suya y entierro; y el cruzero de la Iglesia Catedral le hizo de nuevo porque temía alguna desgracia con su ruina, y hizo una cerca a la Iglesia, solicitando para dicho efecto, la cobranza de deudas que por su antigüedad eran incobrables, y en memoria de estos beneficios perpetuamente se obligaron el Deán y Cabildo de esta Santa Iglesia, a decil[r]le una Misa cantada todos los años al Señor San Juan Bautista en su día, de quien era tan devoto, que jamás dio el nombre para la guardia y custodia de la Ciudad, que se acostumbra en la milicia dar, sin haber hecho oración en esta Iglesia a Señor San Juan Bautista su patrón; y desde esta Ciudad fue a la de Panamá con no menos fama de continente que su antecesor D. Enrique Enríquez, y en la edad aun era más mozo cuatro o cinco años. Antes del primero de su presidencia *murió en Puerto Belo,* estando para hacer un templo porque lloraba mucho, que por *donde pasaba todos los años el mayor tesoro del mundo,* no tubiese casa decente Dios; dicen que con sospechas

> Torres y Vargas describes persons he may have counted as family friends. He stresses their piety in the donations made to ensure masses were said for their holy deaths and happy passage to Heaven.

gence about attacks — Tr.] he had received. He [Enriquez] began to build the walls with such concern and hard work that he would not let any work be left for later, and in the end [of his term] he left it with one gate and two platforms. He also built the two other gates that we have mentioned above.

77.   In the days of this Governor Don Enrique[z] (in 1630) the Governorship of the Castle of San Felipe del Morro was separated from the Governorship of the Island, to which it had been up to that time united. His Majesty granted the governorship to the Captain and Sergeant-Major Agustín de Salduendo, a native of Dicastillo in Navarre, who had spent 30 years in his service, by a decree of appointment dated April 30, 1630, with a salary of 600 ducats a year. He died in office seven years later, and because of his death and his services to the Crown his daughter Doña Constanza de Salduendo was granted a gratuity of 3,000 ducats from the vacancy of a Bishopric in the Indies.

78.   Don Enrique Enríquez de Sotomayor was succeeded by Don Íñigo de la Mota Sarmiento, a Knight of the habit of Santiago, a member of the Council of the Estates of Flanders, and a first cousin of the Count of Salvatierra. He was born in Burgos and had been a cavalry captain in Flanders; his decree of appointment for five years was dated February 23, 1635, with a salary of 1,600 ducats [a year.].

He pursued the building of the city walls with such enthusiasm that in the six years of his term he completed them with three excellent gates. He likewise built half the convent of my lord Saint Thomas Aquinas of the Order of Saint Dominic at the expense of the Infantry, on the account of a chapel and burial vault for them, and he rebuilt the crossing of the Cathedral Church because he feared it might fall down and cause a tragedy. He also built a wall around the Cathedral area, obtaining for this purpose the payment of debts so old that they had been given up as uncollectible. In memory of these benefits the Dean and Chapter of this Holy Church obliged themselves perpetually to celebrate him with a Sung Mass every year in honor of Saint John the Baptist on that saint's feast day [June 24th]. The Governor was so devoted to that saint that he never gave the password for the guard and custody of the City (as is the custom in the military) without first having gone to pray in this Cathedral to its patron, my lord Saint John the Baptist. From this City he was transferred to that of Panama, where he had the same reputation for chastity as his predecessor Don Enrique Enríquez, even though he was even younger than him by four or five years. He died in Puerto Bello before the first year of his Presidency, while he was trying

de veneno por ser muy celoso del servicio de su Rey. En esta Catedral se le hicieron honras y fue de todo el pueblo muy lloraba su muerte.

79.   Al Gobernador Don Iñigo de la Mota Sarmiento, sucedió D. Agustín de Silva y Figueroa Caballero del hábito de Alcántara, natural de Jerez de los Caballeros, teniente de la guardia del Duque de Feria en Milán y Capitán en Lombardia (titulo 16 de mayo 1640).

Vino con tan poca salud que murió en esta Ciudad dentro de 5 meses, y así no hizo cosa de memoria más del designio y planta de la casa de los gobernadores de esta ciudad, que se ejecutó por su sucesor en el gobierno. Está enterrado en la capilla de Nuestra Señora del Rosario que para esto dejó señalada Don Iñigo de la Mota.

> The third Duke of Feria was Don Gómez Suárez de Figueroa, governor of Milan 1618–29 and again in 1630–34; viceroy of Catalonia 1629–30. Mota Sarmiento had excellent credentials.

80.   A este Gobernador Don Agustín de Silva sucedió en el gobierno Don Juan de Bolanos, vecino de esta ciudad, natural de Guadix en el Andalucía, capitán que tenían nombrado en el interin,

> *The Auditor, **Juan de Melgarejo**, has the same surname as the interim governor previously sent to Puerto Rico by the Audiencia in Santo Domingo (see paragraph #53), who married a daughter of Juan Ponce de Leon II and then invited his father-in-law to compose the 1582 report on the island. Even if this is not the same person, connections to the Ponce de Léon family may have influenced the appointment. However, an Auditor's training would be in law, leaving him without military background. In contrast, acting Governor de Bolanos was trained in military matters and used his experience as justification for the dispatch. Simple local jealousies ought not be discounted, however.

y la forma de su nombramiento fue una cedula particular que tenia Don Iñigo de la Mota, para nombrar Gobernador en su ausencia, que no pudo extenderse a otro Gobernador alguno, y aunque en el Cabildo de la Ciudad se estendió este punto y a el tocaba nombrar Gobernador, al menos en lo de la paz, se dejó llevar por lo que se debe atender a la de la Ciudad, donde en aquella ocasión no se hallaba sujeto de mucha importancia, por estar vacas casi todas las plazas de la guerra. La Audiencia con la cédula que tiene para nombrar en tales casos en su distrito, envió un Oidor de ella llamado *Don Juan Melgarejo, y en llegando 12 leguas de la Ciudad al lugar del Arecibo, envió Don Juan de Bolanos un ayu-

to build a church there, for he very much bewailed that in a City through which every year there passed the greatest treasures in the world, God should have no decent house. They say he was poisoned because he was so zealous in the service of his King. A funeral service was held for him in this Cathedral [of San Juan] and all the people mourned greatly over his death.

79.   Governor Don Íñigo de la Mota Sarmiento was succeeded by Don Agustín de Silva y Figueroa, a Knight of the habit of Alcántara, born in Jerez de los Caballeros, a lieutenant in the guard of the Duke of Feria in Milan, and Captain in Lombardy (his decree of appointment was dated May 16, 1640).

He arrived in such poor health that within five months he died in this City, and thus he did not do anything worth remembering except for the design and plan of the house for the Governors of this City, which was put into execution by his successor. He is buried in the Chapel of Our Lady of the Rosary [in the Dominican convent of Saint Thomas], which Don Íñigo de la Mota had designated for the Governors' burial place.

80.   This Governor Don Agustín de Silva was succeeded by Don Juan de Bolaños, a *vecino* of this City, born in Guádix in Andalusia, a Captain who was appointed as interim Governor.

The form of his appointment was a personal letter from the King that Don Íñigo de la Mota had, authorizing him to appoint an [interim] Governor if he had to be absent from the Island. This privilege could not be extended to any other Governor, and although the City Council stretched the point, claiming the nomination of a Governor, at least on civil matters [as opposed to military ones], belonged to it, they let themselves be swayed by the need to attend to the peace of the City. At that point this was of no importance, since almost all military positions were vacant. The Audiencia [of Santo Domingo], basing itself on the standing authorization it has to appoint in such cases within its jurisdiction, sent one of its Auditors named *Don Juan Melgarejo. But when he arrived at the village of Arecibo, which is 12 leagues from the City, Don Juan de Bolaños sent an adjutant and some soldiers to put him back on a ship for Santo Domingo, as they did, for he said that frontier garrisons should not be entrusted to people who knew nothing about military matters. This Don Juan de Bolaños went to Spain with a good evaluation to claim rewards, but until now we do not know what success he has had.

dante y soldados que le volviesen a embarcar para Santo Domingo, como se hizo, diciendo que las plazas de frontera no se habían de fiar de quien no entendía la guerra. Fue a España dicho Don Juan de Bolanos a sus pretensiones con buena residencia y hasta ahora no se sabe del suceso de ella.

81.   Al dicho Don Juan de Bolanos sucedió Don Fernando de la Riva y Agüero, natural de las montañas y caballero del hábito de Santiago, con titulo de 23 de abril de 1643, el de 48 le proveyó Su Magestad por Gobernador y capitán general de la Ciudad de Cartagena;

> y luego que vino puso en ejecución la planta que dejó Don Agustín de Silva para la Casa Real que es morada de los Gobernadores, y *al puente de los Soldados lo hizo levadizo* con nuevo reducto con que esta defendía y creó para ella un capitán con titulo de teniente. Devierala la plaza de San Martín la corona Occidental que dio Roma a Quinto Fabio, cuando en la 2° guerra africana, la libró cercada de sus enemigos, si se usaran en estos tiempos los honores de la antigüedad; porque entendiendo el peligro en que aquella plaza se hallaba, la despachó dos socorros tan a tiempo que supieron ser su remedio, y en el 2° que dispuso en veinte y cuatro horas, entró en San Martín a los 16 de abril, el capitán Flamenco Vicente, que perdiendo con ella esperanza, levantaron luego aquel cerco, ofreciéronse plegarias y sacrificios continuos a Nuestro Señor en este tiempo, y así le premió con tal feliz suceso. Temor dió siempre a los prudentes el haber de escribir de los vivos por el riesgo de odio o lisonja, pero en la modestia de Don Fernando de la Riva la mayor ha de ser el no hacérsela.

Quintus Fabius used a scorched earth strategy to thwart the Carthagians under Hannibal, who invaded Italy in the II Punic War. Here, engagements only to delay the enemy's advance is offered as a path to victory and not as a sign of cowardice.

---

82.   El año de *1649 fue proveído por su sucesor en estos cargos el Maestre de Campo, Don Diego de Aguilera. Para concluir con este pliego la breve relación que se ha podido enviar de esta Isla, digo que ha notado la curiosidad, que hasta ahora han sido trece los Obispos que ha habido y doblados los Gobernadores que son veinte y seis, con los que han servido en el interin, y como al principio se advirtió que era esta la primer[a] Isla que fue bendita de mano episcopal ha sido también la primer[a] a el año de 1640 que en todas las Indias hospedó grande de Castilla, pues el Señor Marqués de Villena y Duque de Escalona, viniendo por Virrey a la Nueva España, saltó en tierra en el Aguada, y por memoria de su grandeza, apadrinó un niño hijo de un vecino de aquella población, hechándole el agua el Señor Obispo de Tasxala, Don Juan de Palafox y Mendoza con asistencia

81.   Don Juan de Bolaños was succeeded by Don Fernando de la Riva y Agüero, a native of the Mountains of Castile and a Knight of the habit of Santiago; his decree of appointment was dated April 23, 1643, and in 1648 His Majesty promoted him to Governor and Captain-General of the City of Cartagena.

> As soon as he arrived he put into execution the plans that Don Agustín de Silva had left for the King's House which is the residence of the Governors. He also turned the Bridge of the Soldiers into a drawbridge with a new redoubt to defend it, and appointed a captain for that bridge with the title of lieutenant. If the honors of antiquity were still in use, the fortified town of St. Martin [*now Sint Maarten*] would owe him the Obsidional Crown that Rome granted to Quintus Fabius when, during the Second Punic War, he delivered it from enemy besiegers, because when this Governor came to understand the danger in which this fortress found itself he sent it two such timely aids that they remedied its danger. In the second of these rescue expeditions, which he set up within twenty-four hours, the Flemish captain Vicente entered St. Martin on April 16th, so that the enemy lost all hopes and raised the siege at once. Constant prayers and sacrifices were offered to Our Lord during this time, and so he rewarded him with such a happy success. Prudent men have always been wary of having to write about the living, for fear of coming across as hating them or else flattering them, but such is the modesty of Don Fernando de la Riva that it would be a greater fault not to praise him.

82.   In the year *1649, Maestre de Campo Don Diego de Aguilera was appointed as his successor in all these positions. To conclude in this sheet of paper the brief report I have been able to send about this Island, I will mention that I have noticed a curious fact: to this day there have been thirteen bishops in the Island, and twice the number of governors, namely, twenty-six (counting the interim governors). And just as in the beginning it was noted that this was the first Island [in the New World] that was blessed by the hand of a bishop. [So we should note that] in the year 1640 it was the first in all the Indies to receive a Grandee of Castile, for my lord the Marquess of Villena and Duke of Escalona, on his way to be Viceroy in New Spain, landed for a short time in Aguada, and in memory of his greatness served as godfather to a child, the son of one of the inhabitants of that village. The Baptism was performed by

*See pages 233–34 for why "1649" and not "1647."

de otros Obispos que se hallaron en aquella flota y ocasión, que ha sido el acto de la mayor grandeza que en el profano se ha podido poner en memoria, desde que se descubrieron las Indias. Llamóse el baptizado Don Diego Pacheco como su padrino, y dejóse ordenado que se le buscase cuando fuese adulto para hacerle el favor que le ocasionó su ventura.

Baroque writers viewed an uncanny coincidence in numbers as confirmation of God's presence.

The incident of the baptism does not indicate what happened when or if the child became an adult.

Pacheco is the family surname of the Marquesses of Villena and Dukes of Escalona.

Section #83 may come from the traveler's source, describing Puerto Rico and the Caribbean.

*"Modern" was a word used during the Renaissance to describe itself in contrast with the Middle Ages. Torres y Vargas indicates here that city planning had been used to create straight streets at relatively equal distances making a grid, unlike the haphazard medieval streets with their twistings and turnings.

To be a *vecino* you had to be a householder, so if you moved in with relatives you lost that position in the city. This means that the number of *vecinos* has decreased, but not the population.

---

83.   De las islas pobladas antes de San Martín, es la de Puerto-Rico, la que se halla a barlovento todas, y así para todas ellas tiene la entrada libre, porque a Santo Domingo se va en tres días, a la Habana en ocho días, a Cartagena en seis a Nueva España en veinte, y así a todas las de más partes porque siempre goza de vientos orientales y como es la que tiene mayor elevación de polo, con facilidad se navega a todas ellas y al contrario desde las otras partes se tarda mucho en el viage porque se tiene contra el viento que de ordinario corre que es dicha brisa. La Ciudad tiene cuatrocientas casas de piedra y algunas de tabla, y es la casería muy buena, y en estremo es la Ciudad alegre y bien asombrada, desde la mar o la tierra que se mira, porque esta toda muy bien murada y luego la ciñe una cinta de plata del mar que casi por todas partes la cerca y rodea; su asiento esta superior al mar, y la disposición de calle es a lo *moderno, todas iguales. Los vecinos son quinientos, porque desde que Boduino Enrico tomóla Ciudad, algunos a quienes quemó sus casas, se agregaron a vivir con sus deudos.

84.   Las mugeres son las más hermosas de todas las indias, honestas, virtuosas y muy trabajadoras y de tan lindo juicio, que los Gobernadores Don Enrique

the Lord Bishop of Tlaxcala, Don Juan de Palafox y Mendoza, with the assistance of other bishops who were also in that fleet and event. This has been the act of most grandeur (from a worldly point of view) that can be remembered since the Indies were discovered. The child was named Don Diego Pacheco, after his godfather, who left orders that this child should be sought after when he became an adult, so that he might offer him the favor and protection to which this good occasion entitled him.

83.   Puerto Rico is to the windward of all the islands which were settled before St. Martin, and thus has free access to them all, because Santo Domingo is reached from there in three days, Havana in eight, Cartagena in six, New Spain in twenty, and similarly to all other parts, because it always enjoys easterly winds. Since it is the one with the highest elevation with regard to the pole, it is easy to sail from it to all those others, and to the contrary, the trip is very slow from these other parts, because sailing from that direction the prevailing wind, which is called "the breeze," [*the "Trade Winds" — Tr.*] blows against you. The City has four hundred stone houses, and a few wooden ones, and the ensemble of the houses is very good. The City makes an extremely cheerful and astonishing sight, whether you look at it from land or sea, because it is very well walled, and then surrounded by the sea as by a silver ribbon, which fences and surrounds it on almost every side. Its location is higher than the sea, and the disposition of the streets is in the *modern style, all of them equal. The *vecinos* number five hundred, because since the time of Hendrick's attack, some of those whose houses he burned have moved in to live with their relatives.

84.   The women are the most beautiful in all the Indies; decent, virtuous and very industrious, and they have such nice good sense that the Governors Don Enrique and Don Íñigo used to say that all prudent men should come to look for wives in Puerto Rico. It was like a proverb with them to say, "If you want to marry, come to Puerto Rico." The people of this land are generally quite tall, indeed there is only one family of short people. They have lively wits, and when they go out of their native land they are very active and valorous. Evidence from older days [of their distinctions] is not abundant, (except for a Captain in Flanders, Juan de Ávila, a native of this City, whose deeds gained him a mention in

y Don Iñigo, decían, que todos los hombres prudentes se habían de venir a casar a Puerto-Rico, y era su ordinario decir, "para casarse, en Puerto-Rico." Los naturales son generalmente de gran de estatura, que solo un linage hay que la tenga pequeña; de vivos ingenios, y fuera de su patria muy activos y de valor, que aunque en lo antiguo no se tiene noticia, mas que de aquel capitán de Flandes Juan de Ávila natural de esta Ciudad, que por sus hechos mereció que se hiciera de ellos memoria en la 3ª parte de la Pontifical que escribió el Doctor Babia, y de otro caballero Don Antonio Pimentel que lo fue del habito de San Juan.

85.   De 20 años a esta parte, han lucido muchos naturales que han salido de ella y vecinos de esta Ciudad; en gobiernos de otras ciudades como lo fue **Don Andrés Rodríguez de Villegas**, de la Margarita y de la Florida; **Juan de Amézquita Quixano**, capitán de este presidio, de el de Cuba; **Don Francisco de Ávila y Luga** del de Chiapa; y **Don Felipe de Lascano** del hábito de Alcántara, y capitán y alcaide la Punta de la Havana. **Don Antonio de Mercado**, de esta Ciudad, y alcaide la fuerza de Santo Domingo, **Don Andrés Franco**, natural de esta Ciudad, del hábito de Santiago, y Maestre de Campo general del Reyno de Nueva España; **Don García de Torres y Vargas**, capitán de infantería de este presidio; **Don Alonso de Torres y Vargas**, su hermano, capitán de la plaza de San Martín y luego de este presidio; **Don Matías Otaso**, capitán y Sargento mayor de Filipinas; **Don Iñigo de Otaso**, Sargento mayor de la flota de Nueva España y cápitan de Filipinas; **Don Antonio de Ayala**, Arcediano y canónigo de Segovia e Inquisidor de Valencia; **Don Juan de Ayala** su hermano, Deán y canónigo de Segovia; **Don Alonso de Ulloa**, Racionero de Guadalajara; **Don Diego de Cárdenas**, Deán de Caracas; **Don Fernando Altamirano**, Canónigo de Taxcala; **Don Gerónimo Campuzano**, Chantre de Cartagena; **Francisco Mariano de Rivera**, Racionero de Yucatán; **Don Juan de Salinas**, Tesorero de Caracas; **Gregorio Pérez de León**, catedrático de Maese Rodrigo en Sevilla; y *de ordinaria todas las dignidades y prebendas de esta Iglesia, las gozan los naturales por el patronazgo Real que los prefiere a otros,* y de los que han salido de la patria, se conoce que cualquiera que cumpliere con el mandato que le hizo Dios a Abraham, *"egredo* [misprint] *de terra tua*

This is a list of natives of Puerto Rico who distinguished themselves in church, army and state.

et de cognatione tua," sin duda lucirá adelantando su casa y honrando a su patria y amor dulce como dijo Virgilio, *"dulcis amor patriae laudum inmensa Cupido,"* y que sea la primer[a] nobleza la de esta Ciudad y la de Santo Domingo, lo refiere Antonio de Herrera en su general historia y se deja bien entender por haber sido las fundaciones primeras.

the 3rd part of Doctor Babia's *Pontifical*, and another gentleman, Don Antonio Pimentel, who was a Knight of the habit of Saint John [of Malta]).

The reference to the island's beautiful women and the pattern of Spaniards finding spouses from among the Puerto Rican elite is an important social fact. Since a clergyman would ordinarily be reluctant to highlight these facts, it is likely Torres y Vargas is repeating here things he heard, perhaps when attending social events.

Historia pontifical y católica, (1584) listed Spanish prelates.

---

85.   In the last 20 years many natives of this Island and *vecinos* of this City who have left it have made their mark as Governors of other cities, as **Don Andrés Rodríguez de Villegas**, who was Governor of Margarita and Florida; **Juan de Amézquita Quixano**, Captain of this garrison, Governor of Cuba; **Don Francisco de Ávila y Luga** Governor of Chiapas; and **Don Felipe de Lascano,** a Knight of the Order of Alcántara, and Captain and Governor of the fortress of the Point of Havana. **Don Antonio de Mercado**, Governor of this City and of the Fortress of Santo Domingo, **Don Andrés Franco**, a native of this City, a Knight of Santiago and General Maestre de Campo of the Kingdom of New Spain; **Don García de Torres y Vargas**, Captain of the Infantry of this garrison; **Don Alonso de Torres y Vargas**, his brother, Captain of the fortified town of St. Martin, and then of this garrison; **Don Matías Otaso**, Captain and Sergeant-Major of the Philippines; **Don Iñigo de Otaso**, Sergeant-Major of the Fleet of New Spain and Captain of the Philippines; **Don Antonio de Ayala**, Archdeacon and Canon of Segovia and Inquisitor of Valencia; his brother **Don Juan de Ayala**, Dean y Canon of Segovia; **Don Alonso de Ulloa**, Prebendary of Guadalajara; **Don Diego de Cárdenas**, Dean of Caracas; **Don Fernando Altamirano**, Canon of Tlaxcala; **Don Gerónimo Campuzano**, Precentor of Cartagena; **Francisco Mariano de Rivera**, Prebendary of Yucatán; **Don Juan de Salinas**, Cathedral Treasurer of Caracas; **Gregorio Pérez de León**, Professor at the College of Maese Rodrigo in Seville; in fact, *ordinarily all the dignities and prebends of this Cathedral Church are enjoyed by natives of the Island, by choice of the Royal Patronage, which prefers them to outsiders.* And, as for those who have left their native land, it is evident that whichever of them who obeys God's command to Abraham, ["Go forth from your country and your kinfolk," Genesis 12:1] will doubtless make his mark, promoting his family and adding honor to his sweetly loved native land. As Virgil says,   ["Sweet is love of country and immense yearning of praises."] And as for the top rank of the nobility of this City and of Santo Domingo, this is told by Antonio de Herrera in his *General History* and can well be seen from the fact that these were the first to be founded.

> It is not the god *Cupid*, but the immense *desire* or *eagerness* for praise: "*cupido*" here should be written with a small c. The typesetter probably had no idea that *cupido* could be a common noun in Latin, and capitalized it. —Tr.
>
> The line from Virgil is not exact: although "*dulcis amor patriae*" is a common phrase: Book VI of the Æeneid reads: *Vincet amor patriae laudumque immensa cupido.*—Ed.

ANEXOS AL OBISPADO DE PUERTO-RICO

ISLA MARGARITA.

86.   De las islas que tiene este Obispado, la de más nombre y lustre, es la de la Margarita, distante de la de Puerto-Rico, ocho o diez días de navegación, y de la tierra firme seis leguas. Tiene catorce de longitud que corre el Este Oeste; su terreno escabroso y estéril, requisito que generalmente tienen las tierras que en la mar crían minerales de perlas, que aquí son de mejor Oriente que en otra parte. Tuvieron noticia de ellas los primeros pobladores de las Indias, hallándolas en los indios naturales de Santo Domingo, con quien haciendo aprietos para que las descubrieran, les dixeron se las traían los caribes, y estos, que las había en la Isla Margarita; cuya codicia facilitó inconvenientes, despachando la Audiencia bajeles, que certificados de la verdad, movieron los ánimos de muchos para venirse aun con sus familias a poblar, como lo hicieron, en la Isla de Cubagua, que intermedia a esta Isla y la tierra firme; dista de una parte y otra casi con igual distancia, tres leguas, y tendrá otras tantas de longitud. Tuvo Cubagua por nombre la nueva Cádiz: que cuando más acreditada con la opulencia de sus Ostrales, padeció los eclipses que ofuscan sombra las mayores propiedades, pues la codicia que a sus fundadores, despertó también á franceses piratas que la infestasen, á cuyas inquietudes ordinarias pudo mal resistir, fundada en la playa y sin defensa, a que ayudando la falta de agua y leña que se traía de acarreto, se despobló y mudó a la Margarita en el pueblo de la Mar, que por las mismas causas pasó dentro de poco la Ciudad dos leguas la tierra dentro, que hoy tiene por nombre la Asunción. Sus vecinos serán hasta trescientos españoles, gente de lustre por la mayor parte, y en lo que mas lo muestran es el adorno de los templos, devoción del Santísimo Sacramento y sufragios por los difuntos, que frecuentaban con el aseo y cuidado que pudieran en lugares mas cómodos.

87.   Tiene indios naturales que llaman Guaiqueries, libres de servidumbre por el agasajo que hicieron a los primeros españoles, ofreciéndoseles sin con-

TERRITORIES ANNEXED TO THE DIOCESE OF
DE PUERTO-RICO

> Passage #86 begins the description of the parts of the Puerto Rican diocese on other Caribbean islands that was omitted from the version found in Fernández Méndez (1976). The titles to each section come from Tapia y Rivera. See the Appendix for the dates reported.

The ISLAND of MARGARITA

86.   Among the islands that belong to this diocese the one with the greatest fame and renown is that of Margarita, which is eight or ten days sailing from Puerto Rico, and six leagues from the mainland. It is fourteen leagues across from east to west; its terrain is rough and sterile, a characteristic which is general among the lands whose coasts produce banks of pearls — which in this Island are of better luster than anywhere else. The first settlers of the Indies had notice of these pearls by finding them among the native Indians of Santo Domingo, who, when pressed to tell where they came from, told them that the Caribs brought them. The Caribs said they were found in the Island of Margarita, and greed for them overcame the inconveniences. The Audiencia sent out ships that ascertained the truth of the reports, motivating many to come and settle there even with their families, as they did on the Island of Cubagua, which lies halfway between Margarita and the mainland. It is about three leagues distant from each, and about three leagues long. Cubagua was given the name of New Cádiz, and when its reputation was at its height for the abundance of its oyster-beds, it suffered the eclipses that frequently darken the greatest properties. The same greed that attracted its first settlers also moved the French pirates to infest it. The City could hardly resist these ongoing disturbances, since it was built on the beach and unfortified, not to mention the lack of water and firewood, which had to be brought over from elsewhere. Because of this it was dismantled and moved to Margarita as the Pueblo de la Mar, which for the same reasons was soon transferred two leagues inland, and is now called La Asunción. Its *vecinos* must be as many as three hundred Spaniards, most of them persons of noble blood, who show their class especially in the adornment of the churches, their devotion to the Blessed Sacrament, and their suffrages for the deceased, which they carry out with all the neatness and care typical of places where this could be done with greater convenience.

quistas ni fuerza de armas, no obstante que son de natural belicoso, como lo muestran en las ocasiones de guerra con piratas. Hay fuera de la Iglesia parroquial, que gobiernan un Vicario y dos Curas con copia de clérigos, dos Conventos de Santo Domingo y San Francisco; Una Iglesia de Santa Lucia y un hospital, y en tres sitios de ella, las feligresías cuyos capellanes paga Su Magestad. En una de ellas que llaman el Valle, se venera una Imagen de Nuestra Señora y se cuenta por particular devoción de los vecinos y forasteros, que con patentes milagros esperimentan cada día sus divinos favores.

The devotion to "Virgin of the Valley" originally came from the Toledo region of Spain. A statue of the Virgen del Valle arrived with the earliest settlers of Margarita Island around 1541. Her image is honored by a basilica there. In addition to the many wonders attributed to this Madonna, she is considered a defender of the Venezuelan nation because her protection was invoked at the Battle of Matasiete, July 31, 1817.

The Venezuelan devotion is not to be confused with another of the same name in the Catamarca Province of Argentina.— Ed.

---

88.   y aun que en la Virgen todos son iguales, pondré uno que a nuestro ver es particular; estaban dos mancebos criollos de la tierra lisongeando los orgullos de su edad afirmados con espadas envainadas, y uno de ellos fiado en que lo estaban, se arrojó, de suerte que hallando al otro firme, se metió la contera del contrario por la cuenca del ojo, y sintiéndose herido, al retirarse dejó al otro la espada desnuda y el quedó con la vaina colgando del lagrimal. Acudieron a tirarle de ella, y salió dejando la contera tan metida dentro del casco, que aunque la buscaban con una tienta, cirujanos y un doctor que asistían, no podían hallarla, hasta que después de algunas horas invocando el doliente la Virgen del Valle, y repitiendo en su divino Nombre los cirujanos sus diligencias, la hallaron y sacaron con unas tenazas abriendo primero cisura por donde entrasen, echando para efecto fuera la lumbre del ojo; que vuelto a poner en su lugar, quedo casi sin señal de haber padecido semejante batería. Cuando esto se escribe, lo testifica vivo y sirviéndose de ambos ojos, y la contera colgada en el templo de esta divina Señora.

CUMANÁ

89.   De la gente que para poblar la Margarita despobló a Cubagua, se dividió alguna, y fue a poblar en el rio de Cumaná de donde tomo nombre la Ciudad, catorce leguas de la Margarita, en la tierra firme, que aunque solía ser lugar de

87.   The Island has native Indians who are called Guaiqueries. They are exempt from all servitude because of the welcome they offered to the first Spanish settlers, presenting themselves to them without need for conquest or force of arms, in spite of the fact that they are naturally warlike, as shown when demanded by war with pirates. Aside from the Parish Church, which is governed by a Vicar [General] and two Rectors with an abundance of clerics, there are two friaries, one of Saint Dominic and one of Saint Francis, a church of Saint Lucy, and a hospital. In three other places in the Island there are congregations of the faithful [*chapels-of-ease belonging to the parish in places where regular attendance to the parish church would be inconvenient* — Tr.] whose chaplains are paid by His Majesty. In one of these chapels, which they call [the chapel of] the Valley, an image of Our Lady is venerated, and is considered a particular devotion of the local people and of people from farther off, who every day experience her divine favors.

88.   Although all deeds of the Virgin are equally great, I will write one down which in my view is particular. Two young criollos of that land were showing off the pride of their youth playing with sheathed swords. One of them, trusting in the fact that they were sheathed, threw himself on the other youth in such a way that the metal tip of his opponent's scabbard — which was held firmly — got into the socket of his eye. Feeling himself wounded, he stepped back, leaving the other's sword unsheathed, and the scabbard hanging from the corner of his own eye. People hastened over to pull it out, and the scabbard came away, but left the metal tip so deeply embedded in the eye-socket that it could not be found even by a doctor and some surgeons who were there to look for it with a probe. After a few hours of this, the wounded man called upon the Virgin of the Valley, and when the surgeons repeated their efforts in her divine Name they found the scabbard-tip, and pulled it out with pincers, first making an incision by which the pincers could enter — for which they had to eject the eyeball from the socket. But once this was replaced, it was left with hardly a sign of having suffered such bruising. At the time that this is being written the young man is alive and has the use of both eyes, and the scabbard tip has been hung as a witness in the church of this divine Lady.

CUMANÁ

89.   Some of the people who abandoned Cubagua to settle near the Island of Margarita separated from the rest and went to settle near the river of Cumaná,

menos parte que hoy le ha igualado de años a esta parte, *que* el maesso de capilla sube las voces en la música del mundo, ha subido este lugar, con las haciendas de cacao y otras inteligencias de sus moradores, con pueblos de indios, que encomendados, son los que llevan el *pondus dici & estus* de la codicia humana, y particular en el de las perlas, tan preternatural como arriesgado; y aunque esta ocupas[c]ión es propia de la Margarita, se agregan estos dos lugares en un cuerpo que llaman de Ranchería, gobernados por un Alcalde mayor y cuatro diputados, que un año se eligen de un pueblo, y otro de otro, para sacarlos. El número y porte de sus vecinos es como el de la Margarita; Iglesia parroquial, dos convento de Santo Domingo y San Francisco, y clérigos bastantes para la asistencia de la Iglesia y doctrinas de pueblos de indios, en cuyo catecismo se puede decir predican en desierto, por lo mal que les asienta el Culto Divino y policía, y aun todo lo que no es lo bárbaro de sus costumbres.

90.   Venerase en la parroquial de esta Ciudad, una Cruz de poco más de una vara de medir, guarnecida de plata y metida en una caja de lo propio, cuya ceremonia es que en años pasados dando fondo un pirata con número de naos en este puerto, y marchando hasta reconocer la Ciudad, que dista de la marina dos tiros de mosquete, halló en un serrito que está caballero del lugar, una Cruz, y pegándole fuego tres veces sin que hiciera impresión, mudaron diligencias, pero no la Cruz del lugar donde estaba, tan firme, que hechándole los brazos un cabo y tirando de ella con furor diabólico y... sin poderla mover, la dejaron sin señal alguna de tan heréticos oprobios, y sin esperanzas de conseguir la empresa, los retiro a sus naos el pavor de lo que habían esperimentado; de cuyo lugar la llevó general aplauso a la parroquial, y repartió en pedazos, fabricando del mayor de ellos la que hoy se venera en esta Iglesia.

"Two musket shots" as a distance (about 600 yards) would be a familiar measure to a son in a military family, such as Torres y Vargas.

Stories similar to this one are common in medieval Spain in accounts about crosses or images which the Moors tried to burn at the time of the Reconquest.

"Cut it into pieces" was not desecration but devotion so as to give parts of it to other towns, or to individuals for reverence as relics.

CUMANAGOTO Y NUEVA BARCELONA.

91.   San Cristóbal de los Cumanagotos, población fundada casi consecuente con la de Cumaná, catorce leguas la costa abajo, y la Nueva Barcelona, fundación

from which this City took its name. It is on the mainland, fourteen leagues from the Island of Margarita, and although it used to be less important than it is now, in the last few years it had come to be its equal, for just as a choir director leads certain voices to sing louder in the music of this world, so has this place been raised by the cocoa *haciendas* and other industries of its dwellers, and with Indian villages which, being under the *encomienda*, are the ones who bear the ["The burden and heat of the day." Matt. 20:12] of human greed, and especially the burden of the pearl [fishing], which is as risky as it is beyond human nature. Although this business is more proper to the Island of Margarita, for the gathering of the oysters these two places are joined into one venture which they call the *Ranchería*. It is governed by an Alcalde Mayor and four deputies who are elected from one town or from the other in alternating years. The number and bearing of the *vecinos* is similar to that of those of Margarita — they have a parish church, two friaries, one of Saint Dominic and another of Saint Francis, and sufficient clerics for the service of the church and the missions in the Indian villages. In catechizing, it can be said that they preach in the desert, since Divine Worship and civilization suit them [the Indians] but ill. Indeed, they dislike whatever is not as barbaric as in their own customs.

90.   In the parish church of this City there is great devotion to a cross that is a bit longer than a measuring rod, plated in silver and kept in a box of the same metal. Its story is that some years ago a pirate cast anchor in this harbor with a number of vessels, and marching to reconnoiter the City (which is about two musket shots from the beach) they found a cross upon a small hill that overlooks the town. They tried three times to set it on fire with no success, and then they changed their efforts to moving it away. But the cross remained so firm that even when an officer of theirs wrapped his arms around it and pulled on it with diabolical fury, and [*illegible in the original*] without being able to budge it, and without such heretical insults leaving the least dent in it. And so, giving up hope of obtaining what they had undertaken, the fear of what had happened made them retreat to their ships. To universal applause the settlers then brought that cross to the parish church, and cut it into pieces and from the largest of these they made the cross that is now venerated in that church.

CUMANAGOTO and NUEVA BARCELONA

91.   San Cristóbal de los Cumanagotos, a settlement founded almost simultaneously with Cumaná and fourteen leagues down the coast from it, and Nueva

nueva, legua y media una de otra, pueden reducirse a un pueblo, pues habiéndose despoblado el primero para poblar el segundo, solo han quedado en el, media docena de vecinos, que más por tema que comodidad, se ha retenido en el, si bien con su parroquial *que solían* y una hermita de la Virgen del Socorro de particular devoción. La nueva Barcelona tendrá al pie de ochenta o cien vecinos y no otra cosa particular, por ser tan recién fundada.

SAN MIGUEL DE BATEY.

92.   Este lugar es tan nuevo, que aun no ha tornado estado su fundación. Dos días de camino la tierra adentro de la nueva Barcelona. Sus vecinos pocos. Fundóse a titulo de poner freno con la asistencia de sus moradores, a la avilantez de los indios de todo este país, que con menos sujeción, asaltan las poblaciones y matan por los caminos a sus mismos amos con el veneno de sus flechas, tan raro, que sin habérseles hallado remedio, qualquier picadura por pequeña que sea, es mortal al segundo o tercer día, cayéndose las carnes a pedazos, con intensos dolores, tanto, que en hiriendo a alguno, no dicen hérilo sino mátelo: efecto esperimentado con gran aplauso suyo y daño nuestro.

SAN FELIPE DE AUSTRIA.

93.   Esta Ciudad, que en el nombre solo lo es, y merece serlo, cuando no sea sino por el nombre, ha padecido vaivenes desde su fundación hasta hoy que esta en el más bajo de todos, reducida a tan pocos vecinos, que apenas forman una aldea. Hase mudado a tres o cuatro sitios, retirándose siempre de lo mal seguro de los indios, que no tienen encomiendas, pero sujetos a la nación española. Tiene Vicario, Cura y sacristán, que paga, como en las demás partes, Su Magestad.

> Naming the settlement after the King's patron saint and after the royal house of Austria was a way of invoking special protection and financing from the monarchy.
>
> *Encomiendas* was an institution adapted from Spanish experience in order to include non-Hispanicized Indians into the colonial economy. It had been vigorously opposed in the sixteenth century by Las Casas and officially prohibited. See the Glossary. Torres y Vargas suggests here that the natives on the island had formally accepted status as Spanish subjects, but were ambiguous about their loyalties.

CUMANACOA.

94.   Por otro nombre San Baltazar de los Arias. Doce leguas de la tierra de

Barcelona, a recent foundation a league and a half from it, can both be reduced to one town, since one of them was abandoned so as to found the other. Only a half dozen *vecinos* have remained in the former, more out of stubbornness than for convenience's sake — although they have kept the parish church they used to have, and a chapel of Our Lady of Succor to which the people are particularly devoted. Nueva Barcelona must have about eighty to a hundred *vecinos*, and nothing else worth noting, since it has been founded so recently.

SAN MIGUEL DE BATEY

92.   This place is so new that its foundation has not yet been formalized. It is a two-days ride inland from Nueva Barcelona; its *vecinos* are few. It was founded so that its inhabitants would put a stop to the insolence of the Indians of this whole territory. Less subjected [to Spain], they attack the villages and kill their very masters on the open road with the poison of their arrows. [This poison] is so rare that no remedy has been discovered for it, and any scratch from these arrows, insignificant though it may be, is deadly by the second or third day — the flesh falls off in pieces from the wounded person with excruciating pain. When they have wounded someone they do not say "I wounded him," but rather "I killed him" — an effect that has been experienced to their great glory and our great harm.

SAN FELIPE DE AUSTRIA

93.   This City — which is a City only in name, and deserves to be one in fact, if only because of its name — has suffered ups and downs from the time of its founding until today. It is now in the lowest state of all, so diminished in the number of its *vecinos* that they are barely enough for a village. It has been moved to three or four locations, always retreating because of the unsure loyalty of the Indians, who are not under *encomiendas*, although they are subjects of the Spanish nation. It has a Vicar of the Bishop, a parish priest and a sacristan, whose salary is paid by His Majesty, as is the case everywhere else.

CUMANACOA

94.   Otherwise called San Baltazar de los Arias, [Cumanacoa] is founded upon a very fertile valley twelve leagues from the land of Cumaná. It has been set up many times, but never with success, and therefore, it must be just called a

Cumaná, fundada en un Valle muy fértil. De muchas veces que se le ha dado principio, jamás lo ha tenido, de suerte que se le pudo dar título de lugar, sin haberse asentado salario para los Ministros de su Iglesia a quien sirve algún religioso que va solo a decir Misa, sin más autoridad de administrar Sacramentos.

He presumably could hear confessions and give out communion, but for marriages and baptisms the people would have to go to the parish church. This sort of information was important to Baroque Catholicism because it was a measure of the success of the foundation. The more numerous the inhabitants the more sure their settlement, the more likely it was that they would establish their own parish: such was not the case here.

ISLA TRINIDAD.

95.   Hase esta Isla, cincuenta leguas a barlovento de la Margarita, en las bocas que los hidrógrafos llaman de los Dragos, frontera de las corrientes del famoso río de U[O]rinoco, que juzgando estrecho arcaduz para su desagüe una boca, se abalanza por sesenta y dos en el mar, con distancia de sesenta leguas de la primera a la última. Tiene la Isla de longitud poco más o menos, cuarenta leguas, y poco menos de latitud. Tendida de la forma de un corazón, población antigua de españoles y con el riesgo e inquietud de sus naturales, y vecindad de las naciones del Norte, que diversas veces han asistido en ella con pueblos y castillos formados; no ha levantado cabeza a la altura, que lo fértil y cómodo de su terreno, pudiera haber logrado; pero resistiendo a estas y otras muchas calamidades, se conserva hoy con número de cien vecinos, su parroquial con tres o cuatro sacerdotes, y un convento de San Francisco, cuya pobreza muestra bien la de esta sagrada religión y poco caudal de los vecinos.

SANTO THOMÉ DE GUAYANA.

96.   Está en la tierra firme, sesenta leguas el río de U[O]rinoco arriba; esta en sus riberas. Tiene estendidísimas provincias, pero mal sugetas, y apenas conocidas. Esta poblada de infinitas naciones de indios pero de pocos españoles, habiendo sido sepultura de muchos, conducidos a este rincón del mundo por las noticias de una mentira con que los han paladeado sus naturales, pintándoles una anchurosa laguna entre unos cerros, con una Isla en medio, poblada de gente vestida, con gran numero de ganados y tanta cantidad de oro, que a su capitán o Rey todos los días, después de untado con un betún, lo asperxan todo con polvos del oro, que con facilidad sacan en aquel sitio, por cuya causa han venido a llamarse estos retiros del mundo las provincias del Dorado, y lo peor es, que habiéndose

village. It has no stated salary for the ministry of its church, which is served by a friar who simply goes there to say Mass, with no authority to administer the sacraments.

The ISLAND of TRINIDAD

95.   This Island lies fifty leagues to the windward of Margarita, by the river-mouths which hydrographers call "the Dragons," across from the currents of the famous Orinoco River, which, judging one mouth to be too narrow an outlet for its drainage, rushes into the sea through sixty-two of them, with a distance of seventy leagues from the first to the last. This Island has a length of forty leagues, more or less, and nearly the same width. It spreads out in the shape of a heart, and is an old Spanish settlement which has not risen to the level that it might have achieved because of its fertile and convenient land. This is because of the danger and restlessness of its natives, and the vicinity of the Northern nations [*English and Dutch* – Ed.], who on various occasions have settled there with formal towns and

> Trinidad was to be conquered by the British in 1797, and although English culture and language were installed, vestiges of the long Spanish colonial period are evident everywhere.

forts. But despite these and other calamities it still has managed to have as many as a hundred *vecinos*, a parish church with three or four priests, and a Franciscan friary whose poverty well shows forth both the poverty of that sacred order and the scant wealth of the *vecinos*.

SANTO THOMÉ DE GUAYANA

96.   This is on the mainland, sixty leagues up the Orinoco River, on the river's banks. It has very widespread territories, but is badly colonized and barely known. It is populated by an infinite number of Indian nations, but [only] by a few Spaniards. It has been the grave of many, who were led to this corner of the world after hearing a deceitful report. The natives have enticed their palates, painting for them a wide lagoon surrounded by hills with an island in the middle of it populated by clothed people, with abundant cattle. [They say] they have such a quantity of gold that every day they cover their captain or king with pitch and then sprinkle him all over with gold dust which they easily gather there. On this account, these backwoods of the world have come to be called the Provinces of the Gilded One [*Provincias del Dorado*]. And the worst part of all is that numerous expeditions have come from many directions to search for this implau-

hecho para este descubrimiento, entradas por diversas partes, a buscar este imposible con las mismas guías que lo testificaban, y muerte de los mas que iban a ellas ni el escarmiento de los *muchos* sucesos ni el poco o ningún efecto que han surtido, han dado lugar al desengaño en que hasta hoy los tiene esta patarata.

> This practice of ritually adorning a man with gold dust created the legend of the *Dorado*, "the guilded one." Hearing of abundant gold in the Americas, the popular imagination entertained the notion that the treasure had come from Spain, based on the idea that seven bishops had hidden the gold from invading Moors in 1150 when Mérida had been conquered, perhaps using it to build new cities in the Americas. By 1647, this tale had been discounted.

97.   La población es sola una, y sus vecinos pocos, y aunque tienen encomiendas de indios, solo les sirven para sembrar maíz, que comer y algún tabaco, que siendo del mejor de las Indias, suele malogrársele por falta de bajeles y merchantes, que rara vez suben aquel puerto, infestado de piratas diversas veces, una de las cuales no dió lugar su asalto a que retirasen la Custodia del Santísimo Sacramento, que con sacrílego desacuerdo llevaron a depositar a un lugar cincuenta leguas de este, para cuyo desempeño se aprestó gente y hicieron prevenciones que por justos juicios se malograron, sin poder ejecutarlas (castigo quizá del poco cuidado si es que fue culpable) que pusieron en reservarla cuando debían hacerlo.

98.   Tiene su parroquial con dos clérigos, y un convento de San Francisco que tenía, pereció en una de estas invasiones y aunque la mies es mucha y los operarios pocos, no convida a que haya más, el poco fruto que se ha esperimentado en los indios, porque su natural nunca les ha inclinado a tener siquiera alguna falsa religión de idolatría, encarnizados muchos de ellos en la voraz y nefanda carnicería de carne humana, haciendo armadillas por mar y escuadrones por tierra, solo a título de comerse unos a otros. ¡O piedad divina! que insultos no ha perpetrado la temeridad humana, pues este que al natural horror dificulta imposible, lo ha ejecutado por no reservarse a ninguno, cuando a lo rapante y canino de los demás animales no son escepción de su voracidad los de su misma especie.

ISLA DE SAN MARTIN.

99.   Es una de las que, llaman de barlovento. Quitósela al Holandés, España, y fundó en ella un presidio cerrado para prohibirle sus salinas, cuya esterilidad no ha sufrido mas población que la del Castillo y ese por evitar gastos y otros in-

sibility, guided by the very persons who claimed to have witnessed it. It has resulted in the death of most of those who went in these expeditions, but neither the bitter experience of the ill results nor the little effect (or none) which they have produced, have led to dissuading those who to this day remain in the toils of this ridiculous fancy.

Nothing remains of this settlement. The Guayanas on the South American coastline between Venzuela and Brazil, were divided into three jurisdictions after being taken from the rule of Spain and Portugal. Surinam has been Dutch since 1616; Guyana was formerly known as British Guiana and is an independent nation today; French Guiana, taken from the Dutch in 1667, is an overseas *Départment* of France and was once the location of the penal colony called "Devil's Island."

97.   There is only one town, and the *vecinos* are few, and, although they have Indians in *encomienda*, they are only good for planting maize for them to eat and some tobacco, which, while it is the best in the Indies, is usually spoiled for lack of ships and merchants. They rarely sail to that harbor, which has often been infested by pirates. On one of these occasions the pirates' attack gave no chance to take away the monstrance of the Blessed Sacrament. In sacrilegious frenzy they [the pirates] carried it away to a place fifty leagues away from this one. A troop was made ready for its rescue, but the plans made could not be carried out. By God's just designs, they came to nothing and [were] possibly a punishment for the little care — assuming this was their fault — that they had taken to hide it [the monstrance with the Blessed Sacrament] when they had still been able.

98.   The town has its parish church with two clerics. A Franciscan friary which it also had was ruined in one of these pirate attacks. Although the harvest is great and the laborers few, (Matt. 9:37) the little fruit that has been rendered among the Indians does not attract more [missionaries]. The local Indians' temperament has never inclined them even to having a false religion of idolatry, and many of them are fiercely given to the voracious and unspeakable devouring of human flesh, setting up flotillas of canoes by sea and bands of men by land for the single purpose of eating one another. Oh, Divine Mercy! What insults has human temerity not perpetrated on you, since this one, which our natural disgust renders so difficult as to make it impossible, has here been put into practice so that none would be un-committed, when even the rapine and fierce voracity of the other animals makes an exception for those of its own species!

convenientes, esta mandada retirar su infantería y demoler su fortificación, como se hizo por principios de Enero de 648, con cinco navíos que envió de Puerto-Rico, su Gobernador y capitán general Don Francisco de la Riva Agüero, que llegaron a dicha Isla víspera de año nuevo, hallándola apestada, y a toda prisa embarcaron la artillería y municiones demoliendo las fortificaciones, y se hicieron a la vela, y llegaron a este puerto, en dos días de navegación, a los 20 de dicho mes de Enero, habiendo muerto más de cien personas de la dicha peste, y así mismo hundídose uno de los cinco navíos en que perecieron mas de sesenta personas, escapando seis milagrosamente sobre unos palos; perdiéndose a las nueve de la noche más de cinco leguas de tierra. Atribuyese este desgraciado fin a estar, su Gobernador excomulgado por ciertos agravios que hizo al Cura y Vicario y a otro clérigo.

100.   Este dicho año de 648, por Febrero, la peste que cesó luego que llegó la gente apestada del presidio desmantelado de San Martín, con las plegarias, misas y rogativas que se hicieron, teniendo descubierto el Santísimo Sacramento, volvió con tanta fuerza, que murieron seiscientas personas usando Dios de su misericordia, que nadie murió sin Sacramentos; y habiendo en este tiempo salido un barco para la isla Margarita, se avisa, que les llevó la peste, y ha muerto mucha gente.

In the passage below (#101–102) Torres y Vargas speaks favorably of Bishop López de Haro, undercutting the hypothesis that there was animosity between the two clerics.

It is common to refer to the Bishop and his diocese as husband and wife, and the pastoral ring a bishop wears is a symbol of his being married to the Church of his diocese.

"*Novenario*" was a series of nine Masses said or sung for a deceased person after the funeral, or, as in this case, after receiving notification of the death.

See Glossary.

The canon's choir was towards the middle of the cathedral, not in a loft at the back as more modern churches.

---

101.   En este ano de 648, murió, por Agosto, el Señor Obispo de este obispado, Don Fray Damián López de Haro, en donde estaba entendiendo en la visita espiritual, que por corregir algunas cosas, que necesitaban de remedio y defender su esposa la Iglesia de la Ciudad de Cumaná, padeció mucho por los enemigos poderosos que se le levantaron y referiré un caso notable que sucedió, estando haciendo sus honras en esta Catedral, de que se ha tornado testimonio, y fue así:

The ISLAND of ST. MARTIN

99.   [The Island of St. Martin] is one of those that are called Windward Islands. Spain took it from the Dutch and founded a closed fort there to keep them from its salt pans, whose sterile soil has not allowed more population than the garrison of the castle. Even that (for the avoidance of expense and other inconveniences) has been ordered to be demolished, and its infantry taken away. This was done at the beginning of January of [1]648 by five ships sent from Puerto Rico by its Governor and Captain-General, Don Francisco de la Riva Agüero. These arrived at this Island on New Year's Eve, and found it plague-stricken, so they hurried to put on board the cannon and ammunition and to demolish the fortifications. They sailed away, arriving at this harbor after two days' sailing, on January 20th of that year, after more than a hundred persons had died of that plague. Furthermore, one of the five ships was wrecked, in which more than sixty

> This was the Bubonic Plague or Black Death.

persons perished. Only six escaped by a miracle, holding on to some planks. The ship was lost at 9 PM, more than five leagues away from land. This miserable end is attributed to the fact that the Island's Governor was excommunicated because of some wrongs inflicted on the parish priest and Bishop's Vicar, and on another cleric.

100.   The plague, which had ceased because of the prayers, Masses and processions that had been made with the Blessed Sacrament exposed, came back in February of that same year of [1]648 when the plague-stricken people arrived from the dismantled fort of Saint Martin. The plague returned with such force that six hundred persons died, but God showed his mercy in that no one died without having received the Sacraments. And as a ship sailed at that time for the Island of Margarita, we are informed that it took the plague there, and many people have died.

101.   In this same year of [1]648, around August [24th] the Lord Bishop of this diocese, Don Fray Damián López de Haro, died there, where he was making the Pastoral Visitation. He suffered much there at the hands of powerful enemies that rose up against him because he had corrected certain things that needed to be remedied, and had defended his Bride, the Church of the City of Cumaná. And I will now tell of a notable thing that occurred when we were doing his funeral obsequies in this Cathedral [of San Juan], of which event a witnessed attestation has been written, and it was as follows: On October 21st of that year of

que estando a los veinte y uno de Octubre de dicho año de 1648, diciéndose la primera Misa del novenario, entró una paloma montaraz en la Iglesia, y se puso sobre el coro, en medio de un tirante que cae sobre la silla obispal, estando cantando la música, después de la epístola, el verso, *"in memoria eterna erit iustus abanditione non timebit."* La cual se estuvo allí, hasta que se acabó la Misa, y salieron del coro a cantar el responso, donde estaba el túmulo al lado del Evangelio, junto al Altar mayor, donde es el entierro de los Señores Obispos; y entonces, dió un vuelo pasando por sobre el túmulo y se estuvo allí cuatro días naturales, hasta el sábado después de la Misa del novenario, sin comer cosa alguna. De esto hubo general regocijo en la Iglesia, teniéndolo por buen anuncio de que estaba en carrera de salvación el alma de dicho Señor Obispo.

102.   De la Margarita se avisa, hay hecha información como el Señor Obispo profetizó su muerte, y por carta de su Gobernador se avisó al Canónigo Don Diego de Torres y Vargas. También que se hizo información con mucho número de testigos, que le vieron muchas veces llamar los pájaros y venírsele a las manos. Esta información se remite a España en el patache, y en ella va inserto el testimonio del suceso de la paloma.

> The information below (#103–130) was apparently added to include items that the court historian had requested. They are added without much literary style and in an abbreviated way, suggesting they were written in a short amount of time.

103.   **En esta relación, van algunas cosas que el Señor Secretario Juan Diez de la Calle y el maestro Gil González, avisaron iba falta la que llegó a sus manos, de esta Isla de Puerto Rico, y de los anexos a este obispado.**

104.   Puerto-Rico y Santo Domingo fueron hechas Catedrales, el año 1511 a 8 de agosto, y sufragáneas al Arzobispado de Sevilla hasta el año de 1545, en 31 de enero, que se hizo Metrópoli Santo Domingo.

> That is, an Archdiocese, with Puerto Rico and the other dioceses in the Caribbean area as its suffragans. The "Metrópoli" referred to is the Archdiocese of Santo Domingo.

105.   El escudo de armas fue dado a Puerto-Rico por los Reyes Católicos el año de 1511, siendo Procurador, un vecino llamado Pedro Moreno. Son: un cordero blanco con su banderilla colorada, sobre un libro, y todo sobre una isla verde, que es la de Puerto-Rico, y por los lados, una F. y una I., que quiere decir:

1648, as the first Mass of the *novenario* was being celebrated, a wild dove flew into the church and perched over the [canons'] choir, upon a beam that stands above the bishop's throne, after the Epistle, as the musicians were chanting the verse ["The righteous man shall be eternally remembered; an evil report he shall not fear" Psalm 111 (112):7. *From the Gradual of the Requiem Mass* —Tr.]. This dove stayed there until the end of the Mass, when the canons went out of the choir to chant the Responsorial at the catafalque which was on the Gospel side, where the burial vault of the Bishops is located. At that point the dove flew over the catafalque and remained on that spot for four natural days, until the Saturday after the Mass of the *novenario*, all this time without eating a thing. This caused general rejoicing in the church, being taken as a good omen that the soul of the Lord Bishop was on the road to salvation.

102.   News has been received from Margarita that there is a written document witnessing to the fact that the Bishop had prophesied his own death, and this information was sent in a letter from the Governor [of Margarita] to Canon Don Diego de Torres y Vargas. A document has also been written, with a great number of witnesses, to the effect that he was many times seen to call the birds and they flew to perch on his hands. These documents are being sent to Spain in the mail boat and inserted in them is the attestation of the incident of the dove.

103.   **The following report covers certain points which the Honorable Secretary Juan Díez de la Calle and Master Gil González, pointed out were missing in the report that they received on this Island of Puerto Rico and the regions annexed to its diocese.**

104.   Puerto-Rico and Santo Domingo were made Cathedral cities on August 8, 1511, and were suffragan to the Archdiocese of Seville until January 31, 1545, when Santo Domingo became a Metropolitan See.

105.   Its coat of arms was granted to Puerto Rico by Ferdinand and Isabella in the year 1511, when the City's procurator was a *vecino* called Pedro Moreno. The arms are: A white lamb with a red banner sitting on a book, and all of this upon a green Island, which is the Island of Puerto Rico, and on either side of it, an F and an I, which stand for "Ferdinand" and "Isabella," the Catholic Sovereigns who granted the arms. These are still seen [embroidered] on the Royal Standard of orange-colored damask with which this City was won, and, as Antonio de Herrera says in his *General Chronicle of the Indies*, the King and Queen made this City equal to the Island of Española in all privileges and grants.

Fernando e Isabel: los Reyes Católicos que se las dieron, y hoy se conserva en el estandarte Real que es de damasco naranjado, con que se ganó esta Ciudad, y como dice Antonio de Herrera en su "Crónica general de las Indias", hicieron a esta Ciudad los dichos Señores Reyes igual en todos privilegios y mercedes a la Isla Española. Las armas de la Catedral son: un cordero sobre un islote, con su banderilla, con estas letras alrededor: *Joannes est nomen eius.*

106.   Gozan en ella sus capitulares de Jueces adjuntos, por costumbre inmemorial, y aunque el Obispo Don Juan López Agurto quiso interrumpirles la costumbre, apelaron a la Metrópoli, con que quedo ejecutado en favor de dichos capitulares, por haberse hallado gozaban de ellos antes del Concilio Tridentino.

> This long-standing custom explains why Puerto Rico was not in compliance with all of Trent's decrees.

107.   La dotación de los cien ducados de renta para el catedrático de Gramática, dejo un vecino de esta Ciudad llamado Francisco Ruiz, año de 1589. El general donde se enseña Gramática, y el hosario de los difuntos, están juntos y contiguos con la Catedral, y el año de †1641, siendo catedrático Don José de Jarava, capital de infantería que fue de este presidio, el año siguiente de †1640, puso estos dos disticos sobre la puerta.
   Hic habitant Musae hic servant sua pignora pareae.
   Vivere disce, puer, dogmata disce mori

> Puerto Rico's first school was established in the cathedral.
>
> "Distich" a pithy statement of morality.
>   "*disce*" not "*difce*"

108.   Por cédula de 20 de mayo de mil seiscientos trece, mandó Su Magestad se le diese silla en todos los actos públicos al lado de la del Gobernador, al Capitán y Sargento mayor García de Torres y capitanes de infantería, y no han querido obedecerla. Los Gobernadores hoy se sientan en frente de la Ciudad, al lado del Evangelio, en un escaño como se hace en la Havana.

> In a status-conscious society, where one sat for official events established the rank of personal importance. Torres y Vargas uses the existing practice in the cathedral to signal that the king had offered recognition to his father by awarding a "higher seat."

The arms of the Cathedral are: a Lamb on an islet with its banner, and around it the words: *Joannes est nomen eius* ["John is his name," Luke I:63].

Coats of arms were important because they signified prestige. Torres y Vargas came from a military family where such approbation was prized.

See the explanation posted for paragraph #11 above, explaining Torres y Vargas' confusion about the seal for the city and the coat of arms for the island.

106.   The members of its Chapter enjoy the position of Adjunct Judges by immemorial custom, and although Bishop Don Juan López Agurto wanted to interrupt this custom, they appealed to the Metropolis which found in favor of the Chapter, because it was discovered that they enjoyed this privilege before the Council of Trent.

107.   The endowment of a hundred ducats' income for the Professor of Grammar was left [in his will] by a *vecino* of this City called Francisco Ruiz, in the year 1589. The common room where grammar is taught, and also the ossuary of the dead are next to each other, and joined to the Cathedral. When the professor was Don José de Jarava in the year †1641, formerly Captain of the Infantry of this garrison, he placed these distichs over the door the following year, †1640:

> *Hic habitant Musae; hic servant sua pignora parcae.*
> *Vivere disce, puer, dogmata disce mori.*
> [Here live the Muses; here the Fates keep their pledges/tokens
> Boy, learn how to live (well), by these teachings learn how to die (well)].

In the 17th century this meant Latin Grammar; knowledge of Latin was essential for a career in the Church or any kind of university studies. –Tr.

†The dates seem inverted: 1641 for 1640—Tr.

108.   By an order of May 20, 1613, His Majesty commanded that the Captain and Sergeant-Major García de Torres and the Captains of the infantry should be given chairs next to the Governor's in all public functions, but the local authorities have not chosen to obey this. The Governors sit across from the City Council, on the Gospel side, on a special pew, as is done in Havana.

The next two paragraphs (#109–110) remark on items on the island that have historical significance. The cannon comes from the decisive Battle of Lepanto off the coast of Greece on October 7, 1571, which broke Turkish control of the Mediterranean, a date now celebrated as the Feast of Our Lady of the Rosary. The silver Pyx (See "Custodia" in Glossary) was a gift of the Emperor and is proof that Puerto Rico had merited royal attention. It is in the San Juan Cathedral's collection even today.

109.   En la fuerza de San Felipe del Morro de esta Ciudad, hay una pieza rabona con cuarenta libras de calibre, que tiene las armas del gran Turco, que se dice era canon de Crujia de la galeaza Real que rindió Don Juan de Austria, en la batalla naval. Envió la el Señor Rey Felipe 2°, que en su tiempo se dio principio a esta fuerza.

110.   En la Catedral hay una Custodia de plata, en que se lleva el Santisimo Sacramento a los enfermos, que es de muy primorosa obra, la cual la envió el Señor Emperador Carlos 5°, con una cruz que habiéndose quebrado, no ha habido aquí quien la pueda aderezar. A la parroquial de la villa de San Germán, de las cosas que se recojieron, envió otra cruz de estremada hechura que hoy tiene.

111.   En tiempo del Gobernador Sancho Ochoa de Castro, sucedió que a un islote que esta frente de la boca del río de Toa, que dista por mar dos leguas de la Ciudad, venían infinidad de palomas a nidar y sacar sus crías por cierto tiempo del año, con que los vecinos cojian gran cantidad de ellas; y el Gobernador pareciéndole que esto seda de provecho para Su Magestad, mandó con pregón general que ningún vecino las cojiese en aquella parte, y desde entonces hasta hoy, que ha más de cuarenta años, no han vuelto más las palomas al islote, mostrando Dios en su liberal mano, que quiere gozen todos de sus beneficios, y casos semejantes han sucedido en otras muchas partes de las Indias.

112.   El Gobernador Don Iñigo de la Mota Sarmiento, presidente que fue de Panamá, antes de acabar el primer año de su presidencia, murió en Puerto-Belo estando para hacer un templo. Dixose que con sospechas de veneno fue su muerte, por ser muy celoso del servicio del Rey Nuestro Señor. En esta Catedral como a bienhechor, se le hicieron honras, y fue de todo el pueblo muy sentida su muerte. He oído al padre fray Jacinto Martín, padre de los Dominicos en esta provincia de Santa Cruz, y natural de esta Ciudad, que llevó por su confesor, que era Virgen.

109.   In the castle of San Felipe del Morro in this City there is a short piece of artillery with a caliber of forty pounds that has the coat of arms of the Grand Turk [engraved on it]. It is said that this was the gangway cannon of the Royal Galleass which Don Juan de Austria was forced to surrender in the naval battle [of Lepanto]. His Majesty King Philip II sent it, for it was in his reign that this castle was begun.

110.   In the Cathedral there is a silver pyx in which the Blessed Sacrament is taken to the sick; it is of exquisite workmanship, and was sent as a gift by Emperor Charles V, although with a broken cross that no one here has been able to fix. He also sent the parish of San Germán (out of the things that were gathered) another cross of outstanding workmanship which that parish has to this day.

111.   In the days of Governor Sancho Ochoa de Castro it happened that an infinite number of pigeons came to nest and bring up their fledglings in an islet that is in front of the mouth of the Toa River, about two leagues from the City by sea, so that the *vecinos* of the City caught a great many of them. The Governor, supposing that this would be of some profit to His Majesty, ordered by a general proclamation that no *vecino* should catch pigeons in that area. But since that time (more than forty years ago) the pigeons have never come back to that islet, and in that God showed his liberal hand, which desires that all should enjoy his gifts. Similar cases have occurred in many parts of the Indies.

The entry #111 reflects the Baroque fascination with the marvelous quality of coincidence because it always suggested the presence of God, working in history. The upper classes showed their piety by making generous gifts to the church (#112–#113).

---

112.   Governor Don Íñigo de la Mota Sarmiento, who [later] was President of [the Audiencia of] Panama, died in Puerto-Bello before he finished the first year of his presidency, when he was about to build a church. They say that his death was under suspicion of poisoning, because he was very zealous about the service of the King our lord. Obsequies were celebrated for his soul in this Cathedral, since he had been its benefactor, and his death was greatly mourned by all the people. I have heard from Father Fray Jacinto Martín, a priest of the Dominicans of this Province of the Holy Cross and a native of this City, whom he took with him as his confessor, that the Governor had kept his virginity.

> The Antilles Province of the Dominican Order was headquartered in Santo Domingo. Celibacy for a layman was considered a sign of great piety. Although the seal of confession prevents communication about sins, it was common that confessors — here understood as a spiritual director — would disclose the sanctity of an individual after death.

113.   El Gobernador Don Agustín de Silva, en los seis meses no cabales que vivió, hizo a sus espensas en el hospital de Nuestra Señora de la Concepción, dos altares colaterales al de Nuestra Señora, y en el uno colocó un Santo Cristo muy devoto que indecente estaba en la Sacristía, y en el otro a Señora Santa Catalina mártir, de quien era mártir, de quien era muy devoto, adornando este Altar con un retablo que le costo 600 ducados. Había ofrecido a los religiosos de Señor San Francisco dar principio a la obra de su convento con el año 1642, y cuando murió que fue por Navidad de 1641, trataba de salir a pedir limosna por el lugar, deseando imitar y seguir los pasos de su antecesor Don Iñigo de la Mota Sarmiento, en las obras que hizo en

> The phrase "*de quien era martir, de quien era muy devoto*" makes no sense because he was **not** killed for his devotion to her.
>
> A typesetter probably duplicated the word *martir* in the line about the saint in the line with *devoto* about the governor and repeated the phrase instead of substituting for it.—Tr.

los templos; que en estas partes de las Indias, un Gobernador sin poner de su casa mas que el cuidado y solicitud basta eso para que se hagan grandes cosas y se allanen muchas dificultades, como se echo bien de ver en la obra de la Iglesia mayor de esta Ciudad y del convento de Santo Domingo, en la relación antecedente referida; que teniéndose por casi imposibles, el hacerse por lo pobre de sus rentas y de esta tierra, se hicieron con gran facilidad obras tan Reales, tomándolas a su cargo el Gobernador Don Iñigo de la Mota Sarmiento.

114.   Dicho Gobernador Don Agustín de Silva, era grande ingeniero y arquitecto, y así estaba por orden de Su Magestad, fortificando a Gibraltar, cuando le hicieron merced de este gobierno y del de Cumaná, para que escojiese, y eligió este por ser el de mas reputación de las Indias, como lo dice S. M. en sus Reales cédulas referidas en el primero pliego de la relación, que llegó, sus fechas en agosto de 1643 y en mayo de 1645.

> *Cofradías*, literally "confraternities" were important to Baroque Catholicism because they linked prayer and good works together for lay persons, under the guidance and instruction by the Tridentine clergy. The clerical influence was more pronounced in the Baroque than it had been in pre-reformation times. The vitality of a local diocese was often measured by the number of *cofradías* and the total membership of each. See Glossary.

113.   In the less than six months that he lived [here] Governor Don Agustín de Silva paid out of his own pocket for the building of two side-altars in the [chapel of the] Hospital of Our Lady of the Conception, flanking the [main] altar of Our Lady; in one of them he placed a very moving Crucifix which had been kept indecorously in the sacristy, and in the other he placed [an image of] my lady Saint Catherine the Martyr, to whom he had a great devotion, adorning this altar with a *retablo* that cost him 600 ducats. He had offered to the Friars of my lord Saint Francis that he would begin the building of their convent in the year 1642, and when he died, which was around Christmas of 1641, he was planning to go out into the City begging for alms [for the building fund], wishing to imitate and follow in the footsteps of his predecessor Don Íñigo de la Mota Sarmiento in the repairs and extensions he made in churches. In these parts of the Indies, a Governor does not have to do much more than show how some care and solicitude, and that is enough for great things to be achieved and for many difficulties to be smoothed over. This was evident in the refurbishing of the Cathedral Church of this City and the convent of Saint Dominic, as told in the original report. The things that needed to be done were believed to be practically impossible, because of the poverty of the endowments in this land. Yet they were done magnificently once Governor Don Íñigo de la Mota Sarmiento took personal charge of them.

> Another reason for the dedication of this altar may have been the fact that the Hospital is next door to *La Fortaleza*, the Governors' residence, into which the *Ermita* of Saint Catherine had been incorporated, which is still known officially as *Palacio de Santa Catalina.*

114.   This Governor Don Agustín de Silva was a great engineer and architect, and as such he was fortifying Gibraltar by order of His Majesty when he was granted the governorship of this City or of Cumaná, to choose whichever of the two he preferred. He chose this one because it was the governorship with the greatest reputation in the Indies, as His Majesty says in the decrees we mentioned in the first part of this report, and which arrived in August of 1643 and May of 1645.

115.   In this City there are twelve confraternities. In the Cathedral there is the Confraternity of the Blessed Sacrament, the Confraternity of the Souls in Purgatory, that of Our Lady of Mount Carmel, that of Our Lady of Altagracia, that of my lord Saint Anthony, that of my lord Saint Peter, that of the Sweet Name of

115.   Hay en esta Ciudad doce cofradías. En la Iglesia mayor la del Santísimo Sacramento, la de las Animas del Purgatorio, la de Nuestra Señora del Carmen, de Nuestra Señora de Alta gracia, de Señor San Antonio, de Señor San Pedro, del dulce nombre de Jesús y de San Miguel; y en el hospital, la de Nuestra Señora del Rosario, de Nuestra Señora de la Soledad y la de la Vera Cruz; y en el Convento de Señor San Francisco, la del Señor San Diego. Todas son pobres pero las que se sirven con algún lucimiento son la de Nuestra Señora del Rosario, la de Nuestra Señora de la Concepción, la de Nuestra Señora de la Soledad, la del Santísimo Sacramento y la de las Animas.

> The confraternity of the Conception was not listed as one of the twelve above; it may have met in the Hospital, of the same name, but it could also have been located in the Cathedral, or in the Franciscan convent, since that Order was particularly devoted to the Immaculate Conception. See Glossary.

116.   La de Santísimo Sacramento, tiene veinte y cuatro hermanos, los doce eclesiásticos que con su compañero secular, cada dos a su costa, el tercer domingo del mes que les toca, celebran la fiesta, con Misa, procesión y sermón, teniendo descubierto el Santísimo Sacramento, y asistiendo todos los hermanos con sus cirios encendidos, *procurando unos a otros aventajarse en su fiesta* en el adorno de la Iglesia, música, olores, predicador y flores que se van regando por donde pasa el Santísimo Sacramento. Los principales estatutos es, celebrar todas las fiestas del Santísimo Sacramento, a que acuden como arriba esta dicho, y que piden limosna los dos hermanos todos los jueves del mes que les toca hacer la fiesta, para que la cofradía pague a los sacerdotes que van cantando y llevan el guión, varas de palio y incensario cuando va el Santísimo Sacramento a visitar los enfermos. Tiene prefecto a quien se jura de obedecer, mayordomo, diputados y secretario que se elige todos los años.

> It was the custom in Spanish churches to carry an equivalent of the Royal Standard before "His Divine Majesty," as the Sacrament was often called; this would be emblazoned with Eucharistic symbols instead of the Royal Arms. The staff would often be covered with silver, and in many places the "flag" would also be a sheet of silver shaped like a banner.
>
> When the Sacrament was taken to the sick or the dying it was the custom to carry it in solemn form, with canopy, incense, etc. Persons who met this procession were expected to fall on their knees in the street until it had passed, and to join it with a lit candle if they were free to do so. In Puerto Rico this lasted until it was discouraged by the American governors.

Jesus, and that of Saint Michael. In the hospital, there is the Confraternity of Our Lady of the Rosary, that of Our Lady of Solitude [the Sorrowful Mother], and that of the True Cross. In the convent of my lord Saint Francis there is the Confraternity of my lord Saint Diego. All of them are poor, but the ones which are served with some distinction are the Confraternity of Our Lady of the Rosary, that of Our Lady of the Conception, that of Our Lady of Solitude, that of the Blessed Sacrament and that of the Souls in Purgatory.

116.   The Confraternity of the Blessed Sacrament has twenty-four brothers, twelve clerics each of whom, together with his lay counterpart, takes care on the month which is assigned to them of the expenses of the feast that is celebrated every month on the third Sunday. This celebration consists of a Mass, a procession and a sermon, during all of which the Blessed Sacrament is exposed [in a Monstrance], and all the brethren of the Confraternity attend this feast with lighted candles in their hands. Each pair of brethren try to outdo the others on the feast that falls to their turn, in terms of the adornment of the church, the music, the incense, the preacher chosen, and the flowers that are strewn [on the street] where the Blessed Sacrament is to be carried [in procession]. The principal statute [of this

> In section #116, Torres y Vargas apparently expects all readers to understand that cofradías had to be composed of at least 24 members; 12 clergymen and 12 laymen; that way there would be one cleric and one layman to take charge for the events of each month.

confraternity] is to celebrate all the feasts of the Blessed Sacrament, which they attend as mentioned above, and two of the brethren ask for alms around the City every Thursday of the month whose feast is allotted to them, so that the Confraternity can pay the priests who do the chanting from the money collected. They [the brothers] bear the Standard, the rods of the canopy that is carried over the Sacrament, and the censer when the Blessed Sacrament is taken to the sick. They have a Prefect whom they swear to obey, a Steward, Councilors, and a Secretary, who are elected every year.

117.   The Confraternity of the Souls [in Purgatory] also has a brotherhood of twenty-four brethren, but with no rule that half must be clergy [and half laymen]. They celebrate a service for the Souls in Purgatory on the third Monday of each month with two of the brethren in charge of it [each month], with a [Requiem] Mass, a procession and a sermon; a catafalque is set up in the middle of the church upon two steps, decorated with 48 candles and many *bulas de difuntos*. All of this is at the expense of the two brethren who are in charge of that month's

117.   La cofradía de las Animas, tiene otra hermandad de veinte y cuatro hermanos, en que no hay el orden de que sean por mitad eclesiásticos, celebran fiesta todos los terceros lunes del mes por las animas del Purgatorio, cada dos hermanos, con Misa, procesión y sermón, puesto un túmulo en medio de la Iglesia con dos gradas, adornado de 48 luces y muchas bulas de difuntos, a costa todo de los dos hermanos que hacen la fiesta, y la cofradía reparte cera entre los hermanos y cófrades para la Misa y procesión y piden limosna dichos dos hermanos, todos los lunes del mes que les toca, para pagar las demás Misas y procesiones que se dicen y hacen los demás lunes del año, y un día después que muere cualquier hermano, se le dice su Misa cantada.

The narrative here returns to the traveler or navigational source to detail the rivers in Puerto Rico and some of its fruits. The "*naranjos agrios*" or "bitter orange trees" produced fruit (*naranja*) not usually eaten except as marmelade or by animals; the sweet oranges people preferred to eat came from China. Today in Puerto Rico, people often refer to the naranja or orange as "*una china*," meaning a sweet orange.

---

118.   *Ríos*.— Tiene esta Isla 26 ríos principales que salen al mar sin algunas quebradas, y los ríos que salen a la parte del Norte son los más caudalosos como el río Guadalete que sale al punto de Santa Maria en España. Los cuales son diez y se llaman como se sigue: Rió grande, Luisa, Puerto nuevo, Gu[B]ayamón, Toa, Sebuco, Manatí, Arecibo; y en el Aguada hay dos ríos, el uno no tiene nombre, el otro se llama Calvache; y así mesmo dos quebradas sin nombre, en espacio de una legua, que hace una ensenada, *y aquí es donde hacen agua y toman refresco las flotas de Nueva España* y algunas veces galeones, por ser tan acomodado el sitio, que en las mismas bocas de los ríos y quebradas esta dulce el agua. Este paraje esta a sotavento de Puerto-Rico 18 leguas, y es tan ameno y lleno de muchas arboledas y árboles frutales, y especial de naranjos agrios y dulces y limones, que los navegantes lo alaban diciendo que no han visto cosa más deleitable en el mundo, que la naturaleza echó allí el resto. La palabra Aguada en lengua de indios según Gómara en su *General historia* hablando de este sitio, quiere decir jardin.

According to the Royal Academy, in Spanish the word "*Aguada*" means "A place where there is drinkable water, and which is convenient for provisioning oneself with it," while "*hacer aguada un buque*" means "a ship provisioning itself with potable water." This would seem the more probable origin for the place's name.

Since the language of the Taínos had many words with the "gua" sound, "Aguada" could be the Spanish approximation of what they heard in the foreign tongue, even if the natives did not refer to water.

celebration, and the Confraternity gives out wax [candles] to its brethren and members for use in the Mass and procession. The two brethren [*whose turn it is that month* —Tr.] ask for alms every Monday of the month to pay for the Masses and processions which are held on the other Mondays of the year, and also for the Mass, which is sung for each brother of the Confraternity the day after he dies.

> Just as Thursday was considered a special day for honoring the Blessed Sacrament each week, and Saturday was for honoring the Virgin Mary, so Monday was associated with special prayers or the souls in Purgatory.
>
> A bula de difuntos was a sealed papal document granting certain indulgences on behalf of the dead.

118.   *Rivers.*— This Island has 26 principal rivers that flow out into the sea, plus a few brooks. The rivers whose mouths are on the North side are the ones that carry more water, like the Guadalete River which flows out at Puerto de Santa María in Spain. These rivers are ten, and their names are as follows: Río

> The text has *punto de Santa Maria*, which is likely a misprint for "Puerto" or Port. —Tr.
>
> There is no Calvache River in Puerto Rico today, but the Rio Grande of Rincón is fed by a brook with that name.
>
> Aguada was the last place a ship on the way to Spain could fill its casks with fresh water before the Canary Islands, and the first after the Canary Islands for ships sailing from Spain to Veracruz.

Grande, Luisa [Loíza], Puerto Nuevo, Gu[B]ayamón, Toa, Sebuco, Manatí, Arecibo. In Aguada there are two rivers, one of which has no name, and the other is called Calvache; as well as two nameless brooks, all within a league of each other, which make a cove. Here is where the fleets of New Spain take water and fresh provisions, and also some times the galleons, because the place is so convenient that the water is sweet even in the very mouths of the rivers and brooks. This place is 18 leagues to the leeward of Puerto-Rico [*the City of San Juan* — Tr.] and it is so pleasant and full of groves and fruit trees, especially of orange trees (both sweet and bitter) and lemon trees, that sailors praise it saying that they have never seen a more delightful place in the whole world; that here Nature gave everything possible. The word "*aguada*" in the language of the Indians, (as Gómara says in his *General History* speaking about this place) means "a garden." This place is twelve leagues away from the town of San Germán, and is the most fertile land within that town's jurisdiction.

Esta de la villa de San Germán doce leguas, y son las más fértiles tierras de su jurisdicción.

> San Juan and San German were the two original municipalities in the island, and were divided by a diagonal line running from the Northwest to the Southeast. Aguada was on the Northwest end of the San Germán jurisdiction.

119.   A la banda del Oeste, salen los otros tres ríos que son Guaraibo, Mayagüez, Guanaxivos. Este último río pasa por la villa de San German. A la parte del Sur salen otros varios ríos que son los siguientes, Guanica, río de Ponce, Jacagua, río de Coamo, Guayama, Maunabo, Guayanes, Candelero, Jumacao, Cristóbal Alonso, Nagua[bo]u, Río Santiago, y en la ensenada donde sale el río Guanica hay una buena salina de sal. A la parte del Este sale solamente el río Faxardo, dos leguas de la cabeza de San Juan, que así se llama el principio de esta Isla. Estos veinte y seis ríos referidos son los que salen al mar, que sin exageración son más de doscientos los ríos y quebradas que entran en ellos, antes que salgan al mar, por ser la tierra por el medio muy doblada de Serranías.

120.   Tiene la cerca de la Ciudad tres puertas principales, la una al Este que cae a la parte de tierra y se llama de Señor Santiago, con una capilla encima, en que está el glorioso Santo de bulto sobre un caballo de buena escultura, y en ella se celebra Misa en su día y en otros del año. Las armas Reales tiene encima labradas de piedra, y a los lados dos escudos pequeños con las armas del Gobernador Don Iñigo de la Mota Sarmiento, en cuyo tiempo se hizo la cerca y debajo de dichas armas este verso. *"Nisi dominus custodierit civitatem frustra vigilat, qui custodit eam."* La segunda puerta está a la Marina, sobre el Sur, y *es donde los navíos descargan, dan carena y cargan,* por ser lo mas abrigado de los vientos. Llamase de San Justo y Pastor, con capilla encima y armas como la otra, que los Santos estan pintados en lienzo y tiene este letrero. *"¿Dominus mihi adjutor quem timebo?"* La tercera puerta está a la parte del Oeste a la entrada del puerto, donde surjen los navíos luego que entran, llámase de Señor San Juan Bautista. Con capilla y armas como esotras puertas y el Santo en lienzo, de pintura de buena mano. *Celebrase también Misa como en las demás* y la letra que tiene es este verso. *"Benedictus qui venit in nomine domini."*

> **"Puerta de Santiago,"** also known familiarly as Puerta de Tierra, or the "Land Gate;" was about where the Plaza de Colón is now located.
>
> St. James (Santiago) was believed to have appeared on horseback and with a sword to aid the Christian knights during battles fighting larger Moorish armies; for this reason he was invoked as Patron of Spain.

119.   Three rivers come to the sea on the west side of the Island; they are the Guaraibo River [Añasco], the Mayagüez, and the Guanaxivos. This last one runs through the town of San Germán. A few other rivers reach the sea on the South side, which are the Guánica, The River of Ponce [Río Portugués], the Jacagua, the River of Coamo, the Guayama, the Maunabo, the Guayanes, the Candelero, the Jumacao, the Cristóbal Alonso [Antón Ruiz], the Naguau [Naguabo, i.e., the Rio Blanco], Río Santiago, and in the cove at the mouth of the Guánica River there is a good salt pan. The only river that comes to the sea on the east side of the Island is the Faxardo, whose mouth is two leagues from the Cabeza de San Juan, as the first cape of the Island [*as you sail in from Europe* – Tr.] is called. These twenty-six rivers I have enumerated are the ones that open into the sea, for without exaggeration, there are more than two hundred rivers and brooks that flow into these rivers before they enter the sea, because the land in the center of the Island is rippled everywhere with mountain ranges.

120.   The city walls have three principal gates, the first of which is on the east and faces the land, and is called after my lord Saint James. It is crowned by a chapel with a statue of that glorious Saint on a horse, well carved, and Mass is celebrated there on Saint James' Day [July 25th] and on other days during the year. The Royal Arms are carved over the gate, and on either side of them there are two smaller shields with the coat of arms of Governor Don Íñigo de la Mota Sarmiento, in whose time the walls were built, and under these arms this scriptural verse: ["Unless the Lord watch over the city, in vain do those who guard it keep vigil." Psalm 127:1]. The second gate faces the waterfront, to the south of the City, which is where ships load and unload as well as go on dry-dock, because it is the part most sheltered from the winds. This gate is called the Gate of Saints Justus and Pastor and it has a chapel on its top, with the two saints painted on canvas and the coats of arms carved as in the other one, and these words carved on it: ["The Lord is my helper, whom shall I fear?" Psalm 27:1]. The third gate is on the west side, at the entrance of the harbor, where the ships come forth after they enter it; it is called the Gate of my lord Saint John the Baptist. It has a chapel and coats of arms like the other gates [*no longer extant* —Tr.] and the Saint is painted on canvas, by a good hand. Mass is celebrated there as in the other gates, and the inscription is ["Blessed is he that comes in the Name of the Lord" Psalm 118:26, Matthew 21:9 and parallels.]

The San Juan Gate is the only city gate still extant after most of the city walls were torn down in the nineteenth century; it is next to La Fortaleza, and the street that runs through it leads directly to the main door of the Cathedral. Incoming Governors were formally received at this gate, and then walked in procession to the Cathedral for a service of thanksgiving.

Justus and Pastor were Spanish boy martyrs in the persecution of Diocletian.

121.   Hay en la fuerza de San Felipe del Morro y plataformas y baluartes de la cerca de la Ciudad, cien piezas de artillería, las ochenta y seis de bronce, y las catorce de fierro colado.

122.   En las ocasiones que el enemigo ha acometido a esta plaza, se han mostrado muy valerosos sus vecinos en defenderla, y en la del conde Jorge Cumberland, el año de 1598, que se apoderó de ella, al lado del capitán Bernabé de Serralta, de quien va hecha mención en la relación remitida, murieron muchos vecinos y naturales en el puente de los Soldados que esta media legua de la Ciudad, donde se les resistió con gran de esfuerzo, hasta que caído en tierra dicho capitán de un mosquetazo que le dieron en un muslo, y acometidos de nuevo por otra parte, perdiendo una nao pequeña el enemigo que hizo parar en el Boquerón sobre las penas, se retiraron a la Ciudad antes que les cortasen la retirada: sólo se acuerdan los antiguos de los valerosos hermanos que allí murieron, llamados Juan y Simón de Sanabria que hoy tienen vivos hermanas y parientes.

123.   En la ocasión del año 1625 así mesmo se señalaron muchas personas, y en particular el Capitán y Sargento mayor García de Torres, natural de la villa de Vélez y vecino de esta Ciudad. Hombre de conocida nobleza y valor, como lo mostró en Flandes; dicen los que se hallaron en esta ocasión, que no hubiera el enemigo saltado en tierra, si mal aconsejado no le hubiera mandado retirar el Gobernador Juan de Haro, de la playa, donde se había fortificado en una noche, para impedirle no echase en tierra su gente, y que dicho Sargento mayor respondió con harto sentimiento, que como le mandaba retirar sin saber el poder que traía, que él lo haría a su tiempo, y animando a sus soldados les decía, "para esta ocasión nos ha estado sustentando Su Magestad tantos años ha; en defensa de esta plaza hemos de morir como leales vasallos, y yo os prometo ser el primero," y así sucedió, como en la relación remitida mas largamente va referida su muerte.

121.   In the Castle of San Felipe del Morro and in the platforms and bastions of the City walls there are a hundred pieces of artillery; eighty-six are bronze and fourteen are cast-iron.

122.   On those occasions when the enemies [of Spain] have attacked this City its *vecinos* have shown themselves very brave in its defense. In the attack of Earl George of Cumberland (1598) — who took the City — many *vecinos* and natives of the City died together with Captain Bernabé de Serralta (who was already mentioned in the report originally sent) on the Bridge of the Soldiers, which is half a league from the City. The enemies were resisted with great vigor until that Captain fell from a musket shot that hit him in the thigh. Then, being attacked from a different angle, after the enemy wrecked a small vessel which they made to run aground on the rocks of El Boquerón, they withdrew to the City before their retreat could be cut off. Old people only remember [by name] the brave brothers Juan and Simón de Sanabria, who died there and to this day have surviving sisters and relatives [in the City.]

123.   In the [Dutch] attack of 1625 many persons also distinguished themselves, particularly the Captain and Sergeant-Major García de Torres, a native of the town of Vélez and a *vecino* of this City. He was a man of well-known nobility and bravery, which he had demonstrated in Flanders. Those who were present on that occasion say that the enemy would not have been able to set foot on land if the ill-advised Governor Don Juan de Haro had not ordered him to withdraw from the beach, where in a single night he had fortified himself so as to prevent their landing. The said Sergeant-Major had replied with all too much feeling that that he would do so in his own good time, since the order to withdraw came without his knowing on what authority he had been ordered. Encouraging his soldiers, he said to them, "It is for times like this that His Majesty has been supporting us for so many years, and for the defense of this City we must die like loyal subjects. I swear that I shall be the first." And so it happened, as is told more extensively in the previous report.

In developing the theme in this addition to the first draft, Torres y Vargas again (#123) describes the heroism of his father. Earlier in the narration of the Dutch attack (#72), he compared his father and two army brothers to the Horatii brothers, triplets who died defending Rome against the Albans in 669 B.C. (Livy, *Ab Urbe Condita*, Bk. I, 24–25). *See also paragraphs # 85, 108 and 125 below.*

Old Spanish "*ha*" for "*hay*" in the citation of his father, García de Torres.

124.   En esta ocasión murieron muchos vecinos, y otros quedaron estropeados y se les hizo merced de plazas muertas de soldados, como fueron **Blas de Mesa**, **Francisco de Navarrete**, **el capitán Luis de Larrasa**, **Domingo Vélez**, y otros que se han quedado sin premio por su flojedad y que tenían con que comer. También se señaló valerosamente **Juan de Amézquita Quixano**, capitán de Infantería española, que era en aquella ocasión, y después murió Gobernador de Cuba, y en particular el primer domingo de octubre de dicho año de 1625 que con menos de cien hombres, de las nueve a las diez del día, acometió al enemigo y lo puso en huida ganándole las primeras fortificaciones, matándole mucha gente y entre otros oficiales al Sargento mayor, de que hizo gran sentimiento el enemigo, y trató de retirarse. Hízole Su Magestad merced de quatrocientos ducados de ayuda de costa.

125.   En esta ocasión como en muchas otras que se ofrecieron, en los treinta y nueve días que estuvo sitiada esta plaza, que fue desde 24 de setiembre hasta 1° de noviembre día de todos Santos, las personas que mas se señalaron son las siguientes: **El capitán Don Antonio de Mercado y Peñalosa**, natural de esta Ciudad que murió alcaide de la fuerza de Santo Domingo, la española. Era hijo del Gobernador Alonso de Mercado y en esta ocasión alférez. **El Doctor Don Juan de Salinas**, natural de esta Ciudad, a quien Su Magestad hizo merced de Canónigo de Santo Domingo y hoy vive Tesorero de la Iglesia de Caracas, con gran ejemplo de virtud. **El Capitán Don García de Torres y Vargas**, hijo del Sargento mayor arriba referido, a quien hizo Su Magestad merced de una com-

To forestall rebellion, Spanish policy was usually to grant positions of authority only to persons who were not native to the region.

The idea that Puerto Ricans would be entrusted with the important military command on the island is noteworthy because it indicates the loyalty of the natives to Spain and the trust that the monarchy placed on these Puerto Ricans. Torres y Vargas mentions here his own family as one that earned this distinction.

124.   On this occasion many *vecinos* died, and others were crippled. They were granted the salaries of vacant positions in the garrison — for example, **Blas de Mesa**, **Francisco de Navarrete**, **Captain Luis de Larrasa**, **Domingo Vélez**, and others who were left unrewarded because they did not bother to claim rewards, since they already had enough to sustain themselves. **Juan de Amézquita Quixano**, who was a Captain of the Spanish Infantry at that time, and who died as Governor of Cuba, also stood out for his bravery, especially on the first Sunday of October of that year 1625, on which he attacked the enemy from nine to ten in the morning with less than a hundred men. He put the Dutch to flight, capturing their first lines of fortification and killing many of them, and among other officers he killed their Sergeant-Major, which caused the enemy so much grief they were forced to try to retreat. His Majesty rewarded him with four hundred ducats for his expenses.

125.   In this occasion, as in many others that occurred during the thirty nine days that the City was under siege from September 24th to November 1st, which is All Saints' Day, the persons who most distinguished themselves were the following: **Captain Don Antonio de Mercado y Peñalosa**, a native of this City, who died as Governor of the fortress of Santo Domingo, Española; the son of Governor Alonso de Mercado, an ensign at the time of this siege, **Doctor Don Juan de Salinas**, a native of this City, whom His Majesty made Canon of Santo Domingo, and who is now Treasurer of the Cathedral Church of Caracas, where he gives a great example of virtue; **Captain Don García de Torres y Vargas**, son of the Sergeant-Major we mentioned above, to whom His Majesty granted a Company of Infantry in this garrison in spite of his being a native of this City; **Alderman Francisco Dassa y Bastida**, a native and *vecino* of this City, and a descendant of a brother of Bishop Don Rodrigo de la Bastida, who was mentioned in the list of bishops above; and **Captain Don Sebastián de Ávila**, an alderman and *vecino* of this City, a native of Jeréz de la Frontera, and one of the Ávilas of that town.

pañía de infantería en este presidio, sin embargo de ser natural de esta Ciudad. **El regidor Francisco Dassa y Bastida** vecino y natural de esta Ciudad, descendiente de hermano del Obispo Don Rodrigo de la Bastida de que fue hecha mención en la sucesión de los Obispos. **El capitán Don Sebastián de Ávila**, regidor y vecino de esta Ciudad, natural de Jerez de la Frontera y de los Ávilas de allí veinte leguas por tierra hacia la parte del Sur, y esta de la mar donde tiene puertos dos leguas, como más largamente consta de la relación remitida.

126.   **El capitán Don Juan de Bolanos**, vecino de esta Ciudad y natural de Guadix en Andalucía, hombre noble, y en esta ocasión servia plaza sencilla de soldado, y en el año de 1642 gobernó esta plaza por muerte de Don Agustín de Silva que era el propietario, y así va puesto en el número de los Gobernadores. **El alférez Antonio Moreno de Villa Mayor**, vecino de esta Ciudad y natural de Llerena en la Estremadura.

127.   **El capitán Juan Lugo de Sotomayor**, vecino y natural de esta Ciudad y de lo noble de ella, a cuyo cargo estuvo el impedir por la parte del puente de los Soldados, que estaba apoderado el enemigo de ella, no entrase par los campos en la fuerza todas las noches.

128.   La población de San Felipe del Arecibo, *no es villa sino valle;* y está a sotavento de Puerto-Rico, once leguas, sita en las riberas del río de Arecibo de quien tomó nombre. Fundose siendo Gobernador Don Felipe de Beaumont y Navarra, por el año de 1616.

129.   El valle de San Blas de Coamo, falta por poner en el memorial, y noticias sacras y reales que ha impreso el Sr. Juan Diez de la Calle, de que fue hecha mención en la relación remitida, y dicen sus vecinos tienen hecha merced de villa, aunque no les ha venido la cedula, avisándome lo que hay en esto. Los alentaré a que envien lo necesario para el despacho de ella. Dista de esta Ciudad dicho valle, veinte leguas por tierra hacia la parte del Sur, y esta de la mar donde tiene puertos dos leguas, como mas largamente consta de la relacion remitida.

> The seaports which were then in the jurisdiction of Coamo are now municipalities in their own right, for example Salinas, Santa Isabel, and especially Ponce.

126.   **Captain Don Juan de Bolanos** is *vecino* of this City and a native of Guadix in Andalusia, a man of nobility who on this occasion was serving as a private soldier, but who in 1642 governed this City because of the death of Don Agustín de Silva, the appointed Governor. He is therefore included in the list of Governors given above. **Ensign Antonio Moreno de Villa Mayor** is a *vecino* of this City and a native of Llerena in Extremadura.

127.   **Captain Juan Lugo de Sotomayor**, a native and *vecino* of this City, and from one of the best families of it, was in charge of ensuring that the enemy should not enter the fortress through the fields at night from the direction of the Bridge of the Soldiers, which they had taken.

The three entries #128–130 seem to correct misunderstandings about statements in the first draft. Apparently "*Valle*" (valley) was written as "*Villa*" (town). Fernández Mendez notes in his text (ftn. 40) that although it would be requested in 1690, official status as "*villa*" would not be granted to Arecibo until 1778 (#128). Distances and political rank are clarified in the note on Coamo (#129). Torres y Vargas notes the mistake of *pesos* for where he had *reales*, almost equivalent to stating five dollars for five cents. He rejects the practice of bribery that was somehow understood from the first submission of this report (#130).

---

128.   The settlement of San Felipe del Arecibo *is not a town, but a valley,* and is eleven leagues to the leeward of Puerto Rico [*the City of Puerto Rico, i.e., San Juan* —Tr.] on the banks of the Arecibo River, from which it takes its name. It was founded during the governorship of Don Felipe de Beaumont y Navarra, around the year 1616.

129.   The valley of San Blas de Coamo was missing in the report, but sacred and secular notices have been printed by Señor Juan Díez de la Calle, as mentioned above in the report that was sent. Its *vecinos* claim that it had been granted the category of a town [*villa*], although the royal decree has not arrived; they have notified me of the facts. I will encourage them to send what is needed for the decree to be dispatched. This valley is twenty leagues from this City by land, in a southerly direction, and it is two leagues away from the sea, where it has ports, as is more extensively explained in the report that was sent.

130.   El estanco del tabaco de esta Ciudad no vale más que ocho mil reales cada año y fue yerro de la imprenta, porque está puesto ocho mil pesos. Tampoco en los oficios de la Ciudad viene puesto el alguacil mayor.

The selling of official postitions was a major source of income for 17th century governments.

This is the unceremonious ending of the report by Torres y Vargas. As noted, these last sections (#103–130) were inserted as notes to the editor, correcting misinterpretations or editorial mistakes in the first version.

130.   The state monopoly of tobacco in this City is worth not more than eight thousand *reales* a year [*about $960* — Ed.], and it was by a misprint that the final report gives its value as eight thousand *pesos* [*about $8,000* –Ed.]. Also, the Bailiff does not have the right to sell positions in the offices of this City.

CHRONOLOGY FOR THE LIFE OF
DIEGO DE TORRES Y VARGAS

1614–1615 (?)	Birth in San Juan
1625	Dutch attack on city: death of his father, García
1635	Enrolled at the University of Salamanca in Spain
1639	Graduation with a Bachelor's degree in canon law
	Ordination to the priesthood in Spain
c.1640	His brothers, García and Alonso, killed while in military service
1641	Appointment as Canon of the Cathedral of San Juan
1642	Return voyage to San Juan before the hurricane of September 12th
1644	*Arrival of Bishop Damián López de Haro*
1645	Synod of Puerto Rico
1646	Founding of Carmelite Convent in San Juan
1647	Composition of the *Descripción* undertaken for Gil González Dávila
	Portuguese troops sent to dismantle St. Martin colony
	Refusal to excommunicate ex-Governor Guajardo Fajardo of St. Martin
1648	**Treaty of Westphalia**
	Death of Bishop López de Haro while on visitation at Margarita Island
	Completion of the *Descripción* and its likely dispatch to Spain
1649	Addendum completed for *Descripción* after review of the printed entry
	Arrival of Bishop Lobo del Castillo
1651	*Executor of will of Bishop Lobo del Castillo (as Vicar General).
1652	Judge in case of attempted assassination of Puerto Rico's governor
1653	*Bishop Francisco Naranjo refuses See of Puerto Rico*
	Assigned as judge in case involving Bishop of Santo Domingo

	Conducts canonical inquiry for two Carmelite novices
1654	*Elected *Vicario Capitular*, April 17th (*may be a second election*)
	Censure from Spain for 1653 Santo Domingo judgment, April 27th
	*Rome confirms him in administrative powers *sede vacante*, July 3rd
	Judge in case of Swedish refugees
1655	Promoted to *chantre,* June 21st
1658	Named Dean of the Cathedral, July 25th
	Attempt on his life by a deranged priest
1659	*Arrival of Bishop Francisco Arnaldo de Isasí*
	Peace signed with France
	Donativo taken up for King of Spain
1661	*Vicar of Diocese upon death of Bishop Isasí
1664	*Arrival of Bishop Benito de Ribas*
	Decree of sanctuary for runaway English slaves
	Named Ecclesiastical Governor by Bishop de Ribas
1668	*Vicar of Diocese upon death of Bishop de Ribas
1670	Death in San Juan, between April 5th and 15th

He functioned as interim administrator and Vicar of the Diocese for approximately thirteen years: 1651–59, 1661–64, 1668–1670.

QUESTIONS OF CHRONOLOGY

As noted in the first essay, the list of bishops and governors of Puerto Rico provided by Don Diego Torres y Vargas has chronological errors. His mistakes in dates or in their sequencing may be attributed to the lack of reliable texts and documents in Puerto Rico at the time he wrote his report. Some persons omitted by Torres y Vargas were local officials and civil authorities (*los gobernadores letrados*) who are counted as governors in more recent histories of Puerto Rico, like those of Figueroa and Silvestrini and Luque de Sánchez (1987). It may be that in the instructions sent from Madrid for the proposed *Teatro Eclesiástico* by González Dávila only royal appointees were to be listed.

The reader should not dismiss the historical value of the work by Torres y Vargas on account of such mistakes or omissions, however. As already noted, Torres y Vargas relied greatly on supplemental information from sources as diverse as oral histories, personal recollections or simple observations taken from close-up examination of engravings, tombstones and the like. The information he provided about these historical personages contributes enormously to our knowledge of this earliest history of Puerto Rico. While we can correct errors in dates or sequence by simple comparisons with contemporary works, Torres y Vargas' original insights about the historical circumstances are invaluable and can not be found in any other single source.

While errors in chronology may be easily resolved, there are some more stubborn discrepancies in the text. Torres y Vargas cites (#82) that there were thirteen bishops and twice that number, or twenty-six governors, when counting both those appointed and the interim governors. This observation comes in a paragraph that begins by listing Governor de Aguilera as the official appointed in 1649. Counting de Aguilera along with the others named in the *Descripción* by Torres y Vargas, however, produces twenty-seven, rather than twenty-six governors. Thus, not only does mention of de Aguilera contradict the numerical observation Torres y Vargas made in the first part of the *Descripción* (#1–102), it also offers a date that would place the composition of the first installment of the work too late to have been seen by González Dávila, who delivered the published edition of the *Teatro Eclesiástico* to the King on Good Friday, April 2, 1649.[1] In his published text, González Dávila states that he has read the report by Don Diego (2004 edition, pg. 518), rendering 1649 dubious as the year for the completion of Torres y Vargas' first installment.

---

[1] See Paniagua Pérez and Vifocos Marinas, 2004:63ff.

If this one line that mentions de Aguilera is removed, however, the problem disappears because the completion of the first installment becomes the fall of 1648 and the number of governors remains twenty-six as indicated in Don Diego's text. Thus, there is reason to believe that this one line on de Aguilera was not in Torres y Vargas' original manuscript. One suspects that it might have been added after the *Descripción* was received in Spain. Perhaps a clerk wished to update the information given to the Royal Historian and failed to take into account the numerical curiosity of thirteen and twenty-six mentioned in Torres y Vargas' text. He may have simply inserted notice of the recent nomination of the current governor in the place where it seemed to best fit in chronological order.

Not only do we need to take care in fixing the date for the completion of the *Descripción,* however, we also must ask questions about when Don Diego began to write it. The cover page indicates that Torres y Vargas' manuscript arrived in Spain on April 23, 1647. Yet many of the events described in the first part of the work occurred as late as October 21, 1648 (see #101; also, #81, #99, #100). Even if it is supposed that the reference to the 1649 appointment of Governor de Aguilera was not in the original first installment, the date of 1647 on the title page remains an issue. In as much as this title page announces the date the report arrived in Spain, it could not have been recorded by Torres y Vargas, who had sent it from Puerto Rico. Medrano Herrero (1999) simply states in a footnote (p. 127–28, ftn. 4) that the title page is wrong. Could the clerks in Spain have mislabeled the report? Was a handwritten "9" misread as "7"?

Mistakes abound in the book published in Madrid, as indicated by Viforcos Marinas and Paniagua Pérez in their introduction to the 2004 critical edition of the *Teatro Eclesiástico*. For instance, the chapter on Puerto Rico included a paragraph that belonged to the entry on Cuba (p. 70). They also note that González Dávila did not always wait for the information he had requested from the colonial churches before completing his manuscript (p. 33).

Before settling on an explanation of sloppiness, however, we should note that the first volume of Gonález Dávila's work received official permission to be published on September 18, 1647. Two other later permissions were received in June of 1648,[2] even before the events of October 21, 1648 cited in the first installment of Torres y Vargas' work. One possibility — that can only be suggested, but not proven — is that the 1647 date refers to an acceptance letter from Torres y Vargas, consenting to provide information on Puerto Rico for the *Teatro Eclesiástico* and offering a description of his proposed contents. Conceivably,

---

[2] Juan Diez de la Calle, the Royal Secretary gave his permission on June 4, 1648 and the ecclesiastical permission was dated June 8, 1648.

González Dávila wished to convey to the authorities as early as September 1647 that his completed work would include information on Puerto Rico. Notice of a letter from Torres y Vargas that arrived earlier in April of that year would have confirmed the scope of the work and helped González Dávila secure permission in the fall of 1647. Perhaps this cover page with the date for the initiation of the project remained as label for the work completed in 1649 with the second installment. Obviously, this is only conjecture.

There are also some ambiguities about the materials sent from Spain to Torres y Vargas for corrections and which occasioned the second installment (#103–#130). Don Diego writes (#130) that the manuscript he reviewed had an error in the "printing *(imprenta)*." Yet, the final printed work of Gil González Dávila did not include any citation from the *Descripción* of Torres y Vargas, only a sentence praising its quality. Additionally, the printed error cited by Don Diego that confused *reales* with *pesos* (#130) is not found in the entry on Puerto Rico eventually published by González Dávila.

If Torres y Vargas was asked to correct mistakes and add some details to his report in order to help complete the *Teatro* published in 1649, what printed document was sent to him from Spain? It is highly improbable, if not also impossible, that Torres y Vargas was sent a printed version of his own *Descripción*. The time between October 21, 1648, when the last entries of his first installment were composed in San Juan and April 2, 1649, when the *Teatro* was published in Madrid, is simply too short a period. How could Torres y Vargas have mailed his work from San Juan, have it arrive in Spain, have the whole text of the *Descripción* typeset and printed, then mailed this printing back to Puerto Rico, have it reviewed with data added in the second installment of Torres y Vargas (#103–130), then conclude with return shipment to Spain for inclusion in the work of González Dávila — all within six months? Even today with computers and Internet, such a brief turn around for publishing is seldom seen.

If the printed data on Puerto Rico reviewed by Torres y Vargas was not his own *Descripción,* then what was it? The most likely answer can be taken from the analysis of Paniagua Pérez and Viforcos Marinas (pp. 32–33). They focus on a similar issue of author's review for an entry in this same volume of the *Teatro* for the Diocese of Michoacán in Mexico. These scholars note that González Dávila sent to Mexico certain printed pages from another author's work published in 1645. Intending to incorporate this source into his own work, they conclude that he sent the printed pages of the relevant data as a gesture of goodwill towards the cleric who had authored that text. This supposition regarding printed materials sent to a contributor while compiling the *Teatro Eclesiástico* is supported by the review procedure the Royal Historian had followed for his earlier work on the dioceses of Castile. It falls within the the practice of incorporating other texts into one's own work without attribution which was characteristic of the age, as noted above in "Notes on the Text" (pp. 87–88).

Thus, it would seem that the materials where Torres y Vargas finds a "misprint" [yerro de la imprenta] (#130) were not from his own report. Rather, González Dávila had sent to Puerto Rico some already published materials about Puerto Rico that he was consulting. Torres y Vargas, it would seem, was not being asked to correct his own composition, but verify facts cited in another source.

The misprint in question may have been taken from a work of Juan Díez de la Calle. This official had produced in 1646 a document that contained information on Puerto Rico and was entitled, *Memorial y noticias sacras y reales del Imperio de las Indias Occidentales, La Nueva España y el Perú* [Recollection and notices both sacred and governmental of the Empire of the West Indies, New Spain and Peru]. Since Torres y Vargas mentions this author in his second installment, Díez de la Calle may have been the source of the printed materials sent from Spain.[3]

Thus, it seems that a few printed pages were sent to Torres y Vargas from sources the Spanish Royal Historian already had about Puerto Rico, likely from the published work of Díez de la Calle. As remarked above in the section of "Notes on the Text," it is not clear if Tapia y Rivera — in the nineteenth century — consulted a hand-written report or a printed one, but these considerations incline one to conclude that Tapia y Rivera had only a codex from Torres y Vargas. The definitive resolution of these issues, however, awaits future scholarly research.

---

[3] Extensive commentary on the communications between Díez de la Calle and Bishop López de Haro are found in Medrano Herrero (1999), 76ff.

Sources For The Text

Torres y Vargas, Diego De. 1647. *Descripción De La Isla y Ciudad de Puerto-Rico, y de Su Vecindad y Poblaciones, Presidio. Gobernadores y Obispos; Frutos y Minerales. Enviada por El Licenciado Don Diego De Torres Vargas, Canónigo de La Santa Iglesia De Esta Isla en El Aviso Que Llegó A España En 23 de Abril de 1647.*

Reproduced In:

Tapia y Rivera, Alejandro. 1854. *Biblioteca Histórica de Puerto Rico que contiene varios documentos de los siglos XV, XVI, XVII, XVIII.* Imp. Marquez.

Boletín Histórico de Puerto Rico, ed. Cayetano Coll y Toste. [Published in Puerto Rico starting in 1914–1927]. Issued in a collection by Kraus Report (New York), 1968. Tomo IV, pp. 257–293.

Biblioteca Histórica. 1945. Instituto de literatura puertorriqueña: San Juan. pp. 457–489 and 496–503.

Obras Completas. 1970. Instituto de Cultura Puertorriqueña: San Juan. Tomo III, pp. 537–595.

Fernández Méndez, Eugenio, ed. 1976. *Crónicas de Puerto Rico*, Editorial de la Universidad de Puerto Rico: Río Piedras. pp. 172–217.

Other Relevant Sources

Arrom, José Juan. 2000. "A propósito de la palabra chévere." In *Estudios de Lexicología Antillana.* Editorial de la Universidad de Puerto Rico: Río Piedras. Second edition: 147–154.

Bernstock, Judith. 1980. "Bernini's Memorial to Maria Raggi" *The Art Bulletin.* 62:2 (June 1980) 243–255.

Figueroa, Loida. 1972. *History of Puerto Rico.* Anaya Press: New York.

González Dávila, Gil. 1649/2004. *Teatro eclesiástico de la primitiva iglesia de las indias occidentales, vidas de sus arzobispos, obispos, y cosas memorables de svs sedes (Nueva España)*. Tomo I. 1649 **original edition**, Talleres de Diego Díaz de la Carrera: Madrid.

Facsimile edition, 1982. CONDUMEX: Centro de Estudios de Historia de México: Mexico.

Critical edition, 2004. Edición, introducción notas e índices por Jesús Paniagua Pérez y M.ª Isabel Viforcos Marinas. Fijación y traducción de textos latinos por Juan Francisco Domínguez Domínguez. Universidad de León: Consejería de cultura y Turismo, Junta de Castilla y León. Colección Tradición Clásica y Humanística en España e Iberoamérica.

Herrera y Tordesillas, Antonio de. 1601–1615. *Historia General de los Hechos de los Castellanos en las Islas i Tierra Firme del Mar Océano 1601–1615*. Madrid. (*The first four decades were printed in 1601 by Juan Flamenco. The last four decades, from 1532 to 1554, were printed in 1615 by Juan de la Cuesta.*) Recent edition in Spanish with a study by Mariano Cuesta Domingo, 1991. Universidad Complutense: Madrid.

Huerga, Alvaro, OP. 1989. *Los obispos de Puerto Rico en el siglo XVII*. Universidad Católica de Puerto Rico: Ponce.

Matovina, Timothy. 2003. "Guadalupe at Calvary: Patristic Theology in Miguel Sanchez's Imagen De la Virgen María". *Theological Studies* 64 (4): 795–811.

Medrano Herrero, Pío. 1999. *Don Damián López de Haro y don Diego de Torres y Vargas, dos figuras del Puerto Rico barroco*. Plaza Mayor. San Juan (Puerto Rico).

Medrano Herrero, Pío. 2003. "Damián López de Haro y Diego de Torres y Vargas ¿Escritores encontrados?" Focus II, 2 (2003) 29–42. This article cites: *Cuestionario para la formación de las relaciones geográficas de Indias: Siglos XVI–XIX*, a 1988 publication from the Consejo Superior de Investigación (CSI), Madrid.

Murga Sanz, Vicente. 1959. *Ponce de León*. Editorial de la Universidad de Puerto Rico: Río Piedras.

Murga, Vicente, and Álvaro Huerga. 1988. *Episcopologio de Puerto Rico*. Tomo II: "De Rodrigo de Bástidas a Martín Vázquez de Arce (1540–1610)". Universidad Católica de Puerto Rico: Ponce.

Murga, Vicente, and Álvaro Huerga. 1989. *Episcopologio de Puerto Rico*. Tomo III: "De Francisco de Cabrera a Francisco de Padilla (1611–1695)". Universidad Católica de Puerto Rico: Ponce.

Peck, Douglas T. 1998. "Anatomy of an Historical Fantasy: The Ponce de León-Fountain of Youth Legend," *Revista de Historia de América*, 123 (1998), Instituto Panamericano de Geografía e Historia, Mexico City.

Perea, Salvador. 1972. *Historia de Puerto Rico, 1537–1700*, Editorial de la Universidad de Puerto Rico: Río Piedras. Universidad Católica de Puerto Rico: Ponce.

Silvestrini, Blanca G. and María Dolores Luque de Sánchez. 1987. *Historia de Puerto Rico: Trayectoria de un pueblo*. Editorial Cultural Puertorriqueña: San Juan.

Stevens-Arroyo, Anthony M. 1998. "The Evolution of Marian Devotionalism within Christianity and the Ibero-Mediterranean Polity." *Journal for the Scientific Study of Religion*. 37:1 (Spring 1998) 50–73.

Stevens-Arroyo, Anthony M. 1993. "The Inter-Atlantic Paradigm: The Failure of Spanish Medieval Colonization of the Canary and Caribbean Islands." *Comparative Studies in Society and History* 35:3 (July 1993) 515–543.

Glossary Items

*(Identified with entry numbers in the text, its translation
or an explanatory sidebar.)*

Agora = ahora

Alcaide / #66 = The alcaide or alcayde (#57), not to be confused with alcalde (see below), governs a military fortress as a sort of comptroller. This role is different from the commander or general of the troops, but the upkeep of the building and the administration of its supplies has military consequences. The governor of civil affairs was over the alcaide, but if the governor of civil affairs was absent, the alcaide was next in line to assume the duties of colonial administration. The title was hereditary and was given to the Ponce de León family which a descendant became the alcaide of La Fortaleza and later of El Morro. The contemporary use is mostly as "warden" of a prison.

Alcaldes / Sheriffs – #11 = Officials appointed yearly by the City Council (*Cabildo*) to investigate and punish crimes committed outside the city. The word is used today for "mayor."

Alcaldes ordinarios / Mayors-in-Ordinary – #11 = Residents (*vecinos*, see below) who enjoyed jurisdiction in their own names as sheriffs.

Alcaldes de la Santa Hermandad / Sheriffs – #11 = Santa Hermandad was an institution popular in late Medieval Spain that allowed ordinary citizens to become partisans bearing arms during war or periods of lawlessness. The term here roughly corresponds to deputy sheriffs when ordinary citizens were recruited as volunteer police during a crisis, somewhat like the leaders of a posse in the 19th century Wild West of the United States.

Alférez mayor (from the Arabic. *al faris*) / Bearer of the Royal Standard – #11 = In Medieval Spain, it was the paladin for the army, as for instance, the famous El Cid. In Spanish America, it designated the person in charge of presenting colors, i.e. official flags during events of legal importance. *Alférez* (by itself) is sometimes translated as "Ensign;" however, it was a rank between a noncommissioned and commissioned officer rank and may be more akin to today's Warrant Officer.

Alguacil mayor (from the Arabic *al wazir*, vizier) / Bailiff – #11 = A legal officer to whom some degree of authority is committed such as that of making arrests as might be done by a constable and transporting prisoners under sentence.

Arcediano / Archdeacon – #13 = The Archdeacon was once one of great importance in Catholicism as a senior official of a diocese. It has fallen into disuse, and its duties are now part of the work of such officials as the Vicar General and Episcopal Vicar, the Vicar Forane and Deans. Technically, the rank still exists as one of the dignitaries of a Cathedral Chapter.

Asi, ansi, assi = various forms of *así*

Barlovento – #1 (see "sotavento" below).

Beata / Literally, "Blessed." – #24 = The term was common in the 16th and 17th century Spanish Catholic world to refer to pious women, some with reputations for visions and great holiness, who dedicated much of their lives to prayer and devotions *without* being members of a nunnery. They could, but need not be, members of the Third Order of the Franciscans, Dominicans or some other order of friars.

The Third Order was a lay confraternity (*cofradía*) open to men and women (single or married) that followed the spirit of one of the orders of friars (most commonly the Dominicans, Franciscans or Carmelites) while living in the secular world without vows. They wore a modified version of the "First Order's" (friars') and the "Second Order's (sisters) habit at meetings and processions, and are still considered by Canon Law as true Religious Orders and not mere confraternities.

Caballero / cavalier – #59 = It was an inner fortification in a fortress, which is higher than the others, and thus can cover soldiers with its fire, either to protect them when attacked, or to harass the enemy if it has taken the lower fortifications.

Cabildo (Eclesiástico or *Catedral)* / Cathedral Chapter – #18, 28, 78, 80. (From the Latin *Capitulum*. The name derives from the fact that in monasteries the analogous meetings began with reading a Chapter of the Rule). = The corporate body of the Canons of a Cathedral, whose principal duties are the daily celebration of the Liturgy of the Hours in the Cathedral, serving corporately as the Bishop's counselors (whose advice and consent he is bound to obtain in certain cases) and electing a Vicar Capitular to rule the diocese if the Bishop dies or is transferred, until the new Bishop takes possession. The head of the Cathedral Chapter was its Dean (see below) and while the post required approval of the crown, it also offered a salary.

Cabildo (Civil) / City Corporation – #11, 18, 23, 60. (The name *Cabildo* was given to it by analogy with the Cathedral Chapter) = Its functions were to oversee the governance of the city, to control the budget and account for city taxes. Its members were persons whose social prominence came from inherited family ties, commercial wealth and/or military reputation. Its members were designated as *regidores* (aldermen, see below) and election among members of the cabildo could also bring other titles such as *alcalde* (see above). In some instances, membership was inherited; in others, it could be bought. The *cabildo* had additional responsibilities for ensuring quality control of city water, reliability of market wares and the administration of justice for civil violations.

*canongía [*modern, canonjía*] & Canónigo* / Canonry & Canon – #13 = The most accurate definition of a Cathedral canon is "a member of a chapter." The name can be traced to the norms, that is the canons, of community life that were followed by certain clerics without vows and which distinguished them from others who did not live in community. Assignment to a Cathedral also provided an income or prebend (see below) for some canons, as well as certain rights in regard to the government of the diocese. In reacting to abuses, the Council of Trent (Sess. XXIII, XXIV) redefined the role of the canons as one of exemplary holiness meant to enhance the piety and reform of Catholicism. Loyalty to the church and ecclesiastical training were prime requirements for appointment, but on certain issues the canons could and would legally stand up to the Bishop in dissent.

Capellanías / Chantry Chaplaincies – #14, 42 = A *Capellanía* was an endowment set up in a deed or a testament by which a priest received an income and was bound to celebrate Mass for the soul of the founder and/or of his family on certain stated dates (e.g., once a week, or once a month, or on their anniversaries). Such masses might be said anywhere, or could be connected to a particular church, chapel or altar, depending on the deed of foundation.

Capillas / Chapels – #13 = These could be "side chapels" annexed to a larger church or cathedral, but more often were houses of worship that did not have the same canonical status as parishes. Often built with private donations, these chapels usually were dedicated in honor of some mystery of the Faith (e.g., the Passion) or of some saint. In cathedrals and other churches that had many side chapels, the area around the High Altar (in English the "Sanctuary") would be called *la Capilla Mayor*.

"casas matas" / casemate – #73 (Modern Spanish renders as *"casamata"*) = A reinforced vault for artillery in the walls of a fortress.

Castellán (Latin *Castellanus*, derived from *castellum* 'castle') Castellan – #12 = Duties included supervising the castle's domestic staff as might a mayordomo, but also allowed for execution of some military functions such as maintenance of the defensive installations. The functions were practical ones and unlike the office of alcaide (see above), were not inherited.

cavalier see *caballo* above.

Chantre / Precentor – #13 (From the Latin meaning "the one who sings before" or alternatively, "first singer.") = One of the dignitaries of a Cathedral Chapter, the original function was to intone antiphons, psalms, hymns, responsories for the singing of the Liturgy of the Hours, i.e., the Divine Office, on Sundays and greater feasts. By the time of Torres y Vargas, the title and dignity allowed the delegation of the singing function to persons of greater musical talents, rendering the duties ambiguous. The title continued to bring a stipend, however. In some cases, the precentor would serve in the liturgical installation of canons and the like.

Convento / convent – #14 et passim = Strictly speaking, "convent" was used for both men and women under vows who were not monks, but rather friars and sisters. Monasteries have ecclesiastical restrictions of cloister not operative with convents of friars or sisters; in the latter, the religious had more freedom to conduct apostolates in the general society.

Custodia / (*Custodia* ordinarily refers to a monstrance). – #110 = The vessel given by Charles V to which Torres y Vargas refers (and which is still in the Cathedral Treasury) is actually a Pyx, that is, a gold or silver box for carrying the Sacrament to the sick. (Lat., *pyxis*, from the Greek, *pyxis*, box-wood receptacle, from *pyxos*, box-tree / Pyx).

Cofradía / Confraternity – #115–117 = This was a pious association, usually formed around a particular title of Christ, the Blessed Mother or one of the saints. Members of the confraternity pledged themselves to honor the devotion for which their group was founded, ordinarily by organizing a procession or other observance. In practice, the cofradía also supplied for some social needs, such as ensuring a burial place, mourners, and at times, the money necessary to properly conduct a funeral, marriage or Baptism. Many of the Third Orders such as for the Franciscans functioned like a cofradía. Reacting against some of the purely social functions of the medieval cofradías, the reforms of Trent began to reconstruct the institution as a "sodality," a more purely pious association founded to promote the spiritual and corporal works of mercy among members aspiring to deepen their spiritual life. The Society of Jesus was instrumental in establishing sodalities among students in Jesuit schools.

Deán / Dean (of the Cathedral) – #13 et passim. There is reference to an ecclesiastical dean in the Rule of St. Benedict (c. xxi) as a title for a monk placed over ten others with the duty of oversight for their tasks and observance of the Rule. The Dean of the Cathedral was the highest ranking dignitary of the Chapter, and would preside over its meetings unless the Bishop was present. His ordinary duties were to supervise the affairs of the Cathedral, including matters of income and upkeep. See *Cabildo Eclesiástico* above.

Depositario general / Receiver General – #11 = The treasurer or trustee in charge of financial records.

diputados (of church and hospital) / Trustee – #18 = An elected post of responsibility. In reference to a hospital, it corresponds to a trustee on a Board of Directors. Currently, in much of Latin America it is used to designate a legislative representative.

Dixo, Roxas, etc. where x is pronounced as j; e.g., "Xavier" is also "Javier."

Ducado / ducat – #12 = A gold coin worth about 11 silver *reales* or about a dollar and a half.

Encomienda – #97 = An institution adapted from feudal serfdom in Spain in order to include non-Hispanicized Indians into the colonial economy. The natives were obligated to work the land in a status similar to that of serfs, and the encomienda should not be seen as the legal equivalent of slavery. In contrast, an *encomienda* of the Military Orders was a manor house (in Spain) and its territory, which produced an income for one of the Order's knights. Such a knight was called a *comendador* (knight commander), while the holder of an *encomienda* in the New World sense was called an *encomendero*.

Escribano (público) / Scrivener – #23 = A public functionary authorized to witness written documents signed in his presence. The official had secretarial and administrative duties such as transcribing dictation and keeping official records. The post evolved into something similar to a Notary Public.

Escudo de Armas (insignia) / coat of arms or simply "arms" – #105; #13, 30, 59 = Used to designate a family of noble heritage. At times a coat of arms was granted as a reward for service to the crown, akin to a knighting of a prominent personality. Cities, universities, dioceses and other corporate bodies are also granted a coat of arms, since any official or entity which used a seal for its documents was expected to have one on its seal. For this reason in the Catholic Church, bishops who do not already have an inherited family coat of arms are entitled to a coat of arms.

Esperimentando, esaminar, Estremadura, etc, where s is equivalent to x

Executor (ejecutor) / Executor – #11 = The person charged with finalizing a legal task.

Fortaleza / Fortress – #54, 57 = Here it refers to a specific building in San Juan that was the principal fortification of the city before the buiding of El Morro, and is used today as the Governor's residence.

Fortín / Fortification = Less complex than a *Fortaleza*, a *Fortín* was a defensive position.

Galeón / galleon – #67 = A galleon was a large, multi-decked sailing ship, representing design improvement of the caravel and carrack (or *nao* – #74). The galleon was made longer, lower and narrower to better negotiate ocean travel.

Galeaza / Galeass – #109 = Vessels for Mediterranean warfare that combined features of galleys and the sturdier full sailing ships. The Galeass was about 150 feet long, 27 feet wide and 9 feet deep. It depended upon oarsmen for some of its locomotion, but was among the first vessels to employ cannons firing through gun ports.

Guaiqueries – #87 = Original inhabitants of Margarita Island off the coast of present day Venzuela. Their language is sometimes identified by some as related to the Cumanagoto and by others to the Garao (Warrau). The name, Guaiqueries, has been adopted in contemporary Venezuela as the name for a basketball team.

Hábito de Santiago / Habit of Santiago – #76 et passim. *hábito de Alcántara* / Habit of Alcántara – #85 = The habit of a military order consisted of a white cloak (*manto capitular*) bearing the particular cross of that order, which was worn over one's regular clothes on formal events of the order. On other occasions, the cross of the order was embroidered or appliquéd on one's doublet and cloak.

In the time of Torres y Vargas this was an honor conferred by the crown that added to one's prestige among the upper classes and made one a candidate for an *encomienda* in the order's lands in Spain and the pension which that commandery's income produced. (See *encomiendas* above.) The monarchy often used the conferral of the habit to reward persons from the nobility or near nobility.

The **Order of Santiago** or the **Order of Saint James of Compostela** was a 12th century military order (*see #45 for an idea of how it was associated with service to the monarchy*) named after St. James the Greater, the patron of the *Reconquista* that combated Muslims for control of the Iberian Peninsula. The Order of Santiago adopted the rule of St. Augustine.

This, and other military orders which were associated with the crusades, represented an effort by Catholicism to ensure that war for a just cause would not fall into the pattern of exaggerated violence and the use of force to extract either tribute or the taking of booty after battle. By the 16ᵗʰ century, the order comprised several affiliated classes: canons, charged with the administration of the sacraments; canonesses; religious knights living in community, and married knights.

The cross of Saint James that was the order's symbol was a red cross whose three upper arms ended in fleurs de lis, and the bottom arm in a point (*cross* fleury fitchy in heraldry), thus producing the image of a sword which recalls their title *de la Espada*, and a shell (*la venera*) a sign of the pilgrims to Santiago, was also associated with the order.

Order of Alcántara = This military order followed the severe rule of the Benedictines of Citeaux, written by St. Bernard of Clairvaux for the Knights Templar. Like the Order of Santiago (above), the purpose of the military orders disappeared in 1492 when the Muslims lost control of their last kingdom in Spain. The Order of Alcántara dispensed with the vow of celibacy and the common life in 1540. Thus, in the time of Torres y Vargas, the order was little more than an honor that conveyed an endowment.

The insignia of Alcántara is a green cross fleury; a (Greek) cross with equal arms, each ending in a fleur de lis, whose "petals" by the baroque age had become quite curlicued, later interpreted as the letter M (for Mary).

Hermitas / chapels – #19, 23, 91 et passim (for translation and explanation as "hermitage" see #22; see #40 as "shrine") = These were not parish churches, but more like shrines. That is, places where devotion suggested that passers-by stop and pray. The distinction in English between "chapel" and "hermitage" rests upon remoteness from the parish church. Traditionally, a hermitage was located in the countryside and was more likely a place for prayer than for the celebration of Mass. (See *Capellanías* and *Capillas* above.) Some hermitages were built to commemorate a favor from heaven, as was the case reported in Hormigueros (#22). These remote buildings in holy places were sometimes cared for the beneficiary of the heavenly wonder and family members of the same.

Las Indias (Occidentales) – #3, 5, 6, 11, 27, 35, 46, 49, 54, 61, 72, 82, 84, 86, 97, 105, 111, 113, 114 = A term for all the Americas.

Infante / a prince (*infanta* = princess) of a royal house – #75 = Younger children had fewer prospects of becoming king, but the title of *infante* would therefore convey the importance in royal rank even without right of succession.

Inquisición / Inquisition #13 = A special ecclesiastical institution for combating or suppressing heresy. Ordinarily, the Inquisition was made up of ecclesiastics versed in theology who shaped the process of investigation about doctrinal matters. Physical punishment, which might include execution by burning for major crimes against the faith, was left to civil authorities.

In the Americas, the Inquisition was expected to be watchful for apostasy among Indian converts and relapse to Judaism or profession of heresy among settlers. Bishop Alonso Manso of Puerto Rico may have accepted the post of Inquisitor, as also jurisdiction over the islands of the Eastern Caribbean, partly because the added responsibilities provided additional income to the new Diocese of Puerto Rico. The title was passed on to the Bishops of Puerto Rico, although seldom invoked until the time of Bishop Ramos who had ordered executions for witchcraft still remembered in the time of Torres y Vargas (#27, 32).

Kalinago = The name (for themselves) used by peoples who inhabited many islands in the Eastern Caribbean. A Cariban-speaking people, they are generally known in history as the Caribs and from them has come the name of the Caribbean Sea. Despite atrocities committed against them by Europeans, they continued to survive throughout the area, including the Island of St. Kitts in the time of Torres y Vargas.

Legua / League – #1, 2, 3, 86, 89 et passim = Originally, this was a loose definition for the distance that can be traveled in an hour. The Spanish League or *legua* was fixed as 5,000 *varas* (a measuring rod fixed at 0.82 m), or about 2.6 miles (4.2 km). Abolished by Philip II of Spain in 1568, the league was still used as a measure of distance, especially by mariners.

Maese (Maestre) de campo / General – #12 = A superior officer who commanded more than one Tercio of an army.

The Tercio was a military formation very much like the Swiss' Pike square. It consisted of about 3,000 pikemen and musketeers in tight formation. Used by the Spanish for the wars in Flanders, the tercios relied on professional soldiers of superior discipline and high morale during the 16th and 17th centuries.

Magestad = Majestad (also *"muger"* for *"mujer"*) etc.

Maravedí – #50 et passim = It took 34 *maravedís* to make one silver *real*, which itself was only an eighth of a dollar or about 12 cents. Grants and salaries were usually reckoned in hundred-thousands of *maravedis*, which sounded impressive, but 300 *maravedís* amounted to about a dollar.

Mayordomo de Ciudad / Administrator of finances. #11

Mesmo = mismo see #6.

Nao / Carrack – #70, 74 = A three- or four-masted sailing ship developed in the Mediterranean in the 15th century. The Santa Maria of Christopher Columbus was a *nao*.

Novenario / Novena – #101 = A series of prayers said for nine days in preparation for a feast, or in petition for a favor. Particularly nine Masses said or sung for a deceased person after the funeral, or, as in this case, after receiving notification of the death. In Puerto Rican popular devotion, especially in places where priests used to be scarce, is often replaced by nine rosaries said on consecutive days. Commonly used today as a "novena."

Portero / Doorkeeper – #13 = The person, much like an usher, who oversees the people entering and leaving the house of worship. He has responsibility for the keys that open and close the church doors.

Penitentes see #51 = The name of a type of *cofradía* (see above) dedicated to Holy Week processions. The most famous organizations of this type are based in Seville. During the procession, in which the marchers perform penances, they mask themselves so as not to turn their display of sorrow into vainglory. The distinctive garb masking one's identity is the distinctive pointed hood (*capirote*) in the colors of the particular cofradía. Ironically, the notorious Ku Klux Klan of the American South adopted a similar garb to shield its members from prosecution. **It should be emphasized that there is no connection or sympathy between these groups and the Ku Klux Klan.**

Pertiguero / verger #13 see "verger" below.

Prebendados, #13 see *Racionero* / One who receives a prebend. = This was a benefice, or ecclesiastical post with an endowed income. Appointment conferred a right to share in Cathedral income.

Presidio (Lat. Præsidium) / Fort – #85 = A Presidio was a type of fortress built by the Spanish during the 16th century to protect against pirates or other non-military marauders. It was a fortification that protected living space for non-soldiers within.

Procurador general #11 = Attorney General.

Quintal (Arabic, *qintar*) – #7 = The *quintal* or centner is a historical unit of mass with many different definitions in different countries, but usually it is 100 base units of mass, e.g., pounds. In Spain it is still defined as 100 *libras*, or about 46 kg.

Racioneros / prebendaries – #13 = Literally, a person with a "share = *ración*" in Cathedral income. (The difference between a *Prebenda* and a *Ración* was that a *Ración* was a **share** in the Cathedral income that could vary with revenue, while a *Prebenda* was an **endowment** with a generally fixed sum. Also, the endowment gave the recipient full and exclusive rights to the funds.)

Real (silver) see #7, 13, 130 = about 12 cents.

Real Audiencia de Santo Domingo – #50, 52, 80, 86 = An appeals' court established in Española to process complaints of crimes in the Indies. Translated here as "Audiencia." Judges of the Audiencia were referred to as *Oidores* or Auditors.

Regidores / Aldermen (Members of the cabildo) #11 – #48 = The larger the jurisdiction, the more aldermen chosen. Sometimes the position was afforded to the founder or his family as an inherited title, and appointment of some kind was required, but members of prominent land-holding families were generally included as a matter of privilege. Late in the history of Latin America, the positions were put up for sale.

Residencia / "Audit" or "evaluation" #48, et passim = The *Juez de Residencia* was a judge sent to call to account an outgoing magistrate for the way in which he had exercised his position. During the review of decrees and examination of fiscal and other records of administration, the outgoing official was required to remain in that jurisdiction until the residencia was completed. Aggrieved parties could offer testimony to the judge drawing up the residencia if they had been previously impeded or intimidated by the out-going official.

Torres y Vargas gives a long list of governors involved in this process (#50, 51, 61, 69, 74, 80), including one where the spouse (and relative of Torres y Vargas) suffered depression on account of her husband's bad evaluation (#48).

Revellín / ravelin – #59 = A triangular embanked salient outside the main moat of a fortress.

Sargento mayor / Sergeant Major – #12, 55, 125 et passim = This was the immediate office under a Colonel. After the creation of the Spanish tercios in 1534 (see *Maese* above), the post grew in importance, since the Sergeant Major was the chief field officer. During battle, he transmitted the General's commands. He was often closer to the soldiers than the commander because responsibilities included training and housing of the men. This is how Torres y Vargas describes his father, who held the title (#71–72).

Sotavento – #118, 128 = The Leeward Islands (French: Îles Sous-le-Vent; literally "Islands Under-the-Wind"). The **Sotavento** Islands are found where the Caribbean Sea meets the western Atlantic Ocean. The prevailing winds for these islands blow from the northeast. Thus, these islands are downwind from, or in the lee of, leeward of, the southeastern-most Windward Islands.

The **Barlvento** (*also* **"Barlovento"**) Islands – #1 = (literally, the *Windward*) first meet the trade winds, and the term refers to the side of a sea vessel turned to the direction from where the wind blows. The concept is also used for islands in the Cape Verde archipelago.

The prevailing trade winds in the West Indies blow east to west. This means that for sailing vessels in the time of Torres y Vargas, the trans-Atlantic currents and winds that provided the fastest route across the ocean brought these ships to the rough dividing line between the Windward and Leeward islands. Ships engaged in the Atlantic slave trade, for instance, would depart from the African Gold Coast and Gulf of Guinea and their first American encounter would be on the southeastern-most islands of the Lesser Antilles. This would serve to mark course for final destinations in the Caribbean and North and Central America.

Studium Generalis – #15 = Institutions of collegiate rank were termed *Studia Particularia*, to distinguish them from the wider study signified here, which became proper to what is now termed a university. Originally intended to prepare the friars for ordination, it sometimes allowed other students to study along with the seminarians.

Subteniente / Lieutenant – #63, 79 = This term indicates a function, rather than a military echelon since "Lieutenant" was not a rank in the Spanish army as *teniente* was. The *Subteniente* of the Governor at the Castle of El Morro kept whatever rank he already had in the army, and would substitute for the Governor when necessary.

Suffragan diocese – #39, 104 = A suffragan diocese in the Catholic Church is ruled by its own bishop, with direct and ordinary jurisdiction, but is indirectly supervised by a "Metropolitan." The metropolitan bishop is always an archbishop who governs a diocese strictly his own, while he presides at the same time over the bishops of a well-defined ecclesiastical province composed of his suffragan dioceses.

Synod (Greek *synodos*, an assembly) – #43 = Ecclesiastical gatherings convened with hierarchical authority to formulate policy in matters relating to faith, morals, or church discipline. The scope of such meetings is usually rather wide, embracing more than just several particular issues. Synod decrees are promulgated before taking effect, and a waiting period of two months is allowed for redress.

Tercio see *Maese* above.

Trapiche (Latin, Trapetum) #7 = A trapiche is a six spoke wheel or cog used in processing sugar cane and usually turned by a yoked horse or mule. Brought to Spain from 11th century Sicily, where it was invented, it found its way to the Canary Islands, where a sugar industry was established by the 15th century. In 1515 the first trapiche was constructed in the Caribbean by sugar-masters from the Canaries. The first sugar cane farm in Puerto Rico was established by King Ferdinand in the "Hato de los Reyes Catolicos" (the cattle ranch of the Catholic Kings) known today as Hato Rey.

Urca / A kind of cargo frigate – #71 = Although mainly intended to carry cargo, it carried guns and served double duty as a warship. Often used in shallow waters, the cargo space was without partitions.

Vara / Staff of justice – #49 (symbol of official rulership) = This corresponds to the ceremonial mace made of decorated metal and wood, carried before a monarch or official to represent authority. However, regidores, alguaciles and other municipal officers carried a slim rod in their own hands as a sign of their authority, as do certain Palace Officers in England. The formal academic graduation today may feature a mace bearer to lead the faculty members.

Vecino - #11 et passim = An adult resident and property owner in a city. The 16th century meaning of the term is difficult to translate into English. It is not just a "resident," but one with property and social status. A typical vecino could live with children and servants under the same roof and none of them would be considered "vecinos." On this account, the number of vecinos is usually considerably less than the total population, sometimes by as much as a factor of 6. People of social or military station could also move to a city like San Juan and acquire the status of vecino (#126).

In colloquial Spanish today, it means "neighbor."

Verger - #13 (See *pertiguero* above) = The person, often a layperson, responsible for the material upkeep of the house of worship. Attention to material needs such as sweeping, cleaning the furniture and storing sacred vessels. The office of verger is no longer a part of Catholic organization, having been replaced in functions by a sexton or senior usher of large churches.

Vicario / Vicar = A canonical position that confers power to act for the Ordinary, or bishop.

Vicario General /Vicar General = A priest appointed by the bishop to help him in the government of the diocese with ordinary power and jurisdiction

Vicario Capitular / Vicar Capitular = An ecclesiastical dignitary elected by the Cathedral Chapter to govern a diocese between the death of the bishop (or the acceptance of his resignation, or his acceptance of a promotion to another diocese) and the arrival of a new bishop. During this period the Vicar Capitular has the complete ordinary jurisdiction of the diocesan bishop, but may not take decisions (such as appointment to irremovable positions) that would bind the new bishop when he arrives. As in the case of Diego de Torres y Vargas, a capable Vicar General working under a bishop would be a logical choice by the canons to continue the administration as Vicar Capitular while the bishopric was vacant (*sede vacante*).

Visitation (canonical) of the diocese – #16, 40, 41, 42, 101 = A Tridentine reform stipulating a visit by a bishop to each parish every two years. "Patriarchs, primates, metropolitans and bishops shall not fail to visit their respective dioceses either personally, or if they be lawfully impeded, by their vicar-general or visitor; if unable on account of its extent to make the visitation of the whole diocese annually, they shall visit at least the greater part thereof, so that the whole shall be completed within two years, either by themselves or their visitors."

Yuca – #28 = "Manioc" or *Manihot esculenta* of the Euphorbiaceae (spurge family), which is a tuber plant, once basic to the Taíno economy. *Yuca* was ground up to be made into casabe, or cassava, a bread, common among the Taínos and still popular in the Caribbean. In some sources, the *yuca* plant itself is called "cassava," although that is not the original meaning of the word. Neither should yuca be confused with "yucca," which is a species of perennials, shrubs, and trees in the family of Agavaceae.